Hopes and Dreams ...and Buster Too

John Dickson

Published 2019 by Creativia (www.creativia.org)

Cover art by Cover Mint

Edited by Elizabeth N. Love

Dedicated to Mary, Stephen and Kathleen.

Hopes and dreams can come true.

Table of Contents

Foreword

When I started to write this book I realised a surprising number of people in my life were and are called John! And quite a few Marys too. So, to avoid confusion I've changed some names and amalgamated a number of the characters in our lives to help the story flow; I've also taken some liberties with times and dates and combined some events. I hope you like the result.

The book features a young John Dickson's sometimes hilarious exploits over a ten-year slice of his life. Starting with a drama in the Campsie Hills... Who fired those shots?

The story gives an insight into a Scottish baby boomer's *Hopes and Dreams.* Progressing with humour and drama through John's later teens and into his twenties, his challenges evolve from schoolboy angst to getting married and leaving his four brothers behind. Moving from city to country life where *Buster,* the madcap Labrador, becomes a central disruptive character. Later, John has to cope with real grown-up dilemmas and making life-changing decisions. There are loads of escapades such as a hang-gliding attempt over Loch Lomond, a very close encounter with some brown bears, and an unexpected police car chase. And you can't imagine what chaos a trailer full of haggises can cause... Enjoy the journey.

Chapter 1
Camping in '66

We were fifteen years old, three lads from the east end of Glasgow in the mid-sixties. The three J's; Jim Lang, Joe Slyder, and me, John Dickson. We formed a 'band' called LSD after our initials...honest! That's how naive we were. The band only lasted one gig, so we didn't have to explain the logic too often.

The Summer of '66 I fondly remember as mainly warm and balmy. That magic time in your life even before the pressures and expectations of having to 'find a girlfriend' mattered very much. We didn't really care about passing exams. We'd sat our 'O' Levels, and the results would be out in the middle of the summer holidays. It wasn't like these days when the kids are expected to get 7 or 8 good Standard Grades. If we got 2 or 3 'O' Levels that would do. No grades. You either passed or you failed. If you failed, you had another go next year. Didn't matter. It was summer.

We decided to go camping. None of us had ever been proper camping on our own before. I think maybe Jim had been in the Scouts or Cubs, although that doesn't explain how he had a tent. A three-man tent. *With a sewn-in groundsheet.* It shouldn't have mattered, but it did. The idea of millions of creepy crawlies invading my sleeping space was something I wasn't keen on. Of course, I didn't mention that to the other two. Fifteen-year-old boys aren't allowed to be squeamish.

Lots of plans. Gathered equipment from around our respective houses. My mum never did catch on why her oven had only one shelf after that. I had figured out that it would be essential as a prop for our campfire cooking. It was! Worked a treat.

Meeting up at Dundas Street Bus Station. Comparing our borrowed ex-army knapsacks, we were first on the bus and banged our way to the back seat, where we spread out.

Getting off was more problematic. Pots and pans jangling and bumping against passengers' heads as we manoeuvred ourselves out from the back seats of the Lennoxtown Bus as it drew into Milton of Campsie.

"For God's sake! Yiv jist walloped ma' Granny's heid wi' thone fryin' pan! Whit the Hell are you plonkers trying tae dae? Mow us aw doon before ye get aff the bloody bus? It's awright, Granny, it's a good joab we wur goin' tae the doctor's anyway. Jist two more stops… You'll make it. Away ye go, yah bunch a' eejits!"

It's very difficult to scuttle quietly while clattering off a bus and apologising as we stumbled onto the pavement.

"Well, that was a good start!" Joe's eyes were popping.

This was as far as we had travelled on our own, and definitely the first time we would be staying away from home without our parents.

I don't remember any particular angst or worries from our mums and dads. We were going on an adventure for a whole weekend in the exotic Campsie Hills!

Where were we? We had studied maps, and Jim seemed to know about some legendary camping area in the foothills of the Campsies. It all sounded brilliant to me.

We needed supplies. We had brought a Frae Bentos Steak and Kidney Pie in a flat tin and various cans of beans and soups. Joe Slyder had real potatoes, and I had tins of pears and packets of biscuits. We all had tea and sugar 'cos that was essential.

There was a pub in the middle of the village, with an Off Sales.

"Right." Jim took the lead. "What are we going to ask for? My dad drinks heavy when he goes to the pub, although that's not very often."

Joe looked thoughtful. "My dad drinks McEwan's Export, I think. What about your Dad, John?"

I'd never seen my dad drinking in a pub… I was too young to be allowed in.

"Who's gonna order the drinks? John, you look the oldest. It's got to be you!"

After much more deliberation, we walked in. It was early afternoon, and the pub was empty. I was pushed to the front of the bar as I had the most obvious bum fluff on my face.

"Erm, two pints of heavy and a pint of export, please," I muttered. This had finally been decided after much arguing in the street.

"Same thing." The knowing barman looked straight at me.

"Okay then…" big intake of breath. "Three of them then," I managed, trying to keep my face from turning bright red.

To our amazement, the barman started to pour the three pints. We tried not to look at each other as I handed over the ten-bob note we had prepared as we hadn't a clue how much a beer was.

"That'll be five and thruppence."

That was more than my whole week's dinner money. Four and ninepence bought me five nourishing, if rather tasteless, school lunches. The only thing I liked was the caramel cake and custard we got on a Thursday.

My God, this booze was expensive stuff.

After we sat and pretended to enjoy the 'heavy exports,' we gathered ourselves and said thanks to the barman in the still empty pub, which probably explained our 'getting away with it.' After popping into the wee shop next door for more essential supplies such as a few cans of either heavy or export, *(why did they call them different names if they were the same?),* we started our long march through the village and up the dirt path towards our campsite.

We tramped up quite a steep hill, through woods and spindly trees then open ground to the brow of the hill where we could look back down to the village. We trudged onwards and eventually came to a very pretty area with small lochs and a gurgling stream leading from one wee loch to lower lochs. I now know they were abandoned reservoirs which had become overgrown. They're still there and still as pretty.

We managed to erect the tent. Jim was the practical one. He would study things and prepare. He reckoned we'd need loads of wood for the fire as we had a lot of cooking to do. So, while Joe volunteered to build the fire, Jim and I scrambled around picking up lots of deadwood lying among the trees.

Joe had a worrying fascination with fire. He was the innovative one. He had aspirations of becoming a scientist and had proven this by concocting some noxious chemistry experiment in his 'laboratory' in the loft of his council house. The result had been an explosion that blew the slates off the roof!

We had managed to buy some fresh rolls in the wee shop in the village after our success in the pub. So, Joe came up with the novel idea of toasting the rolls by simply setting fire to the paper bags they were in. It actually worked. Jim and I were impressed.

The tent and the fire looked the business. We had our cooking utensils all laid out with pots balanced precariously on borrowed oven racks and potatoes possibly baking in the stone 'oven' Joe had constructed at the edge of the fire.

Ach, life was good.

The sun set properly with golden clouds and red to pink skies. There was no moon, but the stars were beginning to sparkle. The fire looked even better in the darkness with our glowing faces grinning as we munched our way through the culinary delights of steak and kidney pie and all the trimmings. If our Mammys could see us now! We were coping… and feeling good about it.

As time eased on, the fire settled. We were still enjoying the camaraderie of achievement, as well as the cans of illicit beer we had managed to buy along with our fresh rolls.

Joe had gone down to the stream for a bit of privacy…

We heard a splash followed by a cry of dismay.

"Ma bloody shoes are soaking!" Jim and I looked at each other and grinned.

"Told ye to take the torch, Numpty," Jim called out.

"That wasn't so clever," I said as he squelched back to the camp.

"Ach, no problem. I can fix them".

Joe pulled off his sodden black shoes. He stuffed them with bits of paper then laid them right beside the fire.

"That's a bit close," I said.

"Well, ye need the heat to dry them oot," he said and looked at me as if I was daft. He lit a match to the paper stuffed inside each shoe...

‘ "Are ye nuts?"

“You'll see. The toasted rolls worked, didn't they? They're leather inside and out. They'll dry in a couple of minutes. Just wait. Ah need dry shoes!"

We all three stopped and stared at the black school shoes as the flames licked around the outsides and smoke started billowing up from their insides.

“That doesn't smell right,” Jim said.

“I'm awfy glad they're no mine,” I said.

“Nae problem…”

“Oh shit!"

The black shoes gave the game away. They suddenly folded in on themselves, and a very worrying black plume of plastic pollution engulfed us. “'They said they were made of leather!"

“Was it no' maybe leatherette?"

“Whit's the difference?"

“No shoes!"

“Ah well, at least we were entertained,” I said. “Here, you can borrow the gym shoes I was keeping as spares."

Once the shoes had completely burned out, the fire began to fizzle out. It was too early for bed. Solution? More wood. Jim reckoned it was Joe's turn to go traipsing back over the hill to look for more fuel. He'd had the relatively easier task of building the fire with all the wood we had gathered earlier. But Joe wasn't for moving. He was in a bit of a huff about his lack of proper shoes.

I volunteered to carry the large coal sack Jim had brought as a container. So, up we climbed in the pitch-black darkness to the woods we'd climbed through earlier. We had one torch between us and a small axe which was okay for splitting dead wood but useless for chopping trees down. We realised we had been pretty productive previously and already gathered most of the fallen wood. We would have to work harder for more fuel.

We figured we'd have to break off branches from trees that were still standing. Spotting an obvious target in the middle of the woods, we both grabbed the low branch and heaved it towards us. It snapped with an extraordinarily loud CRACK! We fell over. As you do when you're fifteen had a couple of cans of beer and a bit of nocturnal exercise.

We found quite a few. My God they made a loud noise! Especially in the deep quiet of the dead of night. After a bit we began to have fun. As we pulled back the dry branches, they finally snapped, and the noise echoed over the stillness of the hills.

Getting tired and with a full bag, I heaved it over my shoulder while Jim carried some longer branches.

Then the torch went out.

Total blackness.

Voices! Back among the trees.

My nerves tingled. I could barely make out Jim's silhouette. A twinkle of starlight reflected the fear in his eyes. We stumbled back up the hill carrying our loads.

Lights behind us! Further down the hill. In among the trees. Shouts!

Uh oh…

Clambering across some open ground, fuelled by adrenalin, we reached the top of the hill. We looked back and could just make out the glimmers of torchlight in among the trees. Looking ahead we could see the dying embers of our once glorious campfire nestling in the starlit gloom beside the loch.

We stumbled into the camp. Fed up waiting, Joe had climbed into his sleeping bag and was happily snoring in the tent.

Jim and I gave up the idea of rebuilding the fire. The adrenalin rush and the early introduction of alcohol had drained us. We poured water on the dregs of the fire and climbed into our bags and zipped the tent shut.

Hard ground but sound sleep.

Woke up to a watery morning. It had rained through the night. The sun was trying to break through but everywhere was damp. Shivers. And a sore head…

“What kept you? You were ages. And what was all that noise?” Joe mumbled as he crawled out of the tent.

We told him about the wood gathering and how we’d had to snap dry branches.

“Well, we could do wi’ a fire now.” Jim looked at Joe.

“No problem.” Joe was back in his element, gathering twigs from the bottom of the bag and making a perfect embryonic campfire in the midst of last night’s debris.

Minutes later we had the beginning of warmth as the fire took hold and then grew into a proper grown-up campfire.

Tinned beans and sausages for breakfast. Just what growing lads need.

We gathered up our stuff, conscious of not leaving any litter, even though we did bequeath a blackened log and plenty of kindling for the next bunch of campers. We buried the melted shoes with full funeral honours before setting off back over the hill.

Finally, arriving back at the village store before our bus was due, we were taken aback by the air of excitement in the tiny wee shop.

“Did ye see them?” The lady behind the counter looked at us.

“Whit? Who? Us?”

“The Poachers!” There wiz lots of poachers up in the woods last night firing shotguns all over the place. The gamekeepers were oot a’ night. But they didnae catch them. They saw wan o’ them with a big bag of game ower his shoulders. But they couldnae catch him. Did you no’ see them?”

We looked at each other.

“Nah… Dead quiet last night. We went to bed early. Pity we missed them, could have been exciting.”

The bus arrived.

We clambered up the steps and made our way to the back, trying not to bang too many heads…

Chapter 2
School Train To Italy

"So," the blond, serious-looking boy seated across from me on the packed Glasgow to London train asked, "How many 'O' Levels did you sit? I sat seven, but I'm not holding out much hope for any great results."

Somehow, we'd both managed to grab a window seat, but the question made me grimace. Recent memories of sitting in the draughty examination hall in Parson Street, staring at the maths paper with absolutely no idea how to answer most of the questions. I was in class 4A2, slap bang in the middle of the spectrum of academic possibilities. I reckoned I was aspiring to mediocrity… If I was lucky!

"Well, I sat six. I'll be surprised if I manage to pass *any* of them. The maths teacher's a pillock. And he used to be our science teacher too. The swots at the front got all the attention. So, we 'normal' blokes were left to rot at the back of the class. My main function was to sit with my back to the wooden pillar in Room 24 to stop it falling off the wall," I replied as the train gathered speed leaving Glasgow behind.

"What's your name, by the way? I've seen you knocking about, but we're not in any of the same classes. I'm John Dickson. Class 4A2."

"Aye, I've seen you too. D'you not hang around with big Jim Lang and that weird guy, Joe Slyder? I heard he blew a hole in the roof of his house! My name's Paul Roberts by the way. Class 4B1".

"4B1? You must be a right clever punter then! Did you get Eddie Edwards, the wee fat maths guy wi' white hair? He likes to brandish that belt a bit. He gave me two wallops last week for not handing in the homework I couldn't do! And I'd already got two of the belt from Wee Bobby Hendry when I came in through the pen, first thing in the morning."

"So, do you enjoy being put in the old Child Guidance Clinic then?" Paul laughed loudly, his face changing from that serious look to a happier expression.

"Och, I seem to spend far too many first periods there. With the design of that Victorian building you've got to go past that wee sadist Deputy Head guarding the only way in. They call it a pen, but it's really a tunnel tae keep us in and the real world out! I blame Glasgow Corporation! If the number 38 bus arrives on Cumbernauld Road in Riddrie for quarter to nine I make it in nae bother. I was just three minutes late! I'm telling you it's a crappy way to start your day with two red weals on your wrist. 'S not fair!"

"Aye, I've been caught myself, but not all that often." Paul relaxed into his seat. The other six boys in the carriage were blethering away. They all seemed to know each other.

I don't know any of these guys. It's a strange feeling being on holiday without Mum and Dad and ma wee brothers. Ah'm fine… Ah'll be fine…

When the opportunity came up to go on a two-week school trip to 'the Italian Riviera' and Rome I had pleaded with Mum and Dad. Jim Lang had said he was going and that was my leverage. Also the fact that I'd had to cancel a previous trip to Biarritz in France in second year gave me just enough emotional blackmail material to get the go ahead. Although I did have to do an awful lot of kitchen tidying and hoovering every week. It was a hard-earned £1 note I handed in every Monday along with my dinner money.

Now we were on our way. It was a pity Jim had pulled out halfway through the year. Something to do with another baby in the house or some such nonsense. So here I was with another twenty-one St. Mungo's Academy's finest on our way to Italy, and I barely knew a soul.

"Did you know some of the sixth years have formed a band, and they've called it The Tardy Host after Wee Bobby's Register Book? You know? The one where he marks a tick every time you're late and draws a wee dog beside your name if you've dogged it!"

"Don't you clever clogs call it playing truant, young man?" I joked. "I've been ticked off plenty of times and had the belt to prove it. But I've never actually dogged it. Well apart from maybe taking an extended lunch hour in Alexandra Park when the pond was iced over. Of course, Joe Slyder couldn't resist walking over it. And he naturally fell right through the ice! Good job it was only three feet deep. He was going quite blue by the time we got on the bus back. He can be a bit of a plonker. But only 'cos he's always willing to have a go. We went camping, and he managed to toast his buttered roll by putting it in a paper bag and setting fire to it!"

The train rattled on down the west coast line as we chatted away. The excitement of our impending foreign travels kept our adrenalin levels pretty high.

We discovered Paul and I had both been playing guitar for about a year, and he liked something called Folk Music. A whole new world to me. I'd bought my first record two years before: "Needles and Pins" by the Searchers. Then, like everyone else, I discovered The Beatles. As we were talking music, I asked Paul, "Do you ever go to the Bundy Club on a Saturday? You know… on Sauchiehall Street. The house band are The Beings. They're really pretty good! An' the talent's no bad either. The lasses from Notre Dame and Garnet Hill are usually there. An' a bunch of us Mungo scruff. I've managed a couple of lumbers. Though nothin' that's lasted ye know? There is one lassie I really like. A pity she's going wi' some boy whose dad's a dentist."

"Aye, well, I did go a couple of times, but I'm not really into soul music and such. My brother Josh was down in London last year, and he saw this brilliant guy called Paul Simon. He was playing in a wee folk club. So, Josh bought his album at the end of the show. It's excellent. A bit like Bob Dylan only more musical. And some of the songs are not too hard to play. When we get back you can maybe come down to mine's and we'll have a jam?"

"Sounds like a great idea. I'd like that." This trip was already reaping dividends.

Thoughts of Mum and Dad and wee brothers were fading…

Blethering gave way to games of cards among all of us in the carriage and the time seemed to pass quickly. Brother Adrian and Mr McRae popped in to check on us. But there was no trouble. We were all in great moods.

I was going on my first trip to a foreign country! And not just one country. We were to change trains in London. Travel down to Dover, before braving the English Channel on the biggest ship I'd ever seen. Compared to the ferry I knew from Greenock to Dunoon, the massive

Townsend Thorensen car ferry we boarded in Calais might as well have been the Queen Mary.

By the time we reached the French coast, it was dark and we were all tiring. Brother Adrian and Mr McRae herded us off the ship, and somehow we found ourselves on an overnight train to Genoa in northern Italy.

Lots of clambering through the Continental-style carriages and grabbing the best seats. Someone told us we were in sleeping carriages, but we couldn't figure out how. Until the guard arrived and magically pulled down slabs of walls and hey presto! Six comfy bunk beds.

The train stopped in the Swiss city of Basle for an hour. Not a long time to do much sightseeing, especially around midnight. But we could say we'd been to Switzerland on holiday.

The last leg of the journey had a strange interlude. We were told we'd be travelling through the very long Simplon tunnel between Switzerland and Italy.

After leaving Basle, we were pretty much exhausted as we climbed back onto our couchettes and fell fast asleep. Then the train came to a stop. There was no noise. No thrum of the engine…

Silence.

We all woke up. Somebody pulled back the curtain to look out of the window.

"Can see nothing out there. We must be in that tunnel."

All the lights went out!

Total darkness.

No emergency lights.

Complete blackness. I couldn't see my hand in front of me.

Very disconcerting…

I think it's now called sensory deprivation.

"Mmm. Not sure about this," a tremulous voice.

“Maybe we’ve broken down. Don’t fancy waiting to be rescued here. I heard it’s twelve miles long.”

“Anybody got a torch?”

“Aye. In ma bag. But Ah cannae see ma bag!”

“Ah really don’t like this!” The beginnings of panic.

Just as suddenly:

Lights!

Yay!

The atmosphere lifted.

The tension fizzled away.

The engine throbbed into life.

The train moved.

“Ah’ll be a lot happier when we’re out o’ this tunnel.”

That was me…

After more herding and shuffling and carrying heavy suitcases, we changed trains in Genoa and finally arrived in Santa Margherita, a very pretty little town cascading down rocks to a sandy beach and a busy fishing harbour.

We’d arrived!

The next few days were very relaxing, after the trauma of six train journeys over forty-eight hours.

We visited an abbey and a castle, but mostly we were allowed to sunbathe on the beach and wander along the harbour watching the fishermen sorting their nets.

As a bunch, we were pretty well behaved. We’d been well warned that we were ambassadors of the school, and apart from one boy who was caught showing off his shiny new flick knife, there was very little need for discipline.

We were with our accompanying teachers, neither of whom took any of my classes. Brother Adrian was a gently spoken, other worldly languages teacher. He spoke fluent Italian which was a real help as our travelling arrangements regularly unravelled. The worst example was the last leg from Milan to Rome when our comfy carriages on the booked express travelled merrily without us. We followed on an hour later squeezed into every corner of the slowest train in Italy. It stopped at what seemed like every hamlet on the way. My battered suitcase finally crumpled after seven hours using it as a makeshift seat.

Once we arrived in Rome, we were bussed to our pensione in a narrow side street. After dumping our bags, we were taken on a brief tour of our surroundings, and boundaries.

"Look. There's the Vatican! It's only round the corner!" Paul was as astonished as I was that we were so close to such a major attraction. Somebody had done something right!

St. Peter's Square was phenomenal in the brilliant sunshine. It looked just like the photos!

After a twenty minutes break to get our bearings, we regrouped back at the hotel to unpack and get ready for dinner.

Having 'bagged' our beds in a room with a view of the narrow street below, Paul and I took the chance to check out any local amenities. It was extremely hot. Someone mentioned 100 degrees. Sticking to the shady side of the street, we stumbled on a cafe just a few doors away. Feeling very continental and sophisticated after our northern Italian experiences, we sat down at a little outside table.

Paul and I looked at each other when we were approached by the loveliest Italian waitress. About our age, with full-bodied shoulder length hair, flawless lightly tanned complexion, and a smile the Mona Lisa would have envied.

Order pad in hand, this Roman angel spoke to us. *"Buon Pomeriggio. Vuoi qualcosa da mangiare?"* We guessed she was asking what we would like to eat.

In my best recently learned pidgin Italian, I replied, "*Due limonate e due torte, per favour, Senorita.*"

My Glasgow accent definitely didn't compete with her lilting Italian, but it did enough to produce a delightful giggle.

"Aye… you're in there," Paul whispered sotto voce.

"I've only ordered some lemonade, for God's sake!" I felt my neck reddening, and it wasn't the temperature.

Just as our soft drinks and cakes were being laid on our table and I had managed to make eye contact again, we were disturbed by a posse of our peers arriving noisily and taking up the seats around us.

"Paul, John. You'll never believe it but another school party arrived after you left… They're all girls! From Coventry! And they're all gorgeous!"

I looked at Paul then looked at our waitress as she demurely placed the two *tortes* between us. *"Grazie"* elicited yet another smile. Who needs females from Coventry? I was smitten.

The next few days were a blur of organised visits to lots of important sites in Rome. The Vatican and the Sistine Chapel, through the Pantheon and the Coliseum, then a formal visitation to the Scots College where St Mungo's had historic connections.

Each evening after our early dinner we were let free. While my contemporaries were pairing off with the Coventry girls, I was determined to develop a Scottish-Italian romance.

I had managed to elicit that the demure young lady's name was *Fiorella* which wonderfully means *Little Flower.*

By the fourth evening, I had become a *very* regular customer in the café, eking out my limited lire on soft drinks and tortes.

I escaped from the rest of the boys and managed to be alone in the cafe.

Plucking up all my courage I let Fiorella know in a mixture of broken Italian and confused sign language that I'd love to take her out…

Anywhere…

Even just "*andare a fare una passeggiat"* (I had been practising from my phrase book and a walk was a good start).

I was overjoyed when she nodded and indicated I should come back to the cafe at nine.

At five minutes to nine, I arrived wearing my best outfit. I'd sourced a small bunch of flowers which I held nervously while Fiorella bustled about within the shop, apparently saying goodbye to her father and the other family members whom I'd seen coming and going.

With a beaming smile, she took the flowers from me and kissed me on the cheek! *"Grazie, Giovanni, sono bellissime."*

My heart melted.

I smiled back and gave a feeble kind of wave to her relatives in the shop. Then I faced Fiorella and shrugged my shoulders, *where to then?*

I proffered my arm, and she took it. *Yay!* We started walking towards St Peter's Square.

I heard a kind of murmuring behind us.

I looked round and couldn't quite believe what I saw.

Ten feet behind us there was a knot of about twelve people noisily chattering to each other. It was obviously a family group as they were all ages.

One of them, a very old lady wearing a black laced shawl over her head grinned at me and waved.

Then I recognised Fiorella's father in the group.

Her whole family's following us!

Culture Shock!

I looked at my beautiful Fiorella and raised my eyebrows.

"My family…Zay look out for me. Si?"

I nodded knowingly.

No chance of a winch up a close here then!

I wonder if all those Coventry girls are taken yet?

Chapter 3
Sweet Sixteen

"Are you up yet, John? There's a big envelope for you here." Mum's voice floated up the stairs into my tiny bolt hole of a bedroom. Just enough room for a single bed, a chest of drawers and a window pole that I could use to turn the light switch off while lying in bed. Not a lot of space, but I was the only brother to have a room to myself as befitted my role as the eldest. Rank has its privileges.

Pulling my jeans on and shuffling into yesterday's slightly grubby tee shirt, I loped down the stairs and across the lobby.

All four younger brothers were up before me. They stopped eating their breakfasts and looked at me as Mum handed me the results of four years' secondary education in one of Glasgow's best Senior Secondary schools.

Thomas rubbed his eyebrows between spoonfuls of All Bran, his eczema a constant irritation. Alan, eyes grinning, stopped munching his corn flakes to say, "Come on, John. Give us a laugh. Open it up!"

"I really don't want to open it, Mum," I said as I held the thick brown envelope secreting my dreaded 'O' Level results.

"So long as you've done your best, John. That's all you can ask of yourself." Mum was sitting at the kitchen table, mug of tea clasped in hand. A warm, muggy air came from the newly washed clothes hanging from the 'pulley' strung up above our heads, the occasional drip finding its way down the length of Dad's pullover sleeve plummeting to the linoleum floor between the table and the sink. A small puddle was gathering which would be attacked with the mop and bucket poised against the wall.

I stared at the envelope. My own careful handwriting stared back at me. Examination Centre 83. Candidate No. 335 in my best capital letters.

I looked at Mum then peeled back the gummed flap.

Easing the single sheet of parchment-like paper, I slowly pulled it past the *Scottish Certificate of Education* heading. Then, unable to resist any longer I whisked out the remainder of the page.

"Well?" Mum looked at me, trying to read my expression.

"I only got three, Mum." I didn't really know how to react. *Was it terrible to fail half your exams?*

"The way I see it you've got the best results this family has ever had. Your dad and I both left school at fourteen and all we got were good attendance certificates. Although I did win a book in my last year!" Mum preened herself. "So be proud of your achievements."

As I stood awkwardly, looking down on Mum, Thomas interjected, "Well, I think you did great! What did you actually pass?"

I felt a bit better as I read out the details on my hard-earned certificate. "I've passed three subjects, English, Arithmetic and Art. There's no grading in 'O' levels, that comes next year with the Highers. God help me! It means I never got Maths, French or Geography."

"How did the rest of your class do? Maybe three's ok," Alan chipped in as he cleared his plate. "I'm going out, Mum. Rory and me are taking the bikes up to Huggie Loch. The sun's shining. I'll see you all later. Bye." With that, he disappeared out the back door and clattered down the stairs to grab the bike he and Thomas shared.

"Oy! That's not fair! I was maybe going out with Marco! Mu-um?" Thomas had missed his chance.

"Can I use the phone to call Jim and Joe, Mum? I won't be long." The use of the phone was always an issue.

"Alright, John, of course you can. And I'll tell your dad when he comes home for lunch. I reckon he'll be pleased."

A couple of short phone calls later and I was in a better mood. Big Jim Lang had only passed one exam, English, while Joe Slyder had managed two. I felt relatively clever. Although, when school returned a month or so later, I realised I had achieved my ambitions of mediocrity and so would have to re-sit Maths and French. Something to look forward to… But before that reality the Summer of 67 beckoned.

xxxxxxxxxxxxxxxxxxxxxxxxxxxxxxxxxxxxxxxxxxxxxxxxxxxxxxx

It was one of those long hot summers that become part of the structure of your life.

As I approached the milestone of my sixteenth birthday, life was sweet. The hiatus of the school holidays gave us time to really relax, soak up the fantastic music that was penetrating our souls and simply enjoy the moment.

One of the musical peaks was a Saturday in mid-May just after our exams, when the BBC Light programme gave us an insight into its forthcoming entry into pop culture when the revolution that was to be Radio 1 went live in September.

The Beatles' music had become part of the background to our adolescence, and when the double A-side "Strawberry Fields" and "Penny Lane" was the first Beatles' single not to reach number one in February, I felt a sense of unfairness. Especially as they'd lost out to the dirge of "Please Release Me" by the ridiculously named Engelbert Humperdink.

Jim was on the phone, enthusiastically enticing me and Joe to join him in what was to become a real musical landmark. "I've turned my bedroom into a psychedelic den. Kenny Everett is going to play a preview of the whole new Beatles' album this afternoon. Let's blow our minds, man!"

Cycling from Riddrie to Balornock was a half-hour climb up Cumbernauld Road, through Provanmill, past the empty fields surrounding Robroyston Hospital where my mum had spent thirteen months when I was a toddler. She'd been caught up in the TB epidemic around Glasgow in the early fifties. As I cycled my heavy second-hand bike past the fifty-year-old red brick buildings, I pictured Mum and her fellow patients trying to make the best of what must have been a terrifying situation. Her older sister, Betty, had died of TB the year before Mum contracted the deadly disease. Still, she'd survived, albeit with a scarred and weakened back. Although, it hadn't stopped her having four more sons after me. A strong woman, my Mum.

True to his word, Jim had made an amateurish attempt to turn his bedroom into an early discotheque. He'd rigged up spinning coloured lights with the aid of a bedside lamp covered in coloured cellophane and a record turntable circling determinedly in the darkened council house bedroom.

With the radio blaring out the opening bars of "Sergeant Pepper's Lonely Hearts Club Band" the three of us were headbanging in unison at the novelty of yet another completely different genre. As the tracks merged seamlessly from one song to the next without any interruptions by the DJ, we were entranced by the psychedelic sounds of "Lucy in the Sky with Diamonds", bewildered by the Indian influences of "Within You Without You" and finally frustrated by the BBC's decision the day before to ban the broadcasting of "A Day in the Life." It made us all the more determined to hear what all the fuss was about.

"I'll bet you Stuart Henry'll play it on Radio Scotland. Those pirates aren't as choosy as the daft ol' BBC!"

Sure enough, we soon heard the tantalising track on the soon to be doomed Radio Scotland with its complement of cheeky chappies and DJs who could properly roll their r's. Then we bought the album as soon as we could, and nearly wore the grooves through the vinyl by repeated playing.

My music purchases were very much limited by how much I could earn. I had a Sunday job standing in the street at a stall in the famous 'Barras' in Glasgow. It sold toys and gas balloons. Sometimes it didn't rain, and sometimes the broken downpipe above the stall didn't have torrents of water gushing onto the tarpaulins covering the stall. My dad knew the owner of the stall, Big Peter, who used to live on Gallowgate near my Granny. No need for a CV and an interview. I got picked up at eight o' clock one Sunday morning, and that was my Sundays taken care off for quite some considerable time. But I did get to hear the latest singles blaring out from the record kiosk behind the stalls in Kent Street.

Sometimes I'd also help Big Peter out at carnivals and Gala days. The extra money helped me to accumulate about half the cost of my heart's desire. Just round the corner from Big Peter's stall was a second-hand motorbike shop. I'd taken to wandering round any time I had a chance. On the pavement outside the small shop were half a dozen machines ready to be roared away by some lucky customer.

One particular scooter caught my eye, a bright red and white Lambretta which seemed a bit bigger than most of the others. And it was a good deal cheaper than the rest. At £35 it represented six months of Sundays at the Barras with all the fun of dodging the broken water pipes with their freezing showers, and the nuances of Big Peter's reprimands every time I burst a balloon, which was not infrequent.

"I've told you a thousand times. Rub the balloons between your hands to warm them up and make them stretchy before filling them with gas. And that gas you're wasting costs money too! And don't lose the feathers off the burst balloons; we'll find a use for them!" Peter's comb-over flapped ever more vigorously the more annoyed he became. "Sorry, missus, it's dead hard tae get decent staff on Sundays! Ah've told him a thousand times, ye know!"

He was right, he had… But balloons do burst if they've been lying in the back of a freezing-cold van from one week to the next. The trials and tribulations of a Barras balloon seller…

"Da-ad?" I was sitting at the kitchen table, Monday's stew and tatties swimming in our plates. All four brothers and Mum looked at me while Dad concentrated on scooping his food onto his fork. He was a very meticulous eater. Someone in his youth had told him it was healthy to masticate food thoroughly. So, he always took a good deal longer than everyone else to finish dinner. Thankfully he didn't insist that we all wait for him. Life was too short!

"What is it, John?" Mum's sense of curiosity was more acute than Dad's.

"You know how I've been working at the Barras since last year and I've been to a few 'gaffs' as Big Peter calls them. Remember the Links Market in Kirkcaldy in April? Trying to sell balloons in a blizzard is really, really hard! But it was four days extra work plus those gala days. So, I've managed to save up twenty-five pounds."

"Ach, that's great, John." She turned to my wee brothers. "See, just get your head down and anybody can earn money."

I didn't quite know how to take that… Especially from my mum!

"What're you gonna do with it, John? You could go to Spain for a week! I saw it advertised in the *Daily Record*." Thomas's eyes were bright at the possibility.

"Or you could buy the top seventy-five records in the hit parade, John! You're rich! Should you no' be giving me pocket money?" Alan always had an angle.

Dad finally finished his last mouthful and said thoughtfully as he looked at his wife, “That’s more money than I had when I married your mum. Are you thinking about getting married, John?”

I felt my cheeks glowing bright red as Mum grinned at my discomfort.

“Don’t be daft, Dad. Erm… You know how I’ll be sixteen in a fortnight? Erm… Well, if I get a provisional licence, I can ride a motorbike or scooter. I’ve seen a Lambretta scooter down the Barras, but it’s thirty-five quid.” The words tumbled out of me as my brothers’ mouths opened wider and wider and Mum’s eyes matched their rate of expansion.

“And I’ve only got twenty-five… So, I thought… I’m your eldest son… and I’ll be sixteen… And I could get the messages for Mum… And I could get up to Jim and Joe’s in ten minutes instead of an hour on the thirty-five bus… And I would save bus fares getting to school…” My exhortations were fading as Mum looked at Dad with a quizzical expression.

I stopped talking and stroked the thickening down that was trying to take root on my chin and upper lip.

A look passed between Dad and Mum, then he said: “I’ll maybe come down next Sunday. No promises mind!”

The table erupted.

Alan shouted, “Ah bags the first backie!”

Phil followed, “Me next!”

Wee Andy piped up, “Can I get a shot when I’m five?”

Thomas was more circumspect, “Do you need lessons before you’re allowed to use it on the streets? You might fall off!”

Feeling quietly thrilled, I tried to brush off Thomas’s concerns: “I’ve talked to the dealer. He says so long as it’s no bigger than 250cc, I just need a provisional licence and ‘L’ plates. He says it’s dead easy, the gears and clutch are on the handlebars. That’s just like the Sturmey-Archer gears on my bike!”

Mum quipped in: “I think there might be a bit more to it than riding your bike, John. But if your dad thinks you’ll cope…”

Dad's eyes widened: "I just said I'll have a look. Ok?"

"Don't worry." I quickly intervened. *Don't blow it!* "It'll be fine. You had a motorbike when you were young, Dad, didn't you?"

Dad's eyes lit up. "That's right. A BSA 250cc B21. I bought it with my demob money after the war. Forty-five pounds it cost. It was a pre-war model 'cos they stopped making anything except military things while the war was on. Aye, I had a few good hurls on that machine. Although it broke down at Balloch one day. I had to get the bus home. My pal came back the next day with his bike and towed me all the way back to Glasgow. That was murder!"

"And then you met me, and you traded it in for that wee car. An Austin Seven? The one we called Jacqueline. I loved that wee car." Mum looked quite misty-eyed.

"Did your dad, Pop, not help you to buy Jacqueline?" Mum recalled.

"He gave me twenty pounds towards it, that's right," Dad confirmed.

"Great," I said "Good ol' Pop! He paved the way! I'll see you down the Barras next Sunday!"

The day came, and Dad arrived just as we were packing up in the late afternoon. After a wee blether with his old pal, Big Peter, we wandered round to the scooter shop.

There it was. The dealer, who by now knew me well, had 'my' Lambretta sitting in pride of place on the pavement.

Dad proceeded to do his haggling bit. It used to embarrass me, but I seem to have inherited that particular gene, and it has stood me in good stead over many years in business. And sometimes just for fun…

The result was a saving of two pounds which went towards a pair of biker's gloves and a basic crash helmet along with two 'L' plates.

Once the cash had changed hands, it was time for my first ever lesson, which consisted of the dealer showing me how to twist the gears while holding the clutch as my right hand revved the throttle.

Two minutes later I'd managed to weave my way through the dregs of the Barras jaywalkers up to the end of the street and turn and come back. *No Bother!*

And that was it… The world was my oyster!

"See you back at the house then, John. Watch out for potholes, and don't kill anybody on your first day!" Dad waved as he made his way back to his car and home.

I've got a scooter! I don't have to pedal! Zip a day doo dah! And off I went, through the side streets and on to Gallowgate, easily squeezing past cars and buses stuck in the post-Barras jams. *This is brilliant!*

After a dutiful showing back home where all my wee brothers clambered over my prized possession, I managed to extricate myself and head for the almost rural outpost of Balornock.

We congregated at Joe's house where, of course, both he and Jim wanted a go.

"I'm not sure about that. My dad said it's only insured for me. What if you crash?"

Jim shook his head. "Don't be daft! I'll keep it slow. You've gotta give me a wee shot!"

I wasn't sure, so they started off taking turns on the pillion while I honed my nascent riding skills up and down Lamont Road and round to the rear entrance of Stobhill hospital. Easy going, great fun.

I finally agreed to let Jim have a go, on the condition that I sat behind him so I could shout instructions in his ear. *And* I bagged to wear the crash helmet…

A bit nervously I straddled the seat behind Jim, holding on to his red woolly jumper as he pointed the machine down Lamont Road.

"It's easy!" Jim shouted as we trundled at a fairly modest speed down the hill to where we came to the junction with Wallacewell Road, a wide suburban dual carriageway.

"Go left, and we can take it round to your house at the end of the road," I suggested.

Perhaps it was the change of road configurations, but when we pulled out onto the empty dual carriageway, Jim twisted the throttle and opened her up big time.

While I was enjoying the thrill I was conscious of the large roundabout halfway along the road. It was an oversized, dome-shaped concrete lump, and it was coming closer by the second.

"Slow down, ya eedjit! Yir going too fast to go round the..."

I don't to this day know what was going through Jim's head as we rushed towards the roundabout. I suspect he panicked and twisted the throttle the wrong way. All I know is he didn't attempt to go round the dome. He aimed straight at it!

The front wheel hit the surrounding pavement causing me to lean back. As the bike tried to climb the dome the front wheel lifted off the ground...

The rear wheel screamed and spun and pushed us up to the top of the mound where we seemed to hover for a millisecond before rushing down the other side and smoothly bouncing back onto the carriageway.

Jim had inadvertently performed a perfect wheelie on his first ever go on a motorised vehicle.

"Bloody Hell. That was scary!" I shouted in his ear, still amazed we hadn't slithered to a sore and expensive wipeout. "Was it deliberate?"

"Are ye daft?" Jim shouted back as he managed to slow down and pull in at the kerb. "A good idea if you take us back, eh?"

Jim's hands were shaking as he pulled the scooter back on its stand. I looked at his face and thought of one of that year's best-selling hits. He definitely was "A Whiter Shade of Pale"...

Chapter 4
Music and Life

Having the scooter made life more fun. I wasn't involved with gangs of mods like those we'd see on TV marauding through seaside towns on Bank Holiday Mondays. I didn't even know anyone else with a scooter or even a moped. It was just a method of transportation that allowed me to get around easier than by bus or bike.

Paul Roberts and I had become good friends after our Italian trip. I did go down to his house in Sandyhills, a similar area to Riddrie with solid semi-detached or four-in-a-block council houses. A nice area about a ten-minute scooter ride or two buses via the city centre.

It felt cool to be whizzing down the road with my guitar on my back. Pulling up outside Paul's house then going in to practise what was beginning to be called folk-rock. We'd listen to The Byrds version of Bob Dylan's "Mr Tambourine Man" then do our best to busk along to it. Sometimes we succeeded…

Then one day. "John," Paul could be quite laconic. "I think we've got our first gig."

"Gig? Us?" I thought we were just jamming. But, apparently, Paul had grander ideas. "But I'm a rubbish singer. Even my mum thinks so! I entered a talent contest in Butlins when I was twelve and my voice was just breaking. I noticed the pianist changing keys as I went from falsetto to bass when I tried to sing 'Blue Suede Shoes.' It was pretty embarrassing, especially when Mum said maybe I'd be better off learning to play an instrument. *I'm still traumatised!*

"Don't worry! We only have to play a couple of numbers. Your voice has been broken for quite a while now, and your singing's not *that* bad. We can do 'Sound of Silence' and 'Homeward Bound.' You know all the chords. I'll take the lead vocals."

"So, where is this gig gonna be then?" I thought to ask.

"Well, my mum's the secretary in the old folk's home in Cambuslang, and they're having a charity night with a variety show.

We're on the bill as Scotland's Simon and Garfunkel. It'll be a laugh. C'mon."

"A bunch of old folk? They'll want Bing Crosby and Al Jolson."

"Do you remember that lassie you said you fancied from the Bundy Club?" Paul's eyes were twinkling.

"You mean Mary? I've not seen her for ages. The Bundy's not the same since the Beings left. I heard she's going out with some ponsy guy who's at Uni. Why are you talking about Mary?" I was confused.

"Well, my mum told me her would-be posh boyfriend, who's called Dennis and who Mum can't stand, is doing a work placement in the home, and Mary's going to be at the charity night to help out. He was boasting about his girlfriend, and Mum recognised her photo from that group Bundy club picture we've all got."

"So, you want me to sing really badly in front of Mary while her ponsy boyfriend is hanging onto her? Not keen on that!"

"C'mon we just need a bit more practice. You know all the chords. Just learn the words!"

Two weeks later, after much zooming up and down between our respective areas of Glasgow's east end, we turned up at the old folk's home sharp at two o' clock on the Saturday afternoon.

We'd been practising our two songs almost every night and even recorded them onto my mum's wee tape recorder. We reckoned we sounded not too bad. I'd changed my mind. This could be a first step to a career as a performer…

We pulled up a few feet from the front door of the old folk's home. It had originally been built as a Victorian asylum, surrounded by slightly run-down gardens. Paul was on the pillion seat holding a guitar either side of the scooter. Totally dependent on my balancing skills and his ability to squeeze his knees tight when we hit the potholes.

We climbed off. We stood on the moss-encrusted gravel and looked at the massive institution in front of us.

"Don't fancy ending up here, do you?" Paul echoed my own thoughts. The place had a dismal air. The corporation green railings on either side of the path matched the open high gates we'd come through.

"Hello, John! Long time no see!" Coming round the side of the building was Mary, open, ankle-length, tan leather coat revealing a very short paisley-patterned mini-dress showing off long tanned legs that seemed to go on forever. She was carrying a tray of cakes.

"Oh hi, Mary. Didn't expect to see you here," I lied. "You're looking great. Haven't seen you up at The Bundy for ages."

My heart throbbed as she gave me her widest smile. "You're looking not bad yourself, John." She turned to Paul. "You must be Mrs Roberts' son. Dennis said you'd be doing a turn, he never mentioned you though, John. I didn't know you could sing. *And* play the guitar. I'm impressed!"

I felt my tongue tying itself in knots but forced myself to reply. *I'd forgotten how lovely she was.* "Aye, well. The singing's not so hot but Paul here talked me into it. So, God help the audience."

Mary laughed, and her long brown hair floated in the soft summer breeze. "I see you're mobile now. Quite a beast you've got there. Must be fun?"

We all looked at the Lambretta, standing proudly on its hind legs.

Paul interjected, "Sore on your bum when you're carrying two guitars by the way."

"I've never been on a scooter or a motorbike before." Mary looked straight at me with those green eyes that I remembered from the Bundy days. Now we were in sixth year I did feel a bit old for the place when I'd ventured back. Too old at sixteen… Who'd have thought?

"More than happy to let you have a shot. I'll take you for a spin just now if you like." *The show can wait,* I thought.

"Sounds great but I can't right now. I'm helping Dennis with the catering for the show. I'm on tea and cakes duty as you can see." She waggled her tray of multi-coloured fairy cakes. "Maybe after the show though. Once you've brought the house down!"

"C'mon, John. Can't keep our fans waiting." Paul handed me my guitar, and I gestured for Mary to lead the way. She elegantly breezed up the stairs and into the gloom beyond.

Once inside, we located Paul's mum who led us through a maze of faded cream and green corridors until we were shown into the small room we were told was the 'dressing room,' which led onto the stage.

My nemesis was there to meet us. Dennis Lamont, who I realised had been head prefect three years ahead of us, was standing in the centre of the room. There were a handful of people dressed in various stage outfits. I spotted the magician rummaging in his top hat while a dishevelled clown was having difficulty with his popping-off red nose. He had a worried look. A very elderly couple were earnestly discussing their *dance* routine with an equally elderly pianist.

"Dance routine? Is there such a thing as a zimmer dance?" Paul whispered as we extricated our guitars from their canvas bags.

Dennis stood tall, though slightly plumper than I'd last seen him. His hair just a bit too long and quaffed to be fashionable. His smug expression reminiscent of his time as the champion of the *Debating Society…*

"You chaps are Academy boys, ain't you. I'm sure I've seen you in Parson Street! Oh, those were good days. But, of course, you must be Mrs Roberts' boy, Paul? I can see the family resemblance." Master Lamont's false Kelvinside accent was annoying. I knew he originated from Drumchapel. That *Desert Wae Windaes* as Billy Connolly was later to define the sprawling housing scheme on the western edge of the city.

"I'm sure we're all going to have a wonderful show today, people." He spread his arms theatrically as he stood on the steps leading out to the stage. I almost expected him to call us all 'Dahlings!'

"What a pillock! No wonder my mum can't stand him." Paul whispered loud enough for some of the other performers to look round. The elderly dancers both nodded in unison.

We all trouped through the door, and I was surprised to realise we were behind a proper theatre curtain on a proper stage.

Nerves welled up.

Hands trembled

Flashbacks of my last public performance in Butlins…

I could hear the pillock, sorry Dennis, giving it laldy on the other side of the curtain. The magician was on first. Someone was playing drum rolls. Badly. There was an occasional pitter patter of applause. Definitely no roar of appreciation.

"I'm gonna have a look," I said as I pulled back the side of the heavy curtain.

The stage was remarkably big for what looked like the Home's dining room. I could see a few dozen tables spread over the room. The window curtains were halfway pulled, letting some of the outer sunshine dribble in. But the main worry was the audience.

Most of them were sleeping…

Heads resting on folded arms on oilskin covered tables.

They looked very comfy.

This must be their normal afternoon nap time. I thought.

What a first gig! Simon and Garfunkel eat your heart out…

I motioned to Paul to look-see… We peered round the curtain like old-time music hall players. Maybe ten or fifteen dazed looking OAP's actually awake. Two or three of them along with the nurses at the perimeter of the room clapped as the magician literally pulled the rabbit out of the hat to a stuttering drum thump.

Paul and I looked at each other, then strained to see who or what was making the terrible noises on the drums.

We tried not to burst out laughing as Oor Dennis stood up from behind the drums and walked to the microphone applauding the poor magician as he bowed to the sleeping audience.

"And now, Ladies and Gentlemen, for your delight, it's my honour to introduce to you, Scotland's answer to Sonny and Cher. All the way from sunny Sandyhills. Please welcome… Paul and John!"

"He's from a different planet, that guy." Paul wasn't impressed. *Which of us did he think was Cher?*

The curtains parted in the centre, and we walked out to the middle of the stage. There was loud clapping from the left, and I spotted Mary beaming at us from beside the tea urn. The rest of the room managed a ripple of desultory applause. I felt my heart sinking. *What the hell am I doing here?*

I looked to my left and was dismayed to see Oor Dennis settling in behind the drum set. *This guy's no' got a clue*.

Paul adjusted the mike. "Hello, Cambuslang, we're going to play a couple of Simon and Garfunkel songs. We hope you like them."

"One, two, three, four."

We both strummed a resounding A minor and launched into the beginning of "Sound of Silence" and then the drums started… out of time… too loud…

Paul and I both turned mid-chorus and glared at the eejit who was oblivious to us. He was on a trip! He thought he was Ringo Starr or maybe even Charlie Watts.

"Left its seeds while I was sleeping," Paul was singing his heart out in spite of the racket from our left.

The eejit had completely lost it now

BOOM!

CRASH!

TINKLE!

As we sang: "*Within the Sounds of Silence."*

Just then a voice from the audience rose up in protest.

"WULL YE STOAP THAT BLOODY RACKET! I'M TRYIN' TAE SLEEP HERE!"

I gulped. *This isn't going well…*

We kept on strumming.

What's the saying? The show must…

"I SAID WULL YE SHUT THE **** UP!"

I looked around in despair as I desperately kept on strumming. Paul was on his own with the singing by this time.

I wandered towards the cacophony. Still strumming, I kicked the high hat out from under the eejit's feet. It fell with a crash. But no more out of time than he was anyway.

Oor Dennis kept on striking the snare drum as he looked at me with a puzzled expression. I took my hands off the guitar and grabbed the drumsticks out of his hand.

His mouth agape. He finally got the message.

"And touched the sound of silence," Paul was still doing his best.

There was a round of applause! Proper applause. They'd woken up!

I looked over to Mary who was in fits of laughter. She looked up at me and raised her hands and clapped… loudly.

Dennis the menace had slumped away. We had the stage to ourselves.

When we finished "Sounds of Silence," our well-rehearsed "Homeward Bound" went down a treat. So much so we ended with an encore of "Ba Ba Rumba!" with our geriatric audience clapping merrily along.

"Aye, well, you managed to turn a disaster into a triumph, Mr John. You really did bring the house down!" said Mary as she strapped my one crash helmet on before straddling the pillion seat behind me.

"Just a wee hurl now. I still have to let Dennis take me home. He's really given himself a bad day. Now, where do you want me to hold on?"

Yay! Mary's on the back of my scooter! She's holding me round my waist!

I drove through the gates and onto the road for the best ride I'd had on my Lambretta, with Mary's arms tightening as we built up speed.

"Yipee dee do da!" I couldn't resist.

"This is great!" Mary shouted over my shoulder.

The ride lasted a mere ten minutes until we skidded back through the gates, with Mary's head resting on my back. *Ahhh…*

Oops. Dennis was standing waiting with Paul. He waved wanly. His shoulders were slumped, and his teeth were clenched.

I could almost hear his teeth grinding as Mary hopped off the scooter and gave me a thank you peck on the cheek. “That was brilliant, John. Now I get the appeal of two wheels.” She turned to Dennis. “You ready to go now, Pudding?”

Aye! A right pudding. Apt nickname, Mary…

Pudding blushed. And rightly so!

This had been a good day…

Chapter 5
Reality Check

Sixth year at school was much more relaxed. The teachers knew you were there voluntarily, so they had little power over you. The days of getting the strap for feeble reasons like talking in class were over. There was always an element of bullying in the use of the strap, but when the pupils were as big or even bigger than the teacher, it seems more prudent to engage and convince rather than condemn and punish.

It was also probably more civilised because the minority of disruptive boys who put the teachers into bad and angry moods were mostly gone. Left school to get jobs as soon as they were fifteen. And getting a job didn't seem to be difficult. St Mungo's boys tended to be streamed towards the civil service, local government and other institutions. So long as you had a couple of 'O' levels including English you could be fairly confident of being taken on as 'Grade 2' civil servant. Or in other words: the tea boy…

Big Jim Lang took advantage of this ease of employment when he applied for a trainee management job with British Railways. Always the guy who liked to hug the radiators in class Jim seemed destined for a sedentary career.

Not letting on to the interviewer his intention to go back to school for a sixth year, he was awarded the position of trainee administrator in Queen Street Station in the heart of the city. Jim had the enviable job of sitting high above the platforms and looking down on the madding crowds as they bustled their way off and on the trains in one of the busiest stations in the country.

Apart from making the tea, he was sometimes given the task of making public announcements over the Tannoy. The announcements that no one comprehends anyway.

The phone rang at home, and I picked it up. "Hi, John, Jim here, how are things? I hear you and Paul Roberts had a good gig at the weekend. I'm sitting in a big empty office in Queen Street, and you'll never guess."

“Okay, Jim. What have you done? I’m just going out for a spin on the scooter. I said I’d pick Alan up at his pal’s.”

“You know how the Railway strike’s been on for nearly a week now?” Jim sounded as though he was getting slightly excited.

“Yeah, I know. You told me you were getting really good at making paper aeroplanes.”

“Well, the boss has just gone for lunch, and his deputy’s on strike.”

“Uh huh. And your point is?”

“I’m in Charge!” Jim sounded as dumbfounded as I felt.

“Of the whole Station? But you’re only sixteen. And you know nothin’!”

“Well, there is a little but important detail… There are no trains… And no staff… And the ticket offices are closed… But I’m in charge!”

“Ok. That’s bizarre.” I was coming to terms with the situation. “Enjoy your moment of glory. Just don’t abuse that Tannoy system too much!” I had visions of Jim winding up the already frustrated passengers with announcements of ghost trains on imaginary platform numbers.

“Don’t worry. I’m not going to risk this job till I give it up when school goes back. It’s the cushiest number ever! I’ve even managed to sneak my guitar in to practise. You still want to have a go at playing in the Cairn next Saturday lunchtime?”

“I don’t mind, but I think we need a bit more practice. By the way, who’s going to play drums?”

“Joe said Gordon Carr fancies a go. Apparently, he’s got a set of drums at home.”

I recognised the name. “That’s the guy who used to go out with Mary, isn’t it? His dad’s a dentist.” *Maybe I should learn to play the drums, I thought.*

Jim replied, “That’s the one.”

“I hope he’s a better drummer than Mary’s current boyfriend. I told you what a pillock he was!”

"Gotta go now. I can see the boss walking across the platform. I'll have to get busy doin' nothing. See you tonight."

The next few nights we practised in Joe Slyder's house. The Cairn pub was at the top of his street, and Joe's dad was a regular. Impressed with his son's guitar playing abilities he'd asked the regular Saturday lunchtime combo if they'd let Joe and his band (that's us, folks!) use their amps and drums to show off our talents.

Joe and Jim and I had long since agreed that if we ever formed a band it had to be called LSD after our initials *Lang, Slyder, and Dickson.* And, of course, it also meant *Pounds, Shillings, and Pence* due to some Latin link to old Roman coins.

The other obvious reference to the well known mind-blowing drug passed over our naive heads. Ironically the main song we were practising for the pub gig was the Beatles' "Day Tripper" which was actually all about John Lennon teasing Paul McCartney for being a '*weekend hippie' or 'Day Tripper.'* But we didn't know anything about that then…

Big Jim, stress sweat pouring down his cheeks, played the brilliant opening bass riff of "Day Tripper"… Then he kind of got lost as the song progressed. My cheap acoustic guitar, crudely adapted with a pickup to electrify it, just sounded tinny. The only true musician was Joe who had a proper Hohner electric guitar, and he was more than competent.

However, Joe couldn't carry the rest of us, and just because he had a drum set at home didn't make Mary's ex, Gordon, a good drummer. We were actually booed off!

"Away ye go ya bunch a weans! Yir rubbish!"

"Get the real band back oan!"

Unlike the previous week, there was no way of turning it around. These weren't sleeping geriatrics. These were paying punters. And like most Glasgow audiences, they took no prisoners.

Very humiliating…

Joe's dad was sitting in the audience with his head in his hands. We couldn't even pretend we were over eighteen and try to drown our sorrows.

"I think I'll stick to folk music from now on," I said as the four of us trudged forlornly back down to Joe's house.

"Well, I'm going to enjoy listening to music even more now I know how hard it is. That was terrifying! This beast is never coming out of my house again!" Jim's face was still smeared with drying sweat as he lugged his solid bass guitar over his shoulders.

"We just needed a bit more practice!" Joe still had his guitar strap on and was playing a mellow blues riff as we walked.

"Well, I sounded far better in the house." Gordon walked across the road towards the bus stop. "I'm gonna catch the next bus. See you lot in sixth year."

As he waved back at us, I asked "How come Mary seems to fancy really crappy drummers? Do you think I should take it up?"

"Well, you said you managed to humiliate her current boyfriend at your last gig. Maybe that's the way to go." Joe grinned

Bang goes the drums idea then…

Chapter 6
School's Out

"All the best, guys! See you around," I shouted back through the pen of Parson Street, home of many wasted first periods hanging about in the *Child Guidance Clinic* after being strapped by Deputy Bobby in my first year in the 'Big School.'

I had finished my last ever exam. Another attempt at Higher Geography. I didn't have high hopes. Sixth year had maybe been a bit too relaxing. Too easy to miss classes and while away hours in the Lido Cafe at the top of West Nile Street. Or the more upmarket Kenco Cafe in Buchanan Street if we were feeling sophisticated. Veritable gathering places for sixth formers and university students from all over the city centre. Occasionally, I'd bump into Mary and her current crowd. We'd chat about 'old times,' and how she'd enjoyed the hurl on the scooter…

But she just had too many things on to have another scooter ride… Ach.

But this was my last day! Jim and Joe and Paul all had another couple of science exams, but I was free to go and never come back.

What was I going to do? I didn't have a plan. I'd thought of becoming an architect as I was not too bad at art. But there had been very little career help in school. My one interview with a 'guidance teacher' who had never met me before resulted in a cursory glance at my mediocre prospects before handing me an application form to apply for a career in, surprise surprise, the civil service. As a tea boy, sorry Grade 2 clerk.

"So, what are you going to do then now you've finished your exams?" Thomas was just home from school.

"Remember you were going to be an astronaut, John?" Alan chipped in.

I sighed, remembering my eleven-year-old self's determination. *So I was…*

"You gonna be an astronaut, John?" Phil stopped wrestling with Andy who was almost giving as good as he was getting.

"Oh, I'd love to, but I think I'm going to be stuck here on Planet Earth for a wee while yet. I reckon someone else is going to beat me to the moon…"

xxxxxxxxxxxxxxxxxxxxxxxxxxxxxxxxxxxxxxxxxxxxxxxxxxxxxxxx

Dad's shop was the main newsagents in the housing scheme. This was before the spread of supermarkets. The local parade of shops offered all you needed for day-to-day living. Two competing grocery stores: Galbraiths and the Co-op. Caldwells the bakers created fantastic meringues. A proper butchers with dead cows and pigs hanging on hooks on the customer side of the counter, so they bounced off you while waiting in the queue. The floor was covered in sawdust to soak up the dripping blood… And for the occasional treat: a ladies hairdresser, with Charlie, the bald barber at the back of the shop, who regularly had a bunch of fidgeting boys waiting for crew cuts. Accompanied by mums who would slap them on the back of their uncut heads if their fidgeting got too rowdy.

Dad's shop was traditionally laid out. Everything had to be served. No self-service, apart from the birthday cards, and they often went out the door in handfuls. With Dad running after the culprits and usually failing to catch them. Not good for blood pressure!

I fell into the routine of working in the shop during the week, while I still helped out Big Peter at the Barras on Sundays. Sometimes Peter would also take me to Highland Games on Saturdays and even had me working in his stall in the Kelvin Hall Carnival over Christmas.

It sounds enjoyable. At times it was crazily busy, with crowds queuing up for gas balloons with feathers sticking out of their heads. Cowboy hats and dangling furry monkeys were remarkably popular. All the fun of the fair!

Unfortunately, on a wet Wednesday afternoon, there would be virtually no customers. I'd be sitting behind the piles of *Kiss me Quick* hats trying to read a book, but the competing music blaring out from the Waltzers and the Hobby Horses, spinning emptily just feet away tended to dull my concentration. Once Christmas and the New Year rush were over, I couldn't wait for January to end. Working until ten o'clock most nights fair put a stop to any social life. But the wages were better than the shop's, so I tholed it.

February finally arrived, and I slipped back into the shop routine. Though Dad now delegated me to run after the birthday card shoplifters, I even managed to catch a couple of them, two of the bunch of would-be hooligans who hung about outside and who were the bane of Dad's life. But there was a terrible price to pay.

"Where's your scooter, John?" Cathy, the charge hand, was just starting her back shift at half-past one.

I lifted my head and looked over my customer's head. "I chained it to the railings up at the Post Office. Sure it's not there?"

"C'moan, John, Ah'm in a hurry an' ye've no' gied me ma ten Embassy tipped yet! Ah'm goin' tae the bingo an' it starts in hauf an' hour"

"Sorry, Maggie," I said to my diminutive regular. "Nancy." I turned to the other charge hand who was cashing up her till as the shifts were changing. "Can you serve Maggie? I gotta check on my scooter."

"Aye! C'moan, Nancy. This might be ma lucky day! Even if it's no' Johns!"

I ran round the counter and out the front door. The pavement was just drying out after a week of heavy rain and sleet that had finally thinned out that morning.

I looked along the parade of shops to the railings I'd parked behind and chained the front wheel to. It was a good solid chain and combination lock that Dad had insisted I bought before using the scooter to commute to the shop.

"You really should just use the bus. That bunch of thieves that hang around the shop will steal anything that they can get their hands on. If you do bring it, get a combination lock that can't be picked. And they'll still manage to steal it. Mark my words!" Dad's warning of a few months before reverberated in my head as I ran towards the railings.

"Lost something, Johnny boy?" I recognised one of the card thieves, walking out of the Post Office. Malkie, a scruffy, sharp-faced teenager, a year or so younger than me. I slowed and glared at him.

"It wisnae me, mate. Ah wiz in gettin' ma granny's pension. See!" He brandished the buff coloured pension book.

Bloody Hell, it's gone then! I thought as I decided not to give him the satisfaction of a reply. I strode over to the railings.

Then I spied it. Lying flat on the other side of the railings was the scooter's front wheel, with the chain and padlock still attached to the fence.

Bastards! I felt sick. I loved that scooter. It was my key to freedom.

I ran across the main road and looked down Boghall Road in case the thieves were still manhandling the one-wheeled vehicle. It would have been difficult to manoeuvre. *Unless they had a van, or a pickup.*

I ran back to the shop where the usual suspects were hanging around a few feet from the door. I looked at them. *They knew.* But they weren't about to help.

"Ah saw them dragging your bike, John." A small voice from behind me. I looked around and saw wee Ronny, one of our regular school kids, about ten years old, who came in every day. "Just five minutes ago. They had a bogey for the front spokes. They were pullin' it towards Huggie Loch. Ye could still catch them!"

"Aye gone yersel', Johnny boy. Let's see ye run!" The sharp-faced thief was enjoying the drama.

"Do you know them, Ronny?" I asked

"Naw. They're no' frae roon' here. Ah've never seen them before. Good Luck, John. Ah'd help ye but Ah've got tae get back tae school. Ah'm late as it is. Ah don't want tae get the belt again."

"No problem, Ronny. Thanks. I owe you a free MB bar. I know they're your favourite."

I ran into the back shop where Dad was on the phone.

"Dad, quick. They've stolen the scooter. Took the front wheel off. If we go in the car we might catch them!"

"Cathy said it was gone. What did I say about them stealing anything that moves?" He couldn't resist the *'I told you so'* as he grabbed his car keys and we hurried out of the shop.

"Ye'll need to set up a siren, Mr D. If yer gonna catch those nasty scooter stealers in your Z car," one of the crowd mocked as we pushed our way through.

I was conscious of time passing as we climbed into Dad's Zephyr, the very model that was used in the TV police drama. Hence the jibe.

We pulled onto the road. A hundred yards away we were going to race down the footpath the thieves had used into Hogganfield Loch.

"Oh no, when was that put up?" I was looking at the bollard concreted into the centre of the path entrance.

"No idea. I've never noticed it before, though I've never tried to take a car down here before either." Dad looked frustrated.

I opened the door. "I'll run down the path. You go round the long way and I'll see you at the tearoom car park. It'll take you at least ten minutes."

"Be careful!" Dad shouted out the window. "Don't tackle them!"

I ran down the path. About a quarter-mile. No one in sight. It was a cold February day. Not many folk would be strolling in the park.

I reached the end of the path where it opened out to the park proper. Hogganfield Loch with its island bird sanctuary lay before me.

Nobody visible this side of the loch, so I started walking clockwise on the perimeter path. I was just in sight of the carpark when I spotted one of our more elderly customers coming towards me walking her wee dog.

"Mrs McLean," I called as I ran towards her. "You been walking round the loch? Did you see anyone dragging a one-wheeled red and white scooter?

Her wee terrier started barking as I approached, so she bent down and lifted it into her arms. "Wheesht now, Scottie. It's John from the shop. You know John, stop your barking." It worked. The yapping stopped. "Well, I did see something peculiar at the other side of the loch. It's funny the things ye see when ye're out for a walk. Just the other day…" I stopped her mid-tangent. "Sorry to interrupt, Mrs McLean. What was peculiar today? Please?" I implored.

"Well, I'm not sure if it was a scooter, but there were two scruffy looking guys footering wi' some kind of machine on the grass at the other side of the loch. Ye know, beside Avenue End Road. And there was a wee car parked on the grass. I just called Scottie back and kept my head down. Ye never know what's going on these days, do you?" She shook her head. "I'm just going home now. I think I'll put the kettle on. I'm beginning to shiver."

I thanked the nice old lady, who liked a blether with Nancy when she was in the shop, and hurried towards the car park. I knew the loch was just over a mile round and Mrs McLean wouldn't have been walking fast. Damn!

"Dad! Dad!" I shouted as he drove off Cumbernauld Road into the car park.

"Old Mrs McLean spotted them footering with the bike at the other side of the Loch. We might still catch them!" Dad looked sceptical as he started to reverse.

"Don't go back out to the road, Dad," I urged "Just drive round the path. This is an emergency!" I ran round the car and jumped in. *This really is like an episode of Z Cars!*

Two minutes later, lights flashing and splashing through puddles, we had reached the other side of the loch just in time to see an old Austin Seven bumping off the far side of the grass onto the road.

"That'll be them, Dad! Follow that car!" *I was definitely on the telly now…*

Dad's eyes brightened as he bounced the car onto the grass and revved the engine. Someone had just let the Austin join the traffic lights queue. They were static.

"Hurry, Dad, we can catch them! They're stopped."

The Zephyr bumped through the knee-high grass for about ten yards then slithered to a halt. Dad banged his fists off the steering wheel. "Ground's sodden. All that rain."

He gunned the accelerator, and the back end of the car slowly travelled sideways as the rear wheels spun. I looked through the back window to see mud spraying into the air.

I couldn't believe it. My heart was racing as I opened the door and jumped out of the car. The traffic lights were just changing to red and amber as I sprinted through the soggy ground.

MBD 419. MBD 419, I repeated to myself as the Austin slowly turned right onto the main road as the lights turned green. We'd missed them!

"Over here, John. Look." Dad was about fifty feet from his mud-splattered car.

As I came closer, I saw what he was looking at. My pride and joy was lying flat in some thick grass. Or at least its skeleton was there. It had been completely stripped to the bones. The engine was missing as was the other wheel. Even the side panels and the seat were gone. It was a sorry sight. *Back to the buses for you, Johnny boy.*

Dad ruminated, "It's been too big to get in that wee car in one piece that's why they've stripped it down. Och, that's a pity. C'mon, son. We'll get the car out of the mud and take what's left to the police. Not that that'll get your scooter back again. It's a hard lesson."

A fair amount of manual effort and we managed to reverse the car out of the mud. Then we manhandled the scooter carcass into the estate car's boot before heading back to the shop. We called the police and reported the crime.

A hard lesson right enough. While the Austin's licence number did help the police to identify the car's owners and our local cop unofficially told us that it belonged to Malkie's cousin, we had no proof as we'd not seen them actually putting anything in the car. They'd got away with it. Definitely not fair!

Still, the insurance company eventually paid out twenty-five pounds, but I decided I'd stick to the buses for a while. It wouldn't be long till I was seventeen and a proper driving licence beckoned…

Chapter 7
Testing an Opportunity

"You'll need to keep your eyes off the pretty girls while you're at the wheel." The driving examiner finished ticking his boxes on his clipboard.

Oh no! He's going to fail me! I must have looked distracted.

I'd started the test feeling very positive. While I hadn't had any formal driving instructions, Dad had let me drive, unofficially, for months. We'd started down at the local football pitches where I'd got the hang of the car's controls. The Zephyr Estate was a big car to learn to drive in, but it was all I knew. Mum had a wee yellow mini, but she was 'no way' going to let me near it until I had formally passed my test.

The scooter experience definitely helped. And a right good cramming of the Highway Code topped up my confidence.

But when I sat in the car to start the test my right leg started shaking. Almost quivering. I couldn't stop it. *That's not going to help!* I pulled into the traffic, and while the quivering continued it didn't seem to affect my control of the car. Even the reversing round the corner seemed to work out.

My shoulders slumped. *I'm going to have to get proper driving instructions after all. It'll be months before I can go out on my own.*

I stared at the examiner, who looked back with a poker face. "I'm pleased to say you've passed." Then he smiled.

"What?" Brilliant!" A wide grin erupted. Two thumbs up to Dad who was standing on the pavement. His grin matched mine. Yay!

I jumped out of the car waving the coveted pink slip in my hand. Dad extended his hand and I shook it enthusiastically. "Well done, John! Now *you* can go to the Cash and Carry!"

I knew there'd be a catch…

My new status as a fully qualified driver opened up an opportunity just a few weeks later. "...I think he's too young for that kind of job." Mum's voice floated into the hallway through the half-open door.

"Well, he knows all the lines. He's been behind that counter since he was a wean. I'm sure he'd be fine."

What are they talking about? I lingered for a moment.

"He's not had his licence for long enough." Mum sounded adamant. *They're talking about me!*

I opened the door fully. "And I'm too young for what job?" I asked. Mum and Dad were sitting either side of the fireplace. Mum looked up, took a final draw from her cigarette, then stubbed it out on the heavy glass ashtray.

"Dad thinks you should apply for the Ronson's rep's job. You know Mr Evans who takes the sweeties order every Tuesday?" I nodded. A genial old guy who always wore a tie even in the hottest day.

"Well, he's retired, and they're looking for a new rep to cover Glasgow..."

"I fancy that!" I interrupted. "Driving about from shop to shop? That'd be better than listening to wee Maggie moaning about losing at the bingo."

"But are you not too young? And you've not long passed your test." Mum looked concerned.

"Don't worry, Mum. I passed first time, remember. With no lessons! I'm a natural. Would I get commission?" I turned to Dad.

"I would think so, I'm not sure. It was Mr Ronson himself who came in this morning; apparently, the rep they had lined up has gone to a rival company. I mentioned you might fancy it even though you are a bit young. He seemed interested." He looked at Mum and shrugged his shoulders. "I know John's been looking for a 'proper' job, his nose is never out of the Daily Record's appointments page."

True enough. I'd even managed to get a couple of interviews: a junior position in a whisky bond, but I hadn't a clue what the interviewer was talking about when he started mentioning distillation processes and the differences between malts and blended whiskies. My blank expression didn't go down well.

I'd also had an interview as a trainee window dresser in Lewis's, the biggest department store in Glasgow. I scrunched up my face at the interviewer's description of 'like working in a hothouse' making displays in the windows on sunny days, and then she stopped. "I think you'd be too tall for this job, John." *Phew!*

But I did need a proper job. While Dad gave me as many hours as he could, it didn't add up to full-time work. And Big Peter's Sunday shifts were drying up too. His son, Wee Peter, was growing up and I was reduced to doing every second Sunday. The idea of a full-time rep's position really appealed.

The interview with Mr Ronson, a worn-out-looking chap in his forties with red-rimmed watery eyes, went as well as I could have hoped. We were sitting in his office. A lot more comfortable than Dad's squeezed-in desk in the back shop. Mr Ronson had a real leather swivel chair!

"We've supplied your father with all his confectionery for nearly ten years now. I understand you've been 'working' there on and off since you were a child. And you look like you've turned out to be a smart young man. Your dad and mum should be proud."

I blushed. I was wearing my grown-up dark blue suit. Picked by Mum out of Goldberg's department store in what's now been transformed into the Merchant City.

"Your dad's a very good customer. So, I would think you'll have a reasonable knowledge of the products we sell?"

This was my chance: "Of course I do. We sell everything from jars of humbugs and soor plooms to Spangles and Mars bars and big boxes of Black Magic and Dairy Box. As well as all the kid's sweets, like sherbet dabs and gobstoppers." I was trying to impress.

"Yes, well. You seem to know what you're talking about, although I must say we stock even more than your father does. But I'm sure you'll pick it up as you go along." He nodded and smiled encouragingly.

“Now. The remuneration is fairly basic. Where you can boost your earnings is in the sixpence in the pound commission. There’s no cap on commission. The more you sell, the more you make. Plus, of course, you’ll have the use of the company car. It’s not the latest model, but I suspect it’s better than what you’re driving now.” He smiled again.

Considering I was only driving Dad’s car to the Cash and Carry, it all sounded brilliant!

I grinned widely.

“Well? Would you like the job? You could start next Monday.” I couldn’t believe it was so easy.

“Of course, Mr Ronson. I’d love to have the job. I’ll see you at nine o’clock next Monday morning. Thank you very much!”

“Welcome aboard, John. A bit of youth will do us no harm. I’m sure you’ll do well.”

Hope springs eternal…

I couldn’t wait to tell everyone I had a job with a company car! And I was only seventeen!

I arrived home an hour and a half later, triumphantly announcing to Thomas and Alan that, yes, I might be able to give them lifts sometimes, so long as it fitted in with my journey times. Boast, boast…

Everyone was pleased for me. Even Mum.

“Well done, son. Just be careful on the road. You know how I worry about young drivers…”

Monday morning came, and I was up bright and early. I wasn’t going to be late. Memories of Wee Bobby waiting in the Parson Street Pen were too recent!

Mr Ronson took me into the warehouse. A big redbrick building, with the only daylight coming from skylights in the corrugated roof. Rows of shelves reminded me of the Cash and Carrys that had begun opening around Glasgow. Dad said they were a threat to the traditional wholesalers, like Ronson’s. Still, not every shopkeeper used them.

Some of them were stuck in their shops all day with no time to travel to go shopping. I decided not to worry about that yet.

I was introduced to my new colleagues: two other reps, both a lot older than me, covering territories outside Glasgow, and two warehouse staff. I was told there were another couple of reps who covered the Highlands and Islands and seldom came in to the office.

Mr Ronson left me with the other reps while he went to take a phone call. I felt a bit lost. “So, how long have you worked for Ronson’s?” I asked one of the older chaps. Introduced as Chalkie; aka Charlie White. Wearing a crumpled grey suit. Fingers dark brown with nicotine stains. He dragged the dregs out of an un-tipped cigarette before stubbing it out on a dirty saucer perched on a cardboard box.

“Been here twenty-one years, son. Started working with Graham’s old man when I was demobbed just after the war. He’s gone now of course. His boy’s not got the same touch. The next generation usually don’t, is that right, Roddy?” He pulled out another Capstan Full Strength and lit it with a match from a yellow Swan Vestas box.

Roddy was a similar vintage, and it dawned on me that Mr Evan’s, who had just retired, couldn’t have been much older than these two.

Roddy spoke. “Ach, yer such a misery guts, Chalkie. The boy’s just startin’ a new job. Sometimes the next generation take businesses to a higher level. They don’t all fail!” He smiled at me encouragingly, before the sting: “Although I’m surprised Graham’s given Glasgow to such a young chappie… But I’m sure you’ll do fine. Here, son. This’ll help you. It’s the travelling salesman’s bible.” He handed me a well-used street map of Glasgow. I could see that coming in handy.

I was living and learning…

Mr Ronson returned. “Right, John, I’ll take you round a few of your customers and show you how it’s done.”

I climbed into the passenger seat of his beautiful Triumph 2000 saloon car. Red leather seats and mahogany dashboard with Triumph’s sporty dials and gearstick. A boy’s dream car.

My new boss drove west towards Blairdardie and stopped outside a newsagent’s not unlike Dad’s. Mr Ronson introduced me to the owner as his new rep. They’d obviously known each other for years, and the shopkeeper had a list of lines required ready for the order. I could do this!

We talked shop for a few minutes once it was discovered I came from a retailing background. It was all very pleasant.

Another couple of shops and similar experiences and all of a sudden it was one o'clock and we were back at the depot.

"Right, John. You got the hang of it? Here's your customer lists and here's what we sell. Just match them together and we'll both be happy. Now let me show you to your car." *Yipee!*

We walked round the back of the building to where a dark green Morris 1100 was sitting. I wasn't sure what I'd been expecting. My pals had speculated I might get a Ford Cortina... But not to worry. It was a car. Bigger than Mum's mini. And it was mine!

"Pop back here when you've finished this afternoon. Good luck!" He handed me the car keys, and we shook hands.

Thus ended my training. Now I was on my own...

Chapter 8
First Job: First Car

"Good for you. Five orders in your second day!" Jane, Mr Ronson's secretary, beamed as she took the order sheets from me. I felt my neck reddening. Jane was in her mid-twenties. Shoulder length auburn hair, and bright green eyes. Compared to the utilitarian dullness of the admin office, she was a colourful tonic. Wearing a multi-coloured mini-dress, she exuded bright, bubbly positivity, the antithesis of the grumpy old reps I'd met the day before.

"I'd have managed more but I got lost trying to read that street map. I hadn't realised Glasgow was quite so big."

"Don't worry about it. You're young, time enough to learn. Are you enjoying the car? I'd imagine your chums will be jealous." She gave me another beaming smile.

I melted. "Well, yes." I tried not to stutter. "I don't know anyone else my age with a car. I'm quite chuffed actually," I confided.

"And so you should be. So, well done again and just drive carefully going home."

Life was good. Apart from getting just a bit lost, I seemed to be doing not too badly. Time for tea.

"So, you're pleased with yourself then?" Mum said as she ladled out the mince and tatties. My four wee brothers were seated round the yellow-topped kitchen table, Phil and Andy giggling at some private joke. *Better than their usual fisticuffs.*

"So, are you going to get promoted then, John?" Alan raised his head from his plate. "If you do a good job, that's what happens, eh?"

"It's a bit early for that, Alan." Thomas was playing the knowledgeable big brother. "John's only been working for two days."

"It's quite a small firm," I said. "There's not much room for promotion. Maybe if I do well, I could get a job in a bigger outfit. After a while of course."

"Just buckle down and get on with the job, John," Dad spoke up. "Don't count your chickens!"

"I hope you lot have started packing for Girvan. We are leaving on Friday morning, aren't we, Jackie?" Mum turned to her husband. Dad was always late in getting away for days out or family trips. It was a continual bone of contention.

"I've got to pop up to the shop then go to the bank, Marie. You know that."

"Well, make it as early as you can then, eh. I told the landlady we'd be there before four. She'll be expecting us." Mum turned to me again. "You're sure you'll be alright on your own, John? If it wasn't for this new job, you could come with us."

"I know, Mum, but I'll be fine. I'm quite looking forward to having the house to myself. I can play the guitar as loud as I like, and I won't have to suffer Phil and Andy's constant fighting. So long as you've left enough tins of food for me. And a wee bit of money for a chicken supper one night?" I really was looking forward to being on my own… I'd maybe have Joe and Jim and maybe even Paul over for a louder than usual jam on the guitars, but no parties planned. I had a new job and I had to concentrate.

The next couple of days were similar to my second day, although as I explored the further reaches of Greater Glasgow, I seemed to find it harder to locate some of the shops. I couldn't even find some of the street names on the map. I found myself asking pedestrians for directions, and I was amazed how many didn't know where their local shops were…

Friday morning came and I said my goodbyes to the family as I left for work.

"Don't work too hard, John. While we're on the beach. Ha Ha!" Alan's parting words as I walked out the door suited and booted.

"Well, how have you enjoyed your first week, John?" the delectable Jane had my full attention. "Mr Ronson says to tell you 'well done.'

Eighteen orders in the last four days. So, what are you going to do over the weekend? Any plans?"

She handed me next week's paperwork. Our fingers touched...

Electric...

Was this an invite? Don't be daft. She must be six or seven years older than you. Calm down, John!

"Well, not too much. I might go for a wee spin with a couple of mates, sorry, friends tonight. But I've... I've no plans for tomorrow... My folks are away..."

"So, you're on your own in a big empty house then?"

Wow!

"Do... do you have any plans?" My tongue was dry.

Jane gave me a knowing look. If she'd worn glasses, she'd have been peering over them. I felt my cheeks suddenly burning bright red.

"Mmmm. I could always change them..." I literally gulped. "Do you fancy a bit of... companionship... in your empty house this weekend?"

Jelly legs really can happen! "I...I...I..." I started to reply.

"You're lovely, John. And I'm sure we could have fun." She almost whispered. Her green eyes stared straight into my heart. Then she looked towards the boss's office. "But I'm already seeing someone. Graham and I have been going out since his divorce over a year ago."

I was shocked! This lovely creature was going out with that decrepit rheumy-eyed old man. *The world is mad! How could she waste her beauty and vitality on someone twenty years older than her while I'm free and single? And definitely younger and fitter. I fantasised...*

"Not at all, Jane. I...I was just answering your question." I tried to recover. "It's none of my business." *Oh, I wish it was!* "Have a great weekend. I'll see you on Monday. Cheerio then."

"Cheerio, John. You have a good one too."

Just then Mr Ronson came through from his office. He looked at me and waved. Jane gave me a wink as I was going out the door. *Did he see that wink? Oh God!* I waved back feebly.

When I got home there was a puddle of money left for me to treat myself. I decided I deserved that chicken supper after my first week's work as a salesman. I changed out of my suit and wandered around the big empty house. It was the first time I'd had it to myself since we'd moved in seven years earlier. A day I remembered well…

I phoned Joe, as I knew Jim was going out with his girlfriend that night. They'd been going together for quite a while and had kind of dropped out of the social scene altogether. *My time will come… Though I suspect Jane's out of my league for the moment…*

"So, do you fancy having a wee drive around in my new wheels?" I knew the answer.

"Ok. I'll get you at eight. We can go into town. See what's happening. Cheers."

"This is a bit of alright. I'm jealous." Joe was playing with the seat while I tuned in the basic radio. But it did play music.

We drove from Balornock into town and soaked up the Friday night atmosphere. Everywhere was busy. It was a nice early summer's evening, and we were enjoying the moment.

We circled George Square then worked our way up to Bath Street and along towards Charing Cross. There was still a lot of motorway construction going on up there, so we cut through Holland Street to get to Sauchiehall Street.

I waited to turn right. The road was clear enough to cross, so I manoeuvred to the other side of the road. A few yards up we spotted some old school friends waiting in the queue for the ABC Cinema. I pulled in and tooted the horn.

"Wow! What's this?" Eddie and Ian were impressed enough to leave their places in the queue.

"How do you like my company car, eh?" I boasted. "Just got it this week. I know it's not a Cortina but it'll do me."

“Ach, yer a jammy bugger. We’re aw still stuck on the buses an’ here’s you wi’ yer ain motor! We’ll need to meet up and go for a spin. How are ye fixed tomorrow?”

I said I’d give them a call and waved them back to their queue. The queue didn’t want to know. Remonstrations ensued…

Joe and I laughed as we decided to cross over and go down Douglas Street. I rolled down my window and waited for a break in the traffic on the two lanes coming up behind me. Then I pulled out and positioned myself in the middle of the second lane and indicated right.

There was nothing coming from the opposite direction, so I moved forward towards Douglas Street and was halfway across the third lane when there was an almighty bang!

“What the hell!” Joe grabbed the dashboard

We slid sideways as a Land Rover coming up on my outside ploughed into my front wing.

I jammed on the brakes but was still pushed a good few feet up the road.

We slithered to a stop, as did the whole of Sauchiehall Street.

Eddie and Ian appeared at Joe’s window. “Are youz alright? That wiz mental! Did you not know it’s a one-way street now? Been this way for weeks!”

Bloody hell. Bang goes my first good week. It might well be my last.

Fortunately, no one was hurt. The other driver was a middle-aged guy on his own, and he just wanted to swop insurance details. His Landover was barely marked. But the 1100 didn’t look in very good shape…

The police arrived but didn’t seem interested in charging anyone. It wasn’t the first time such an incident had happened since the one-way system had been imposed.

I sat in the driver’s seat and was relieved when the engine fired up. However, when I pulled away it was like driving a crab. The whole front had been bent to the left. I wasn’t a happy chappie…

Joe decided to lick his wounds and go home by bus. I limped home to an empty house and a miserable weekend of worry and anxiety. I wasn't looking forward to my second Monday working for Ronson's…

I drove the crab virtually sideways from Riddrie to my new place of employment, with a few double-takes en route. I parked in the yard in the deepest shadow I could find, and then gathered myself to brave the consequences.

Jane greeted me with a voluptuous smile. "And how's my favourite new rep this fine day then?" I felt my shoulders slump. She looked concerned. "Something wrong, John? You're very pale."

"I had a wee bit of a bump over the weekend, Jane. I'll need to tell Mr Ronson." Last week's confidence had been washed away over the previous two sleepless nights.

"Don't worry too much. He's quite soft really." *Well, you would know… Bitterness creeping in.*

Just then Mr Ronson's door opened. "You've crashed the car, John?" *Och, he can hear everything!* "Drive it round to McTaggart's Garage round the corner. Jane'll call them and tell them you're coming. Then take the wee mini-van out today. I'll see you when you're finished. By that time, we should have a report from the garage." He didn't smile. Jane kept her head down as she picked up the phone. *Ohh nooo…*

After shuffling the bent 1100 round to the garage where there was much in- taking of breath and shaking of heads, I reported to the storeman who handed me the keys to the dilapidated minivan that was used as a runabout.

Driving away I found the gearstick was like stirring spaghetti. Sometimes a gear could be found. Then it would just jump into neutral and the car would suddenly slow down. Torture! I missed my proper rep's car as I tried to find my way to that day's list of shops. And I still kept on getting lost.

Eventually, the day was done. I crawled back to the depot, steering with one hand while holding the gear stick in each gear slot with my left hand.

I was a tad tired…

Thankfully I'd stumbled on a couple of really good orders. So, I held my head high as I presented them to Jane. She handed them to Mr Ronson who was standing behind her. Still not smiling.

"How's the car?" I asked tentatively.

Mr Ronson shrugged his shoulders. "It's a write-off. The axle is cracked and they said it's not reparable." He sighed.

This is it. Here it comes…

"I'll give you a second chance, John. But from now on, you'll have to use the mini-van and leave it in the yard overnight. Then we'll see how you get on. Ok?"

I was amazed. He really was a nice guy after all. Jane was right. However, I only survived another six weeks of gear crunching, continually getting lost and subsequent poor sales before Jane, smiling grimly, told me Mr Ronson wanted to give me my pay packet himself.

He fingered the brown envelope and muttered something about not reaching my targets. *Targets? First I'd heard the word.* He was sorry but he'd have to 'let me go,' a phrase I didn't understand, until his sorrowful look helped the penny to drop.

My stomach felt heavy as I realised I'd failed. A rotten feeling when you're seventeen. Perhaps with better training, or even more than that first morning's mentoring, I might have lasted longer. Though I'm sure writing off the car must have counted against me…

He handed me my last pay packet. I was about to become officially unemployed for the first, and last, time. Dad later told me Roddy, one of the older reps, had taken over my patch. He'd covered it years before.

There was a wee postscript to this episode. A few weeks later Mum asked to look at "that street map you were using for Ronson's." She studied it for a few minutes with a puzzled look then turned it over and looked at the small print on the back.

"No wonder you kept getting lost. This map is dated 1951! It's as old as you are. It's not even got the housing schemes in it, never mind the motorway. Where'd you get it?"

Then I remembered the old rep, Roddy, wondering why the Glasgow territory had been given to someone so young and inexperienced. Before helpfully handing me a map that would hardly enhance my performance.

I was definitely living and learning...

Chapter 9
Oblivious Trainee

"Your Uncle Archie just called." Mum came into the living room where my head was buried in a book. I pulled myself away from the trials and tribulations of Don Corleone and Tom Hagen. "Uh Huh? Uncle Archie? Why'd he call? Something wrong with Auntie Margaret?" Mum's sister who lived in faraway East Kilbride.

"Not at all. Margaret's fine. Still involved in the local bowling club in between having babies. She's a busy lassie is our Margaret," Mum opinionated. "No. Something different. You know how Archie's a painter and decorator?" I was vaguely aware. "Well, he's been painting the main branch of R.S. McColl's in Gordon Street and he was talking to the manageress there. It seems they're looking for trainee managers. And he knows you're looking for work. So, he's given me a phone number you can call? Fancy?"

I'd been out of work for three weeks. Autumn had arrived. Dad had filled my old hours in the shop, and Peter's son was getting all the Sunday Barras work. *Because everyone thought I had a great new job.* So, I'd signed on at the Burroo, or Unemployment Exchange as it was officially called. I filled a mountain of forms. Then went to a different building to collect my Two Pounds Ten shillings benefit. The first time I queued for my unearned cash I was dumbfounded to be handed two pound notes and a strange new coin with flat sides.

"That's the new fifty pence coins. They're worth ten bob. It's legal tender. The shops have to accept them." The clerk perfunctorily passed the cash under the window. I picked up the shiny unfamiliar coin and instinctively weighed it. It felt similar to the good old half-crown, but the thought of a coin that could buy two packets of fags with change back made me keen to look after it. I pushed it carefully into the wee coin pocket on my jeans and decided to give it to Mum as my 'keep.'

Duly suited and booted I reported for my interview, which took place in the basement of the Gordon Street branch of the R.S. McColl newsagents' chain. My interviewer, the local Area manager, Mr Bruce, seemed impressed by my hands on knowledge. This time, a few days later, I received a formal confirmation through the post that I had been accepted as a trainee manager, with a view to managing my own branch after I'd passed through their training system. *Yippee! A real job!* A very different and much more professional set up than my last employer.

After a couple of weeks, I was sent to the training office above a branch in the remote wilderness of Carmunnock, a long double-bus ride from Riddrie. *Oh, how I wished I still had my Lambretta! And the freedom I'd tasted.*

It was a three-week course covering everything from how to perfectly wrap a box of chocolates, through merchandising and stock control, to balancing the cash at the end of each day. Finally, the 'class' of twelve assorted trainees were given an assessment test.

While there was definitely an element of teaching a very young granny how to suck eggs, I did learn some better ways of working than Dad's somewhat make it up as you go along systems. In any case I was delighted to be told I was the first trainee to manage a hundred percent pass mark…

"The sky's the limit for you in this firm, John. You could end up as, say, a senior buyer in our parent company, Cadburys. Just do what you know. And keep on learning. You can never have too much knowledge." The trainer's good advice has stuck with me ever since. In theory at least…

Feeling you're good at what you're doing is a great motivator. It transforms the daily grind into something to look forward to. I was energised and enthusiastic as I plunged into the buzz that was the lead up to Christmas in the very busy store. So different from the previous year's lethargy of wet Wednesdays in the Kelvin Hall.

It wasn't all plain sailing. And I learned another life lesson.

People don't all share the same values.

A week or so after Christmas, a new girl, Pauline, started as a full-time counter hand. Ages with me, she had auburn hair and green eyes and reminded me a bit of the delectable Jane of Ronson's. Though not so obviously worldly wise.

We two were the youngsters in the team of around ten or twelve staff it took to run the busy store. The average age was around mid-thirties. I got along particularly well with the manageress, Mrs Forrest, an energetic leader, who ran the shop with a bright, enthusiastic efficiency. She had been very diligent at filling any gaps in my training that I would need for my eventual promotion to branch manager, sometime in the misty future.

Pauline and I had been on the same shift together a few times. She had a bit of spark, and there was a frisson of banter between us. Eventually, I asked her if she fancied going to the cinema. *Butch Cassidy and the Sundance Kid* was on at the Odeon and we could go after the shop closed. It wasn't exactly a date; more a trial run.

Pauline told me she'd only got the job because her sister, Kate, had worked in another branch for years. She herself had hardly any shop experience. I said she seemed to be managing fine and fitting in well with the rest of the staff.

A few days later I went for my lunch in the staff room. A small room in the basement beside Mrs Forrest's office. There were a couple of benches and hooks for the staff's coats and bags, etc. Unusually there was no one else sharing my break time, so I just buried myself in my book.

I finished my sandwich and looked at my watch. Two o'clock. Time to get back upstairs. As I opened the door to the corridor, I was surprised to see Mr Bruce and another stern-faced man I hadn't seen before. Mrs Forrest was there too, looking serious. She asked me to come into her office.

"Sit down here please, John."

"What's the matter, Mrs Forrest?" I was mystified. Mr Bruce and the other chap went into the staff room I'd just left.

"We have to wait for a couple of minutes, John. It shouldn't be long." I could see her stress. "Is there anything you want to tell me?" Mrs Forrest had lost her usual effervescence. She was quite strained as she doodled on a pad on her desk.

I didn't understand the question. What on earth would I want to tell her? That I'd made up the cigarette order as she'd asked? That my ham sandwich was a bit dry? *What was going on?*

Within a couple of minutes, Mr Bruce stuck his head round the door. "All ok, Maureen." He turned and looked at me. "It's all fine, John. I'll see you next time I'm in, alright? We have to go now."

I nodded incomprehensively then turned to Mrs Forrest. "Please tell me what on earth is happening?"

My manageress visibly relaxed, took a breath then explained: "I'm awfully sorry John. You obviously don't know anything about what's been going on. There's been a spate of thefts from staff purses and bags and Mr Bruce brought the security advisor in to try and catch the culprit."

They thought I would steal from my work colleagues? That's horrible!

"I told them I was sure you wouldn't be involved. You're a nice young man who just wants to learn the ropes… but when they discovered you'd gone out with Pauline…"

"Are you saying Pauline did it?" This was getting worse by the minute.

"Afraid so, John. We set the same trap this morning, and she fell for it. A marked five-pound note out of Josie's purse. She's admitted it now. I'm really sorry you had to go through this. You're a good lad. Try to look upon this unpleasant episode as an opportunity. Now the management *know* you're an honest employee. Not many people get a chance to prove that. Now away upstairs and finish your shift." She smiled wanly, obviously uncomfortable with the whole situation.

I didn't know what to think as I went upstairs. Pauline had seemed like such a nice normal girl! But she's actually a thief! Thank God I didn't get any closer; I could have been her victim… But I had a really rotten feeling in my stomach. They thought I was maybe a thief too! And I was honestly oblivious to the concept. Somehow, I felt tainted.

This living and learning wasn't always such a lark.

Chapter 10
Crossed Lines

In the black and white days before everything was digitalised and computerised, telephones, or what are now referred to as landlines, had an intrinsic flaw: Crossed lines, when two people having a telephone conversation would be interrupted by a third party. You'd be in the middle of a deeply personal conversation and completely out of the blue a strange voice would interrupt. "Is that you, Alfie? It's me, Brenda. Where's my money?" Sometimes it would take a fair bit of persuasion by both original conversationalists to convince the stranger that neither of them was involved in any conspiracy, and get them to hang up.

Big Jim had another way of dealing with the crossed line scenario.

He'd take them on…

One of Jim's impromptu performances occurred while we happened to be chatting about cars and their upkeep when an unexpected voice broke in…

"Hello, hello, is that McFarlane's Garage? Rory McTavish here."

Jim couldn't help himself: "Yes, Mr McTavish, this is MacFarlane's Garage. How can I help you?"

I shut up. I didn't know exactly what was coming next but I had a good guess that Jim, an instinctive prankster, was about to wind up some poor unsuspecting victim.

I covered the mouthpiece of my phone. Poor Mr McTavish simply wanted to enquire if his car was ready to be picked up after its annual service and MOT.

"What car did you leave with us, sir?" Jim asked.

"Oh… don't you know me? You must be new. The navy blue Jaguar. My pride and joy. Wonderful condition! I'm really careful how I look after it. I mean I check the oil and water every week and I check the tyres…"

Jim was getting bored. "Oh, now I know the car!" He continued. "Ahh. Mmm I've got your bill here." A loud intake of breath…

"Yes? Yes? Is there a problem?" Mr McTavish was getting anxious.

"Well, you see Mr McTavish. A couple of the younger mechanics took it for a road test at lunch time… Well, more of a spin if I'm honest. It's been such a lovely blue-sky day. They went just a *wee* bit fast over that humpbacked bridge outside Kilsyth… The exhaust kind of snapped when they landed… And brushed the dry stone wall…" Jim broke off.

"Excuse me! Kilsyth? That's twenty miles from here! "

"Well, yes, I know. But it's such a smashing car; I think they got a bit carried away. Anyway, when we add a new exhaust and headlamp and some filler for the dent. The bill comes to..."

I could hear Mr McTavish hyperventilating.

"DO YOU EXPECT ME TO PAY FOR YOUR WORKERS' INCOMPETENCE AND DAMAGING MY CAR? ARE YOU COMPLETELY MAD? LET ME TALK TO PETER MACFARLANE. I'VE KNOWN THE MAN FOR FORTY YEARS! WE GO TO THE SAME CHURCH TOGETHER!"

Jim replied in a soothing voice, "I'm very sorry you feel that way, Mr McTavish. But I'm just the messenger. Mr MacFarlane just popped round to the bookies to place a couple of bets… Why don't you call back in a few minutes? Bye for now."

Jim hung up before the unfortunate Mr McTavish had time to bust another gut. I called Jim back and had a rare old laugh imagining the bollocking whoever picked up the phone in the real garage was going to get…

A year or so later there was a different victim…

"You've to go to the Partick branch at 237 Dumbarton Road for 9 o'clock on Monday morning," Mum informed me one bleak Saturday afternoon. "Thomas got a phone call yesterday from your head office."

I was dismayed but not surprised. As part of my training, I'd been transferred to different branches as relief assistant manager. I'd been in three different shops in the previous three months. My dismay was because I didn't know that branch or that part of the west end and I was enjoying the busy St Enoch's Square branch.

I stared at Thomas's scribbles on the tiny scrap of paper.

Way before mobiles and internet, with no chance of talking to anyone at head office before 9am on the Monday to check, I just had to get up early, get the No 6 bus all the way from Riddrie to Kelvingrove Art Galleries. Then start walking.

That's how I found myself in my good suit striding briskly along Dumbarton Road. Reading off the odd numbers. After a few blocks, I was getting closer. 231, 233, 235… Then… nothing… Eh? No shop. No building! Just weeds growing in a dirty plot of ground. Obviously a demolished building site.

Ach, Thomas must have got the number wrong. I'll just keep walking. Soon come across the R.S. McColl's logo.

I traipsed another three blocks checking both sides of the road. Later, rather than sooner, I asked an elderly lady, with a definite Partick air about her, if she could direct me to the nearest R.S. McColl's.

"Naw, son. There's nae McColl's in Partick. There's a Birrells further along the road an' wee Jimmy's newsagent's jist across the road ower there." She pointed then looked me up and down with mild curiosity.

By this time, I was going to be late. But not sure what to do, I decided to aim for the nearest phone box and wait till 9 o'clock then call Head Office. Something only my store managers were supposed to do… I was tense and worried. Up until that moment I hadn't blotted my copybook.

I got through remarkably quickly in those halcyon days before 0845 numbers were invented.

After nervously asking for the correct address for the Partick branch, I was surprised how nice the girl at the end of the line was, once she understood my predicament.

"We don't have a branch in Partick." I felt sweat gathering.

What the hell?

"Could someone have given you a false address as a prank?" the kindly voice on the end of the line suggested.

Then it dawned… *Bloody Jim Lang!*

Jim couldn't help abusing gullibility.

And Thomas had more than his fair share. So, when Jim had recognised his voice when he'd called, he couldn't resist blurting out the plausible but potentially career-destroying misinformation!

Thankfully my current boss in St Enoch's had a decent sense of humour when I nervously called her with my unusual excuse.

"Ok, John. Now I've heard it all. Just get on a bus and get here ASAP! We've got a queue out the door. Hurry!

However, Jim enjoyed his beer shampoo the next time we caught up…

Chapter 11
Sangria Shakes

After I'd got over Jim's attempt to wreck my career, life settled down to a decent routine. Still playing my relief assistant manager role, I enjoyed the variety of working in different branches, usually in the city centre. Having been employed with McColl's for over six months, I discovered I would be entitled to a two-week break in the summer. With pay! *Yay!*

As it happened, one of Dad's staff, Maisy, and her husband, Billy, were organising a trip to sunny Spain, in a hired minibus. And they had one free space, so I had a chance of going abroad again. Without school rules this time!

"Mum? How come John's getting to go to Spain and we're not?" Phil wondered between mouthfuls of corn flakes.

"Well, one reason is you're all still at school and the holidays don't start for another three weeks." Mum held the table's attention. "Another reason is John is paying for this trip out of his own wages. And the third reason is there's no more room in the minibus."

"Ach, that's rubbish," Alan interjected. "School's a waste of time now. We're supposed to be starting next year's work over these last few weeks. There's no chance I'm gonna remember any of it after the summer holidays! Why can't we all just squeeze into Dad's car and follow John to Spain?"

"That's a great idea!" Andy was excited. "We could overtake John and beat them. Dad's car can go faster than any daft minibus."

"Afraid not, Andy. But I'll be back in a couple of weeks and tell you all about it." I tried to appease my wee brothers as I lugged the big family case out the back door. Billy and Maisy waved from the waiting minibus. I was the last pick up.

"Now, don't you do anything silly, John." Mum held both of my hands tightly as she looked me squarely in the eyes. "This isn't like Rome with teachers looking after you. Billy and Maisy are going on *their* family holiday. You'll have to look after *yourself!* Now give me a big, big hug."

With Mum's warning ringing in my ears, I climbed into the crowded minibus to be confronted by a bunch of happy holidaymakers. *Looks like a fair mixture of folk! I hope I get on with them ok. Ach, I'll be fine!*

"Squeeze in, Big Boy!" One of the two blond young women sitting tightly together on the back seat gave me a big beaming grin. Her companion waved me in and shouted towards the front. "He's even better looking than you said he was, Maisy. We'll need to watch out for our John. The senoritas will be all over him! That's if I don't baby snatch him!" I felt my neck reddening as I squeezed into the last remaining seat behind Maisy who was sitting up front, road map open on her knees.

"Alright, John? Ready for our big adventure?" Maisy twisted round to face me. She was really the only person on the bus I knew, and while I'd met Billy, her husband, and their three kids in the shop, this was the first time I'd been in their company.

"Remember to be careful, John." Mum stuck her head through my open window, her dark curly hair brushing my face as she gave me a last-minute kiss on the cheek.

"Don't you worry, Mrs D. We'll make sure John's looked after! Hello, by the way. I'm Janet, and the rock chic beside me is Marie. We reckon John's worth the watching!" With that, Janet let out a raucous laugh. Mum's eyes narrowed. *My poor boy!*

Billy let the clutch out and we were on our way. Roof rack loaded. Wee brothers running along the pavement waving.

Yay! Adventure time!

In the front seat between Billy and Maisy was a head of wispy, badly dyed ginger hair. "Hello, I'm Mrs Buchanan, but seeing as how we're going to be living together, I suppose you can call me Victoria. How'd you do?" The elderly woman, mischievous glint in her watery eyes, turned and offered me her hand, palm down.

I looked at Maisy who shrugged as if she'd long since given up on her mother's eccentricities. "Meet Mum, John. Mad as a hatter. I think you're supposed to kiss it."

I dutifully held the wrinkled fingers and gently kissed the back of her hand. “Pleased to meet you, Victoria. You seem like fun.”

“Have you ever tasted sangria, John?” The old woman grinned showing a mouthful of uneven teeth.

I shrugged my shoulders and shook my head. “Never heard of it.”

“Oh, you will, John. You will…” chimed the chorus from the back seats.

It was a long and tedious journey down the unfinished motorway network all the way to Dover; eventually, with time to spare, we caught the ferry to Calais.

Billy was visibly tiring as we drove into the bowels of the ship. I had offered my services as a relief driver but had been diplomatically told that the insurance would have been too expensive. “Just you relax and enjoy the ride.”

The next day, after a well-deserved good night’s sleep in a Calais hostel and a very early rise, we motored on down through France.

Hours passed and I dozed off. I felt my shoulder being gently shaken and woke up just as the minibus rounded a wide corner with steep mountains on either side of the road.

Everyone on board burst out of their lethargy as the spectacle of white tipped Pyrenees suddenly spread before us. “That’s awesome!” Wee Billy piped up.

“Not long to go now, people,” Maisy said. “The map says we’re about an hour away.”

Oh, thank God! My bum is numb…

Almost exactly an hour later we reached Santa Maria de Mar, a small fishing village on the Mediterranean coast. Billy gingerly steered the van round tight village corners and very narrow streets.

Billy and Maisy had rented an old bungalow at the back of the village. It had a simple rustic look with a red tiled roof and worn shutters on the windows. Just enough beds, if you count the sofa bed in the living room, I had been volunteered to use…

We unloaded the van as quickly as we could and decided we had time to explore our new surroundings.

The cobbled streets were quiet until we came down to the harbour area where a few locals were ambling along. There was a sprinkling of other touristy-looking folk.

“Now this is nice. There’s a warm gentle breeze coming off the sea and I can spy an open bar just at the end of the harbour. Anybody fancy?” Victoria looked thirsty.

Maisy glanced at her exhausted husband. “Not for us, thanks, Mum. We’ll take the kids and unpack, have a bite to eat, and I know Billy’s knackered. Early night for us. John and the girls can keep you company.”

We strolled to the bar where Victoria took charge and attempted to order her long-awaited sangria while Janet and Marie went to freshen up.

The barman poured four insipid looking glasses out of a jug, and Victoria lifted one and had a sip. Her face screwed up. She raised her voice as if volume equals clarity.

“I said proper sangria! Not that pretendy stuff the weans can drink! I’ve been on the road for two days cooped up beside my son-in-law. I need a proper drink! Comprendes?”

The barman looked bemused as Victoria waved her glass of pink liquid in his face.

“Keep yer hat oan, Vicky, the cavalry’s here… Marie; where’s that phrase book you were carrying?” Janet took charge while I hung back.

“Podemos tener un poco de sangría fuerte por favor.” Marie gave our order to the barman, who nodded and smiled then started busying himself mixing bottles and fruits behind the bar. “I’ve been practising that ever since you told me what you were looking forward to back in Calais.”

Victoria sat at the table and visibly relaxed. She waved me over. “Sit down, John. Now you’ll taste what I was talking about. We’re having a treat. Proper sangria. You’ll love it!”

"There ye go, handsome John. Get that down you." Janet poured a generous tumbler full of the rich looking fruit-filled concoction from the large jug delivered by the barman.

"Salue! To the four amigos!" Victoria raised her glass and we all followed suit, swallowing what tasted like the nectar of the Gods. It was delicious! Sweet and fruity with a hint of spices. So refreshing after the long hot journey.

After the third jug, we decided we should show face at the bungalow. Marie and Janet had been chatting with a couple of French lads who had told them there was a small nightclub in the middle of the old town… Maybe see them later?

We snaked our way back to the bungalow. "I feel all Spanish now I've had a dose of sangria." Victoria snapped her fingers in a poor pastiche of a flamenco dancer.

"I can see you've had more than a dose." Billy pointed out as the two girls and I staggered through the door behind her.

"That's ok, we're going to a nightclub, ain't we, Janet?" Marie started pulling her jumper off as she made her way through to their bedroom. "Gotta glam up quick."

"Time I started unpacking," I muttered as I opened my suitcase.

"Hey, John! You want to come with us glamour pussies?" A shout from the other end of the house.

I looked towards Maisy who just shrugged her shoulders. "You're a big boy, but I'm sure the girls will look after you. Have fun."

A few minutes later the two girls appeared in the hall doorway. They had glammed up very well!

Two blond stunners wearing low-cut, very short mini-dresses and very high heels. Heavy duty mascara completed the Dusty Springfield imagery. They simultaneously pouted their bright pink lips in my direction. "C'mon, Big Boy, let's see what this town's got to offer. Your Levi's are fine. Just change that sweaty T-shirt!"

What red-bloodied seventeen-year-old could resist? Especially after my first three 'proper' sangrias.

Quickly pulling on my best T-shirt, I waved to Maisy and the kids as we went out the front door, a blond on each arm. *Can life get any better?*

The club was small and very dark. Occasional red lights dimly illuminated the bistro tables and booths that surrounded the little dance floor. It was very crowded and I could barely see, but we were waved over to a booth by the two French guys the girls had met earlier. We all squeezed round the table and a waitress appeared for our drinks order.

"I'll stick to sangria." I thought I should wear my Captain Sensible hat. I was still a bit woozy from the bar. Moments later I was sipping a weaker version of the earlier nectar. It would do…

The music changed from some Spanish love song to the Rolling Stone's "Honky Tonk Woman." Janet grabbed me and pulled me on to the floor. *This is nothing like the Bundoran Club!*

Dancing among the sweaty, circling crowd. Then back to the table. Another drink had appeared. It tasted different again.

Both girls got me up and we really rocked to Tommy Roe's "Dizzy!" *A very suitable title,* I thought, sandwiched between two gyrating blonds.

The French guys started dancing with the girls, so I turned and found myself pairing up with a very pretty Dutch girl on holiday with her family. We had a drink at the bar then went back onto the dance floor.

More great music. More great dancing. Then the Dutch girl had to go. She was going home next morning… *Oh well.*

I pushed through the crowd to get back to the booth but there was no sign of the girls. The French guys shrugged their shoulders when I asked for them. *Damn. They'll be hard to find in this light…*

Oblivion…

What's that? Oh no! It's a toilet pan! Where the Hell am I? Very uncomfortably half-lying on the floor of a toilet cubicle. Walls bright orange and dirty white. Floor of stained concrete. Left arm stopping my head from resting on the toilet seat. *This isn't good!*

I pulled myself up and realized I had no trousers on! Bare legs sprawled on the concrete floor. *Where's my shoes? For God's sake! What the Hell's happened?*

I managed to clamber onto the toilet seat to take stock of the situation. Head still spinning, but I could feel myself rapidly sobering up. A panic welled up as it dawned on me that all I had on was my T-shirt and a pair of Y-fronts. My prized Levi's and new tan boots were gone!

As I sat for a moment trying to piece together what had happened, I realised that the thumping music had disappeared. A Spanish voice muttering on the other side of the cubicle door. *Oh, God. Is that my attacker?* I felt all over. I didn't seem to be hurting anywhere. Just my pride! *I gotta get out of here!*

Suddenly, I had a desperate urge to run. I pulled open the door and stared at an old janitor mopping the floor. He stopped muttering and looked me up and down.

"Estás bien?" he asked stepping towards me.

"No chance, mate!" I replied as I pushed past him and through the door to the reception area. There was a cleaner brushing the floor. *What time is it?*

I rushed at the double doors expecting them to be locked, but they gave way and I ran into the street.

I had no idea where I was!

A narrow curving street.

Dark shadows and silence.

The lamps attached to the buildings dropped puddles of light. I looked down at my dirty T-shirt and bare feet. Hide in the shadows.

I crept up one curve. Windows shuttered. Everywhere looked the same! It was a labyrinth. Every corner was a clone of the last one.

I stood still.

A low diesel throb bouncing off the curving walls.

Lights illuminating a corner a block away.

They turned towards me and started flashing.

What now?

I stood trapped like the proverbial rabbit...

The minibus shuddered to a stop in front of me and the side door slid open. Marie and Janet jumped out and dragged me into the van.

"Look at the state you're in, ya daft pillock!" Marie put a blanket round my shivering shoulders. "What happened to your jeans?"

Billy looked round. "Well, at least we've found you. We've been combing these streets for ages. Good job I had a couple of hours sleep. Though I can't say it's great fun to be up at three in the morning."

I felt terrible. "I'm sorry. I don't know what happened, the last thing I remember is looking for Janet and Marie." Billy shook his head as he reversed the van round the narrow corner behind us.

Crunch!

The van had hit something.

Billy threw the door open and marched to the back of the van. Marie peered out the rear window. "Uh oh, he's hit a bollard. He doesn't look too happy."

Billy climbed back into the driver's seat and slammed his door. His shoulders drooped. "Need to try and tap out that dent or we'll lose our deposit."

With that, he revved the engine and bounced over the cobbles. As we were thrown about in the back, we looked at each other and tried very hard not to giggle...

Worse was to come. Waking up the next day it finally dawned on me that I'd not only lost my best jeans and boots, I had my wallet and passport in my back pocket.

I'd lost my lot.

I was penniless and passport-less.

Bloody Hell!

What about getting back through passport control?

Bloody Hell!

"I heard you had quite a night of it, John. Wandering around in your Y-fronts in the dead of night." Maisy smiled at me as she dished out cereals for the kids.

"I've lost my money and passport, Maisy. All I've got is the tenner Mum made me hide in my suitcase..."

Victoria came in stretching her arms and yawning wildly. "Fancy some more sangria, John, eh?" Her laughter lines crinkled.

I explained that I was now completely skint and had lost my passport. There was a general agreement that I had to report the loss to the British Consulate but it was pretty far away, and I could hardly inconvenience Billy any more. So, we went for plan B.

Victoria and I went to the local Police Station where the Sergeant, after a lot of sign language and gesticulations, finally understood the story of how and where I'd lost my passport.

He then spent a good thirty minutes writing the whole report down in unexpectedly beautiful Spanish calligraphy, finishing with the most elaborate signature I've ever seen. He then duly stamped the document with his official local police stamp, stood up, and handed it to me with a flourish and a smile.

He saluted. "Bueno suerte, senor!"

I'd need all the luck I could get...

The rest of our time in Spain blurred into sunny days on the beach and occasional forays to a local hotel's pool. Victoria and I sipped more moderate sangrias while keeping our eyes on the kids. This let Billy and Maisy have some time to themselves and we all settled into enjoying ourselves very pleasantly.

However, the lack of a passport meant the journey home had a couple of moments...

Just before we crossed into France, Billy told me to lie down between the seats while coats were thrown over me. I felt like an escaping prisoner of war in an old war movie.

I held my breath while Maisy handed over a bunch of passports through the window to the French border guard,

Everyone went quiet as he stuck his head through her window and counted heads.

Except wee Brenda, Billy and Maisy's four-year-old.

"Why's John got coats on top of him?"

I gulped. Mouth as dry as dust.

"Hiya, John! I can see you…"

Instant sweat.

I felt the coats being pulled off me just as Maisy started thanking the guard just a tad loudly and Marie distracted Brenda by offering her prized sunglasses…

We started moving… Phews all round!

The UK border wasn't quite so easy. "I really don't want to go to jail because you got pissed and lost your passport!" Billy said as we sat round a table in the big lounge on the ferry. There had been no checks leaving France. Maybe the French reckoned any illegal immigrants were Britain's problem. Maybe they still think that…

"We'll wait just past the off-ramp. If you don't come off the ship, we'll find a phone box and call your mum and dad. Good Luck, Johnny boy!"

After hugs all round, I was left sitting alone at our table. Gigantic butterflies flapping inside. We'd explained my situation to the ship's purser who said I couldn't leave the ferry until I'd been interviewed by *Special Branch!* I thought they were only on the telly!

What'll I do if they don't let me off?

I'm sure I've heard of detention centres for illegal immigrants…

Am I an illegal immigrant?

I could have made the whole story up! And now Maisy and Billy aren't even here to back me up…

This could get heavy…

After what felt like ages with only me and the cleaners in the room, two apparitions came towards me. Two belted trench coats and one trilby. Two square jaws and one clipped moustache. Four narrowed eyes.

They kept their coats on as they sat down.

Moustache spoke. “You say you’re British and your passport was stolen? But you’ve no other ID? Why didn’t you report to the consulate in Barcelona?”

I explained that having also lost all my money I couldn’t afford the transport. We only had one driver, and he wasn’t willing to "*waste a day and a tank of petrol because I’d been stupid.*" I produced the artistically written Spanish police report which I’d been looking after very carefully.

They studied the document, asked my name and address and date of birth. Took neat notes. Stood up.

Moustache looked down on me. “Wait there.” They left the lounge carrying my one tenuous proof of my right to re-enter my home country…

How bureaucratic will they be?

Maybe they have to put me in a detention centre…

They didn’t say how senior they were… Did they?

I might have to be interviewed by other people. Customs and Excise?

Long minutes passed and I was aware of crew members looking at me as they went about their post sailing duties.

What if they don’t let me in!

Will I have to sail back to France?

My God, I’m technically stateless! I can’t live on the ship.

I’ve no money to buy food. Mammy, Daddy!

As I was getting ever more agitated, the two trench coats came back.

Moustache spoke. “Right, Mr Dickson. We’ve decided you’re not a threat to the security of the nation. You can leave the ship. Next time, be more careful, eh?”

He handed me a stamped slip of paper for Passport Control and I walked off the ferry, up the ramp, and ran to the blinking lights of the minibus.

Lesson number umpteen. Alcohol and women begat trouble! Be careful out there in the real world…

Chapter 12
Family Business

"Do you still like working for McColl's, John?" Mum asked as I was eating my toast and tea before going to bed one night.

"What do you mean? Aye, it's fine. I wish the pay was a bit more. But the people I'm working with are nice. I quite like the fact I'm the firm's youngest ever manager. The supplier's reps come in regularly and enjoy a chat. And I'm in charge of the rota. That's a perk!" I gave Mum a questioning look.

"No. It's nothing. I heard your dad talking to Maisy in the shop about their staff shortages. He muttered something about John working for the competition…"

I sat up. "Och, that's not fair, Mum! I left because there wasn't enough work for me. And Dad's shop is over a mile away from Smithycroft Road. It's hardly competition…"

Mum motioned me to calm down. "Don't worry about it. I was just checking. If you're happy there, that's all that matters. Your dad will manage fine. It's not a major issue."

But it rankled. I'd feel guilty going to my easy-to-run shop with all the backing of a major organisation, knowing Dad was having to sometimes work double shifts because of a temporary shortage of suitable staff.

Nothing else was said as summer moved into autumn and both businesses geared up for Christmas. It was also the beginning of the party season and a good time to try out the range of dance halls in the city.

Saturday nights were now about trying out new venues. Joe and I went to the Locarno in Sauchiehall Street and found we were the youngsters there. A heaving place where it was hard to tell what ages the girls were. Lots of heavy makeup and lived-in faces.

Joe called one Friday. "Let's try the Electric Garden. I heard it's a cool vibe. They've got some good bands on and we can check out the talent."

A good plan. The talent was more than good. The music was excellent. Bands such as Tear Gas, who went on to become the Sensational Andy Harvey Band, and The Dream Police, who begat the Average White Band.

The format was more informal than some other venues. While it too was heaving, the clientele had a softer, more agreeable look. The girls would dance in pairs or threes, and it was alright to ask one girl to dance. And if she 'stayed up' after the first dance… A flutter in your stomach, a smile on your face, and a kiss and a cuddle on the way home!

The next stage in the game was maybe a date where we'd meet up for a movie, and, if nothing disastrous happened and the spark was still smouldering, we'd have the true testing date: the ultimate couple's dance hall: Joanna's in Bath Street where the music was loud but smooth. The beat was on! Just that bit smoochier…

Normally relationships could last from just that first date to maybe a couple of months. Then maybe a wee vagueness about the next date. "Not quite sure what I'm doing…" Or even the ultimate humiliation, actually being dumped. The: "I'm sorry, it's me not you" routine…

Shoulders back, good gear on… back to the Electric Garden, or even the Maryland round the corner, and start the process again…

But none of the professional venues ever really replaced the sheltered womb that the Glasgow schools' sponsored Bundoran Club had been.

All early hormones, soft drinks, and a great live band. Brilliant!

Once we'd climbed those two flights of stairs to the scaled down version of the proper dance halls of Glasgow, the traditional rituals were sacrosanct.

The girls in all their glorious variations of miniskirts and kinky boots would gather on one side of the windowless hall. The boys with hair just long enough to annoy their teachers, sporting bell-bottom trousers and paisley-patterned shirts from C&A, eyed up the talent from the other side of the room.

"One, two, three, four!" The drums would beat, the guitars would riff, the sax would fire us up…

The girls would dance in pairs to house band, The Beings, very classy versions of Tamla Motown numbers such as "I Heard It Through the Grapevine" or "This Old Heart of Mine."

We boys had to have a pal so we could ask both girls to dance, as it just wasn't done to leave the *other girl* dancing on her own.

Any boy who tried to peel off one girl and leave her chum without a partner would find himself briskly doing the walk of shame back to the boy's wall.

I didn't meet Mary on the dance floor. That's when she was going out with Gordon, whose dad was a dentist. He was a friend of a friend. We all got to know each other around a Formica table, supping Irn Bru out of wee glass bottles, in the little cafe halfway up the stairs to the dance hall. However, I did recognize that Mary was brighter than most of the girls I had met. And she didn't need to surround herself with girlfriends. She could hold her own if she was the only girl in a bunch of boys. Mary had sparkle! She exuded fun and frivolity.

In between dances, there'd be a break. I'd come down the half-stairs to the cafe and share another soft drink with Mary. We'd play the *Don't Blink First* game… Eyeball to eyeball across that Formica table. Childish, but somehow meaningful. Needless to say, Mary always won. Then she'd go back to Gordon…

Some of our bunch knew some of their group and so there was a natural evolution and widening of our circle of friends. This was way before Facebook. The only way anyone got to make new friends was to *actually* meet them. The system seemed to work…

The various 'crowds' intermingled and drifted apart over the next couple of years. I had seen Mary occasionally, such as the gig in the old folk's home, and with other people in the Lido or Kenco coffee bars. She fell under the radar until I bumped into her in the throes of my second date routine (i.e. going to a movie). It was in George Square, with a blond girl, whose name I can't remember. I'm sure she was lovely.

There was Mary, hurrying to be on time for her own, possibly second, date.

I waved. "Hello. And how the Devil are you? You're looking great!" And so she was. A breath of elegance and joy.

We chatted for a few minutes asking after mutual friends and then my date arrived. A moment of awkward body language. We waved goodbye.

I remember thinking while I was in the cinema. *Mary's head and shoulders above this girl. She's full of personality. And she's got a brain!*

I couldn't wait for the film to end so I could go home and call her.

Looking up her number in an old 'black book.'

Is half-past eleven too late to phone?

What if her mum or dad picks up?

They didn't…

Mary answered.

I was happy.

I asked, "So, how was your date?"

"It was good. We saw *Kelly's Heroes*. A wartime comedy. It was a laugh. Did you have a nice night?"

"Well, we went to see *Catch 22*. I'd read the book. I don't think she fully understood it. She kept asking 'why is he called *Major Major?*'"

Mary laughed. There was no malice. But she got it.

So, I said, "How's about meeting up in the Kenco Coffee House tomorrow at lunchtime? Old time's sake?"

"Sounds like a good idea…"

Aahh… I slept the sleep of hope and excitement.

Would now be a good time to pick up a pair of drumsticks?

The lunch was great. Although we were only eighteen, we had lots to catch up on. I was a tad perturbed to hear some of the stories Mary had to tell about previous dates and boyfriends. Even more perturbed to hear her talk about how well Dennis (the drumming pudding) was doing…

“He’s landed a great job!” Mary said enthusiastically. “He’s working for the BBC as a researcher. Sometimes he gets to go to London to link up with people involved in Top of the Pops. Get’s to go backstage and meet the bands. Brilliant, eh?”

Absolutely brilliant? I don’t think so! Here I am thinking I’m doing well managing a newsagent’s branch. No contest, eh?

I couldn’t resist, “He’s not playing the drums, I hope. Can’t see Keith Moon putting up with such competition. Or even Ginger Baker!”

Mary laughed. “That day when you kicked his hi-hat away? The look on his face was priceless! I think he got the message. Well done you! Though he is still a nice guy, even if he does tend to boast a bit…” She looked inward and then smiled. Delectably.

Aha… A chink!

I took my chance. “Can’t pretend to have the ears of the rich and famous. I’m only the youngest ever manager in R.S. McColls. But I’m here and now. And back in the day when we used to play at ‘who blinks first’ in the Bundy café, there was definitely a connection. Don’t you think?”

Mary brushed her hair from her eyes. “I know what you mean. Actually, that ride on the back of your scooter was pretty good too, you know. Reminded me how cool you were. Do you still ride it?”

I shrugged my shoulders and told her the story. *Bloody thieves!*

I made it slightly more dangerous than the actuality. With me sliding in the mud, hanging on to the back of the scooter as the thieves were kicking me away! But the result was the same. No scooter now. *Had I blown my edge?*

“That’s a shame. Too many rotten people out there. Maybe you’ll get another one someday. This has been great. Thanks for lunch, a real blast from the past!”

Mary stood up and smiled. I felt myself standing awkwardly. Should I try and kiss her?

Mary took the initiative and pecked me on the cheek.

And whispered in my ear…

“Top of the Pops is full of posers. You’re for real, John.”

My neck flushed all the way past my ears.

“Right then... Any plans for Friday night?”

After Christmas, outside forces were conspiring to change my world around in other ways.

I learned that McColl’s were to be taken over by the owners of Birrells, their main competitor.

And that meant my job wouldn’t be the same.

Branch autonomy would go as Birrells operated a centralised distribution system. Company reps wouldn’t need to deal with the individual branches. I enjoyed their chit chat and the freedom of ordering what I thought would sell in my store. And the worst aspect was the rota would be handed down from the new head office. Bang goes my main perk!

I’d go from being the *Branch Manager* to simply being a kind of *Team Leader.* Not the same.

On the plus side, Mary and I had had that follow-up date and Dennis wasn’t really in the conversation. We’d now been going out together for a couple of months and I felt I could talk about my anxieties.

“You told me your dad’s got a job for you if you want it. Why not talk to him? Maybe ask him for a bit more money now you’re a qualified manager?”

I sighed. “Working with Dad is fine, but it’s not the same as working for a big firm. I was told I had prospects. Although I’m not so sure after this takeover…”

“Plus, Thomas is already working with Dad now. We’ll end up tripping over each other.”

Mary kissed me gently on the forehead. “You decide. You’ll be fine whatever you do. I’m sure.”

I swithered and worried for weeks until Dad sat me down and told me his plan…

“I’ve heard Birrells are going to close quite a few of the McColl’s branches. They’ll just walk away from them. I think there could be an opportunity to take one over and run it as an independent shop. If you were back working in the family business, you could apply your corporate training to a new family store. Would that be better than working as a Team Leader?"

I looked at him. "I'm not sure, Dad. I'm not keen on this new format they're bringing in. But if I keep my nose clean, the Area Manager reckons I would be promoted within the next year or so. I might even get a company car. And this time I'd do my best not to write it off in the first week! But you're talking about my own shop? That's very tempting. But it's not for sure yet. What happens if I give up my steady number in Birrells and the new shop doesn't come off?"

Dad laughed. "Well, you could always ask them for your job back, if you really couldn't stand working with me and Thomas that much."

"Och, that's not fair Dad. Although I probably would end up as mad as a hatter after a wee while. That's the thing I'm not happy about. I've got used to being in charge. And I like it. Having you telling me what to do on a daily basis, in the hope that this shop materialises..."

Then I had a thought. "So long as we have a chat about money?"

Dad harrumphed.

We decided to just leave me where I was for the moment and see if Dad's hunch was right.

Dad's ear to the ground was accurate. A few weeks after the takeover they did indeed close loads of branches. And, as luck would have it, one of them was the *Riddrie* branch, along the road from our house.

It closed down a month later. I had mixed feelings. I'd used it for years as a customer, and so immediately missed it along with everyone else who lived locally.

On the other hand, perhaps my future lay behind those rolled down shutters.

I had worked in it as Relief Manager for a couple of weeks, so I had an idea what the turnover was. And while it might be less than a head office accountant's target, we knew we could increase it with a bit of hard work, and some personal service.

But before that we'd have to take over the lease and set up the shop from scratch. Dad's Ruchazie shop had been trading a good few years when he'd taken in over.

I sensed a learning curve on the horizon…

Chapter 13
Mistaken Identity

In the meantime, Mary and I were getting closer. The once a week dates soon became a more frequent occurrence. But I wasn't earning enough to take my girlfriend out on the town more than once a week. So wee walks in the park became a good idea. Long lingering coffees in our old haunts: the Lido Cafe and Kenco Coffee House, let us just be with each other. 'Cos that's all we really wanted.

I had no personal transport. I could borrow Dad's rickety Commer van sometimes, but it was always full.

It was actually Big Peter's stock. Dad and he had come to some sort of arrangement whereby he parked the van in our backyard. Dad seemed to have ownership of the van, but it was full of Big Peter's stuff. Cardboard boxes with cowboy hats and kiss-me-quick hats. Boxes full of bows and arrows and cheap toys. Along with lots of balloons and the cylinders of gas to inflate them. The same kind of stuff I'd been flogging at the Barras just a couple of years earlier.

During the week, the van wasn't being used, so I'd put some petrol in it and trundle over to the far west end and pick up Mary.

Being madly in love, we'd go for a drive out to the outskirts of Glasgow, find a secluded spot, and enjoy a wee kiss and a cuddle...

Then we'd head back to Mary's house and go up to her room which had two marvellously comfortable armchairs and a TV. Maybe watch *Steptoe and Son* or try and catch *Top of the Pops*.

One night, it got a bit scary.

I trundled over to Mary's after work and supper, picked her up and off we went.

"Where should we go tonight then?" I asked. This was Mary's territory.

Mary looked pensive. She'd thought about it while she was in the opticians. I could tell...

"I know we like a wee drive, but there's a new shopping centre this side of Bearsden. It'll be closed now. We could maybe go to the car park for a bit of privacy." She smiled as she leaned over the engine housing between the two front seats and planted me a great big kiss.

So off we jolly well went. Bouncing up the back country roads 'till we came across the dimmed lights of the new shopping centre on the edge of Bearsden.

"There's the delivery area behind the supermarket. That looks quiet."

I glanced across at Mary. She smiled back.

I pulled into the large paved area in the shadow of the concrete shapes of the newly built shops. There were a handful of parked lorries and a couple of cars, well spread out over the semi-enclosed space.

I switched the engine off and looked across at Mary. It was almost dark. She switched the cabin light on. Her eyes sparkled as she reached across to me. I shuffled closer.

We kissed the kisses of passion and youth and love and urgency and joy.

We stopped.

We looked at each other.

We played our old game, from way back in the Bundy days.

Who would blink first?

When two people stare into the eyes of the person they love with unblinking passion, a magic happens. A union is formed.

Welded.

Strong.

Unbreakable.

Invincible.

We blinked simultaneously…

We sighed…

"What's that?" Mary looked at the driver's mirror. I turned and looked. Headlights flashing. From one of the parked cars.

Oh Shit!

"Who the hell's flashing headlights in a car park?" I found myself asking.

"Let's get out of here." Mary was composing herself. "They might want to rob the van. They don't know it's full of silly cowboy hats!"

I switched the engine on and fired up the engine. It gurgled into life.

The car had moved.

The lights were right behind us.

Still flashing.

I hit the accelerator.

Aiming for the exit, I bounced over the kerb as I wheeled round into the service road and roared up the hill.

Mary had her head out the passenger window. "They're following us!"

"For God's sake. Who the hell are they?"

I felt my earlier joy melt away, replaced by a mixture of adrenalin and fear, as I pushed the cumbersome van to its limits along the narrow country road.

"We have to get to well-lit roads!" Mary shouted as I accelerated round a bend.

We suddenly emerged into the outskirts of Drumchapel.

People on the street!

Yay!

We came up to a crossroads. A main road. I had to stop.

The flashing lights closed behind us.

Right behind us.

Mary's eyes widened in fear as she held on to her door handle.

I looked in the mirror as I saw two doors opening in the car which had followed us through country roads for the last few miles.

The passenger mirror showed another two doors opening.

The four men walked up either side of the van.

"Keep your door locked!" I shouted to Mary, ready to gun the accelerator at the slightest provocation.

The first man reached my window.

Scruffy T-Shirt. Balding. Stubble. About forty.

He stared at me and indicated that I should wind the window down.

I shook my head and kept it up.

"Why didn't you stop?" he shouted through the glass.

"Who the hell are you?" I answered.

"We're Police. Undercover. Who the hell did you think we were?"

"God knows! Show me your ID," I shouted back.

He shook his head as if I was being unreasonable then reached into his inside pocket…

I looked across at Mary, whose eyes were wider than I'd ever seen them.

"I don't like this," she muttered. I saw the other two men just outside her window. Mid-thirties, equally rough looking.

Ach, to hell with it!

I pressed the throttle and threw the van round the corner and zoomed away from the possibilities.

Looking back, I could see the men clambering back into their non-descript car.

"That doesn't look like a police car to me." I looked at Mary as we broke all the speed limits the rattling van could muster.

"If they're police, they should have a blue light," Mary reasoned.

Five minutes later we had reached Great Western Road and the bright yellow lights of the dual carriageway.

We felt safer.

Until we reached the traffic lights at Garscadden Road. They changed to red just as we approached.

We stopped.

All hell broke loose.

Two police cars, blue lights flashing, came from opposite sides of the Boulevard, screeching to a stop inches from the front of the van.

Mary and I looked at each other… again.

Not a good time to play the Who Blinks First game…

I looked in the mirror. The non-descript car pulled up behind us.

"Maybe they were police after all," Mary observed.

The two white police cars in front of us emptied their cargo of big uniformed coppers. *No need to ask for their ID,* I thought.

They stood by their vehicles and stared at us.

A knock on my window.

"Now do you believe us?"

I rolled down the window. "How the hell were we to know you are police? Where's your blue light? Where's your siren? Why were you following us?"

I was angry… But trying to be careful.

"Right, sir. My name is DC McLuskey. We were on duty at the shopping centre because we have reason to believe that a burglary was planned there for this evening. Could you please step out of the van and open the rear doors… Sir."

Mary smothered a giggle as I climbed out of the cab and opened the doors.

"Have a look, officers. The goods inside belong to a business partner of my dad's. I'll be very surprised if the shopping centre has anything similar."

DC McLuskey glared at me as his colleague pulled out one of the well-used cardboard boxes and opened it. He lifted out a pile of Kiss-me Quick hats and tried his best not to laugh. He showed them to McLuskey, who grimaced at me.

"So, what the hell were you doing at the back of the shops with a bloody van at this time of night if you're not gonna burgle it?"

"Well, seeing as how you've now asked, I was actually playing a game of 'Who Blinks First' with my girlfriend!"

I stared at him.

And didn't blink.

And said nothing…

He blinked.

Radios crackled. Voices blurred, but I heard. "False alarm. Just a courting couple."

"Right, on you go. I'd advise you to find somewhere else for your blinking games." Then DC McLuskey went back to his crappy car to go on playing cops and robbers, while Mary and I drove back to her house for some soothing tea and Jaffa cakes.

Chapter 14

How Do You Open a Shop, Dad?

"How do you go about re-opening a shop, Dad?" I felt myself at the beginning of that learning curve, as Dad and I sat at the kitchen table.

With his squared exercise book open in front of him, Dad started making a list while he talked me through the mechanics.

"Well, the only shop I've opened from scratch was the wee toy shop I had in the Gallowgate. It had been a pawn shop, and I knew the owner, 'cos I had lived across the road when I was growing up. So that was easy. Mr Peterson was retiring and he let me rent the shop kind of informally. It did ok for a while."

"Oh, I remember that wee shop well. It was like an Aladdin's cave. I loved it when I was a kid. It was full of Tri-Ang bikes and prams hanging from the ceiling. And there were so many toys on the counter, I could hardly see you behind it."

Dad nodded and thought back. "That's right, it was pretty full. Do you remember that miniature real guitar you got for Christmas when you were about seven?"

"Oh yes. I remember it well."

Dad looked thoughtful for a moment then went back to his number crunching.

While he was concentrating, I found myself thinking back to that Christmas morning.

"You try it, Marie. My fingers are sore now. I cannae get them in the right places. I don't understand these instructions at all!"

I could see my seven-year-old, self-watching, open-mouthed as Mum and Dad tried gamefully to follow the book of instructions on how to play my brand-new guitar.

It had come in an unusually shaped container. Narrow at the top and broad at the bottom. I was thrilled as I opened the box which was leaning against the fireplace, beside the long Christmas sock now full of sweets and matchbox cars, an orange, and a shiny shilling lurking at the bottom. I'd helped to pin the sock to the wall the night before. Then let our letters to Santa flutter up the chimney. Mum had helped us write our notes. It was really her and Dad's idea that I ask for a guitar. No mention of it being too dear to sell in the shop!

We were in the living room in 1950s Ruchazie. Thomas was five and Alan just two. They were excitedly playing with Thomas's pedal car and a red Tri-Ang bus that Alan could sit astride.

"Can I get another shot?" I pleaded as Mum plonked the metal strings untunefully while crying "ouch" every time she pressed hard on the guitar string.

"Of course you can. It's your Christmas present. Here's the picker. The book says it's called a plectrum. Just run it over the strings. Let me hang the strap round your neck. There you are! You look just like Elvis Presley!"

Mum positioned my smaller fingers on the frets like the diagram on the instructions. But my wee fingers couldn't hold the strings down either.

I felt frustrated and disappointed. "Stupid guitar!" I'd thought I could play like Bill Haley and the Comets.

Mum would play "Rock around the Clock" to get Alan to sleep. I know it makes no sense, but it worked…

I put the guitar back in its box for a bit and pushed Alan about on his bus. We raced Thomas in his pedal car till he nearly took a chunk out of the phone table in the lobby.

After we came back from chapel, I took the guitar out of the box again to have another go.

I stopped trying to get my fingers to stretch into chord shapes and just plonked the notes one at a time. "Dunk dunk dunk, dunk dunk dunk." It was boring and I could sense Dad doing his best not to tell me to shut up. I mean, it was Christmas!

I tried hitting one string then another. I could hold one *note down at a time.*

Suddenly I recognised a tune:

"Oh when the Saints," my fingers played.

I did it again. "Go Marching in."

Mum came through from the scullery. "That's a proper song you're playing, John. I know that! Play it again."

I tried again. And got it right!

Mum smiled and sang along. Then Dad joined in. I felt great! Thomas and Alan stopped and looked puzzled. Who needs Elvis? Here's wee John and the Parents.

Christmas had worked its magic.

Back in the real world, Dad had worked out what the takings would have to be to make the shop pay. Because I'd worked in it as a relief manager, I knew what it had taken on *those* two weeks. If we managed that, we wouldn't get rich but we'd get by.

Dad was more optimistic. "Those takings were made by just selling McColl's products. If we stock it with loads more lines like we have in Ruchazie, then the takings are bound to be higher. If it climbs to anywhere near our levels, you could save up enough to open a third shop and maybe let Thomas take over after a couple of years. He should be up to scratch by then, surely."

I had my doubts: "That would be great, and I'll do my best, but I don't know if it'll ever be quite *that* busy. Have you told Thomas about this hand-over plan?"

Dad shrugged his shoulders. "Well, your mum and I had a wee blether with him about it the other night, when you were out with Mary. And he seemed keen on the idea."

Of course he did. Hmmm. It's never a good idea to make a promise that you're not absolutely sure you can keep… It's an even worse idea to depend on someone else keeping your promise. Still, it might work out. Nobody knows the future…

In the meantime: The next stage was convincing the Council, our potential landlords, to give us a lease.

Let the bureaucracy begin!

Dad sighed. "You know how much I hate form filling. So, you can enjoy that task, and your mum can write the covering note. More useful than writing all those letters to the *Evening Times.*" He grinned.

"Well, she's had quite a few ten-shilling postal orders for best letter. So she must be doing something right," I said, relieved I hadn't been given that job.

A few weeks later, after much form filling and many phone calls, a brown Council letter landed on the hall carpet. I felt excitement welling.

Thomas was first to grab it. "It's addressed to Dad, John. Da-ad!" he shouted up the stairs. "Letter from the Council."

When Dad opened the envelope with us all standing in the lobby round him, I felt my inside butterflies flapping. Would I be handing in my notice to Birrells today?

But then his face darkened as he read the words.

Mum asked. "What's wrong? All the forms were filled in. I checked John's work and we all checked my letter, talking about how you've been a good tenant for well over ten years. Do we have to do something else? Let me read it."

Dad handed her the closely typed sheet. Mum glanced through then said, "Apparently, there's more than one application for the shop! It doesn't say how many but we're going to have to go through their selection system..."

"Or else walk away. It's probably another chain we'd be up against. With deep pockets." Dad looked fed up.

"C'mon, Dad," I heard myself saying. "We've all done a lot of work and figuring to go for this shop. Can I see the letter, Mum?"

The happy mood of expectation had gone. Alan and Thomas wandered into the kitchen, while Phil and Andy resumed their eternal wrestling on the living room floor. Any minute there would be a "Mu-um! He nearly broke my arm!"

I looked through the letter. "It says here, the rent offered will not be the only criteria. So, it looks like we have to make a case for ourselves. I think we've got lots more to offer that any chain has. That's why they shut the place down. They have to work to a limited formula. We don't!"

Dad visibly brightened. "You're right enough, John. We can give the local customers all they used to get. Plus all the lines we sell in Ruchazie."

Mum nodded. "I feel a good letter coming on. What's their deadline? End of March? Time enough to get our act together."

In the meantime, I was still working in for the 'competition.' While the new systems took a while to settle in, I could see my role becoming simplified. For some strange reason, I craved responsibility. Or maybe just the lure of a challenge?

As time moved on, we were worried that our potential customers would change their shopping habits while the store remained closed. One Sunday as we went to church across the road, I was taken aback to see a chap standing in front of the closed shop with a stack of Sunday papers. And he had a queue! Is this going to make life more complicated? Was he connected to one of our competitors for the shop?

We'd submitted Dad's bid along with Mum's 'good letter,' explaining the range of goods we would have for sale, which was far wider than a traditional newsagents. There would be loads of sweets, a big range of toys, 'cos Dad still had those connections, along with a smattering of everyday items. More in keeping with today's convenience stores, a term that hadn't yet crossed the Atlantic. The supermarket phenomenon was in its infancy. The main grocery store for the area was Massey's next door, still serving butter by the paddle and offering a delivery service via message bike. The other independent shops included a butchers, a bakers, and a dairy. There wasn't quite a candlestick maker, although there was a traditional hardware store where a man in a brown coat could very well serve you 'four candles.' The last shop was the inevitable chippy, for our once a week treat.

I told Mary I felt as if I was in Limbo waiting for some pen pusher's decision on how I was going to spend the next chunk of my life...

Mary gave me a hug. "We're all keeping our fingers crossed. The worst that might happen is you look for a better job with another chain. You're well qualified now. Let's be optimistic. How long till you know?"

A fortnight later a bit of déjà vu as the familiar Council letter came through the letterbox.

Thomas grabbed it again and shouted up the stairs. "Da-ad! Another Council letter. It feels thicker. Is that good?"

We gathered round as Dad prised open the letter and quickly scanned it.

His face lit up.

"We've got it! We've to get the keys on thirtieth April. Now we've got real work to do."

Thomas and I looked at each other. The plan was that I would run the shop for the first two years then move on, and Thomas would take over. By then he would be over twenty, have learned all the ropes, and I should have saved enough to open another shop…

He grinned. "So that means you're really going to be my boss as well as my big brother then?"

I smiled back. "That's Dad's idea."

"I know. I know. Then he says, after two years, it's my turn…"

"That's the plan." I was very aware of Dad's concept.

I wonder if that's what'll happen? I thought quietly to myself.

xxxxxxxxxxxxxxxxxxxxxxxxxxxxxxxxxxxxxxxxxxxxxxxxxxxxxxx

The last day in April arrived with a feeling of excitement and anticipation. Dad returned from the Council offices waving the new shop keys in his hand. "Right, let's see what's to do. Who wants to see inside the new shop?"

The schools had closed at 4 o'clock, so the whole bunch of us piled into Dad's car for the short journey along the road to the scene of my new future.

As Dad threw the roller shutter up then fumbled with the front glass door lock, I felt a quiet excitement inside. *This is going to be our shop. Not a chain store. It's gonna be a lot better. 'Cos I'm gonna be in charge!*

Once we got the lights on, we all trouped in and looked around at the familiar cream walls and wood fronted canopies, hiding the strip lights casting their flickering glare on the empty, dusty shelves waiting for *our* choices of customer delights. A three-dimensional blank canvas!

"Look, John, there's space at the end of the news counter for another counter. Maybe a glass one. We could put gifts in there." Thomas had spotted a possibility.

"That corner's got deeper shelves. We should put groceries there." Mum was on the ball.

"The sweeties have to go over there." Alan pointed to the Formica covered counter to the right.

"We think the toys should go there. We think you should have loads of Airfix models and Jigsaws." Phil and Andy were pointing at the back wall. Andy piped up "Make sure you've got lots of Matchbox cars and Lego. 'Cos all my pals'll buy them."

Mum looked at me. "Happy, John? What do you think? Rather be in Birrells?"

"I'm fine, Mum. Although it's gonna be a lot of work to be open in two weeks like Dad says."

"Ach. It'll be fun." Thomas looked around. "Different punters from Ruchazie. And in two years' time, it'll be mine. I can't wait!"

I smiled as I noticed Mum giving Dad a look that I didn't quite understand.

I felt my bubble of excitement springing a leak.

A burst of communal energy and two days before opening day we were almost ready. Mary and Mum had vied with each other as to who was the best scrubber! Mary reckons she won… The floors, counters and shelves were gleaming. And as the goods were positioned around the walls, it was looking brighter and more colourful every day.

Dad had taken on the role of dealing with the fixtures and fittings and had sourced a glass-fronted counter for gifts as Thomas had suggested. It had been delivered to the house garage before we had the shop keys, so it was one of the last items to be moved into the shop. A wee logistical challenge.

"We'll just have to put it on the roof rack to take it along the road. I'm not going to empty Peter's van for such a short distance. We'll just go nice and slowly." So me, Thomas, Alan, and Dad lifted the fairly heavy counter onto the roof rack bars on the dark blue Zephyr estate.

Once positioned with ropes tightened, we were ready to go. The plan was for Dad to drive at walking pace with Thomas and I walking alongside, just in case there was any movement. There was some chat about a man with a red flag in front of the car…

Alan stared at the unusual combination. "That looks like a double-decker hearse. Folk'll think we're going to a funeral!"

"Aye, you're right, Alan. Maybe we've come up with a new invention!" Thomas exclaimed.

We were all in a buoyant mood. It was only a couple of days until opening day.

"Well, we gotta complete the picture!" Alan said as he quickly climbed the step ladder we'd been using and jumped into the floor of the glass counter; he lay down, closed his eyes, and crossed his hands over his chest. He even managed to suppress his ever-present grin.

We all burst out laughing, then Dad half-heartedly tried to persuade Alan to come down. "That's just a bit morbid. I mean I've heard of black humour but…"

"I cannae come down! Can you no' see I'm deid?"

"Ok then. Just don't fall out!" Dad relented as we started our surreal procession along the short journey to the new shop. We got quite a few funny looks from passers-by and we held up a couple of cars who weren't quite sure what was going on. Thomas and I walked along on either side, giggling like big school kids… Until we came round the corner onto Smithycroft Road.

"Uh oh," I thought. But dared not say anything. Thomas and I looked at each other with horrified eyes, as we slowly passed St Thomas's chapel at a snail's pace. A genuine funeral was ending and the coffin was being held by six grieving relatives, ready to slide it into the back of the hearse!

The world paused. The crowd around the hearse and standing on the chapel steps had a collective intake of breath. The pallbearers almost lost their grip as our caricature of their moment of sadness glided by their grief. I wished I could disappear as I heard the low mutterings of the funeral party grow into rumblings of disbelief. "That's outrageous!" "How dare they?"

All eyes glared at Alan's prone mockery of their newly departed.

Alan, unable to resist his natural devilment, slowly turned his head, opened his eyes wide… then raised his left hand and gave a royal wave to the crowd as the Zephyr crawled past.

Suddenly, two burly black-tied members of the funeral party broke ranks and marched towards us. Being the nearest, I got their full attention.

"What the bloody hell do you lot think you're doing! That's my Granny in that box, an' if she wiz still alive she'd make mincemeat out of you!"

My hands were up. Palms out. "Sorry sir, we'd no idea there was a funeral going on. Just my wee brother joking…"

I didn't get another word out before the second burly relative (not sure if he was a grandson too) pushed the first guy out of the way before rushing towards the still slowly moving car. "Let me get that wee bastard!" he shouted as he tried to heave on the ropes holding the counter onto the roof rack.

Alan was now looking worried as he felt the counter wobble. Thomas had run round the car and was grappling with the grandson, while I was pulling the collar of the second relative. "For God's sake!" I shouted. "He didn't mean any harm. Get back to your funeral. Your Granny would be ashamed of you!"

That seemed to make a difference. He stopped pulling against me. Looked back towards his Granny's coffin, now securely in the back of the hearse along with a floral 'Granny' pressed up against the side window, and dropped his shoulders. He looked towards his companion who at that moment had Thomas in a headlock. "C'mon, Bruv, these arseholes aren't worth spoiling Granny's day." I now knew that he was indeed another grandson.

They straightened their shoulders and strutted the few yards back to their fellow mourners.

Suddenly there was a round of applause from their friends and family. Their strutting morphed into swaggers.

In the meantime, Dad had finally stopped the car. The whole incident had probably only lasted a few moments. He leant across the front bench seat. "What on Earth is going on? These are our future customers! Get Alan down. Now!"

I looked across at the funeral party, some of whom were now getting into their cars. But quite a few were lingering…

I opened the nearside front door. "Not a good idea to let them see us unloading the glass coffin and Alan into the shop right across the road there." I looked across the wide junction and saw Mary standing in the shop doorway, window blinds still down, waving tentatively. I daren't wave back!

"Let's go for a wee hurl," I said as I opened the door and jumped in. Thomas nodded and climbed in the back seat.

"Right, Dad, anywhere but across the road. Let's wait till the funeral goes away."

Dad got the picture and turned down Cumbernauld Road, aiming to turn right into Findhorn Street then go round the block behind the shop.

In the meantime, Alan wasn't so comfortable lying prone in his glass coffin as we moved a wee bit faster than walking pace. He crawled to the front of the counter and on hands and knees stared down Cumbernauld Road.

Dad looked in his mirror. "Uh oh. Look behind you."

I turned round, and the funeral hearse was right behind us. Lights flashing. He wanted to overtake! That's how slow we were going…

"Just pull in, Dad! Just pull in!" Thomas shouted from the back seat.

That wasn't a great idea.

We were pointed downhill. Dad pulled in to the left. But the glass counter had no brakes…

With Alan crouched up at the front, it just kept going, breaking through the meagre ropes that would have sufficed at walking pace.

The counter slid forward. The back hit the car roof as it fell off the rear roof rack bar, climbed over the front bar, then down, over the windscreen, as we gaped in horror, scraping along the bonnet, before teetering over the front grill.

It had all happened in a kind of slow motion.

At this point, Alan, miraculously, clambered out of the open side of the counter, onto the road, just as its momentum slid it the last few inches over the front of the car and onto the road surface.

Amazingly the glass counter didn't shatter into a million fragments. It just kind of lent nonchalantly against the bonnet of the car.

Alan stood erect as the funeral cortege glided by, feet away.

To the sounds of boos and jeers from the collective mourners, Alan raised his arm and saluted.

A very incongruous sight.

The funeral cortege finally passed our sorry predicament, just as Mary reached us. "What the hell were you lot thinking of? What kind of nutters am I getting involved with?" She grinned.

Chapter 15

The Birth of a Business

While we had been waiting for the Council's decision about leasing the shop, one of our favourite pastimes had been trying to come up with a suitable name to put above the door. Dad's shop in Ruchazie had never had a brand name. There was a dusty rusting metal sign, possibly put there by the council when the row of shops was built. It said 'STORE.' Accurate and to the point, but not exactly eye-catching.

Our new shop had competition and everyone, including us, called it McColl's. A very Big Brand. We had to be creative.

In the living room, after dinner and the *Black and White Minstrels Show* (Mum's favourite), we had what would later be classified as a brain storming session.

Thomas had ideas. "How's about 'News and Stuff'? I mean that's what's on offer."

Alan butted in, "I've got it!" He stood up and raised his voice. "The Shop That's Got What You Want! With an exclamation mark of course."

"What if I walk in and ask for a fish supper and a haircut. 'Cos that's what I want?" I asked reasonably.

Alan scowled.

Dad was more prosaic. "Just call it 'The Newsagent.' Everybody knows what that means."

"But the whole idea is we're not gonna be just a newsagent. You already sell everything from shoe polish to bile beans, along with sand shoes and biscuits. 'The Newsagents' really doesn't cover that range." I had made myself clear.

Phil piped up. "How's about 'The Best Shop in Riddrie!' "

"That's not bad," I said. "It would definitely get noticed."

Andy had to get his shot. “I think we should call it ‘Dickson’s Shop’ ‘cos that’s what it’s gonna be, isn’t it? An’ all my pals will know it’s my dad’s and my big brother’s shop.”

Mum gave Andy a sweet smile. “That’s a lovely idea, Andy, but it has to be something different from family names. People have to notice it… It would be good if it was modern. Up to the minute, but mean something… It doesn’t have to say newsagent because there’ll be newspaper boards outside. And the locals know it’s a newsagent. What about ‘Buy Right’? Lets them know we sell other stuff.”

“That’s what I said!” Thomas stood up. “‘News and Stuff’ is a great name.”

“Wait a minute.” I liked Thomas’s idea, but it wasn’t quite right.

Mum’s eyes brightened. She’d had an idea. “Got it.” She grinned. The news is full of ‘Sit Ins,’ ‘Laugh Ins,’ and ‘Love Ins.’ Why don’t we call it ‘The Buy In’? It covers all angles. It’s modern, and folk will notice it.”

And so it was decided.

‘The Buy In’ was born two days after the glass coffin had slithered off the roof of Dad’s car. It was destined to become a fixture in our life and the life of our community for many years to come.

Chapter 16

Cars and Vans

One of the perks of opening the shop was that I could justifiably argue that I needed a car or a van. My transport opportunities had deteriorated after the destruction of my lovely Lambretta. (The wrecking of my company car didn't help.) Once I was working for R.S. McColl's, I was totally dependent on borrowing Mum's wee yellow mini for any social outings. And that was entirely within Mum's gift, mood or whim. Especially after the night she surprised me by offering the car as I was going out the door. I was still eighteen and she presumed I was just going up to Joe's for a jam.

I hadn't quite mentioned that I was actually going to my first stag night…

Not wanting a lecture on the dangers of being in such a situation, I took the car keys. *I'll figure out something later…*

After a great session playing guitar alongside Joe in some backwoods miner's club, with the whole room jumping to "I've Been a Wild Rover," I noticed the line-up of vodkas sitting on the table in front of me, gathering while I'd been far too busy strumming away.

As the club was shutting its doors…

I foolishly scoffed the lot.

Joe disappeared into someone else's car. Disorientated, and having no idea where I was, I realised that the car park was emptying and I didn't have a lift back to Balornock. In desperation, it seemed like a good idea, at the time, to clamber onto the roof of a friend of a friend of a friend's white mini. (I'd parked Mum's outside Joe's door.) As he did wheelies in the club car park trying to whip me off his roof, I remember wishing the mini designers could have been more considerate in the depth of guttering there was for me to cling on to…

I've no idea how I managed to get back to Joe's. The last I recall is compounding my potential predicament by climbing into the driver's seat of Mum's Mini… *I'll have a wee rest…*

The next thing I knew was waking up on Joe's couch the morning after with a bumper headache and a mouth that tasted of gravel.

Apparently, when I hadn't come home by my usual time, Mum got worried. She waited until 1am then called Joe's house. His dad let the cat out of the bag about the stag night, but cranked up the anxiety by telling her that Joe had come home without me!

"Where's the car? He's surely not driving it?" Mum was frantic.

Mr Slyder replied, "No, no, he left it on the street outside. They both got a lift to the party."

Mum had a horrible thought. "Can you look outside and see if the car's still there?"

Joe and his dad spotted me slumped in the car. They dashed out and dragged me into the house, saving me, and God knows who else, from myself. (Though I like to think that if I'd woken up, I would have dredged up enough sense to knock on Joe's door…)

When I finally drove the car home the next day, I sheepishly walked through the kitchen door to be met by a very livid Mother.

For the first and only time in my life, Mum slapped me hard across the face.

"Don't you EVER give me a night of worries like you did last night!"

Oh no! That was sore! That's not gonna help the headache…

She forced me to go to work in the shop I was managing for R.S. McColl's, where I sat at my desk, head in my hands, while the staff tee-hee'd around me

I had *the* most unproductive day ever…

xxxxxxxxxxxxxxxxxxxxxxxxxxxxxxxxxxxxxxxxxxxxxxxxxxxx

Once in a while, Dad would let me drive the Zephyr. But really only for the Cash and Carry and such like. I think he let me use it once for a heavy date. But there's something quite unimpressive about arriving in Daddy's car. That relationship didn't last long.

As Mary and I were seriously 'courting,' I invested in another scooter. The distance between Blairdardie and Riddrie was too long and expensive for frequent trips by public transport. And we were seeing each other nearly every day.

This second scooter was nothing like the big old 250cc Lambretta which had been ripped apart and wrenched from my heart. The new one was still named Lambretta. But it was like an anorexic version. It only had 75cc and sounded like a high-pitched Hoover. It had a D-shaped open body so you could see the tiny engine whining away. It was called a Vega. Bright orange frame and an embarrassment to ride. But it was cheap. Did about a hundred mpg and droned me across the city in half an hour. When Mary, who was very light, was hanging on to me on the pillion seat, we fairly crawled along.

Oh, how I missed my first two-wheeled love!

....

Everything changed with the opening of The Buy In.

Dad had had a big *To Do* list.

Top of the list was the purchase of the shop fittings from my old employer R.S. McColl's.

Next came the stock list of lines taken from Dad's order books.

Then: making contact with all his suppliers to order the products.

After that: Figuring out what staff we'd need and when

Finally: I would need a car or a van.

Yay!

Dad read out the list: "Well, we don't know if the shop's going to make any money, so it'll have to be something cheap. You have a look about."

It took me two days to find the next mechanical character in my life. A six-year-old grey and hand-painted blue panelled minivan. It cost one hundred and eighty pounds which was thirty pounds more than Dad had budgeted.

"C'mon, Dad. We don't want something that's going to keep breaking down. I know it's small but I'm used to driving minis. And it'll be cheap to run."

He eventually gave in and handed me the cash. I'd made a side deal with Thomas that he could have my mini scooter for a knock-down price once the shop was open and he was earning money.

By this time Thomas was coming up for seventeen and had had a couple of wobbly shots of the scooter. So he was keen.

According to the log book, the minivan had previously been owned by a butcher. It must have been him who'd hand-painted the side panels to obliterate his signage. He hadn't managed to obliterate the odour of old meat though, according to Mary.

"I think we're going to miss the fresh air of the scooter. This thing stinks. It'll need a proper scrubbing. We'll do it together at the weekend, eh?"

That's my girl! A proper little…

Chapter 17

The Run up to the Wedding

"I know there's a three-day week; I do read the newspapers so I could hardly miss it. But now we've got an official State of Emergency and even more power cuts, just three days before my daughter's wedding. How will this affect the reception?" My very soon-to-be mother-in-law was in full flow on the telephone. I felt sorry for the poor chap in the St Mungo's Club.

A lot of preparation had gone into our impending nuptials by Mary's mum and Big Aunt Peggy, her widowed sister.

Mrs Heaney continued, "You mean the lights will be off while we're *actually eating*? How will I be able to see my chicken or roast beef?" She nodded to her sister for support. She was sitting on the high-backed chair which would be reclaimed by my soon-to-be father-in-law, Iain Heaney, when he came home from his shift in Rolls Royce across the river.

"I see. You're depending on daylight when the power's off? You do realise this is Glasgow in February. It's already snowing outside. There's not a lot of daylight available at the moment. I really don't want our guests peering through the gloom… Ah, you have *plenty* of candles! You're either very fortunate, or better still, very well organised. The shops around here are completely sold out."

Big Aunt Peggy spoke out. "It's a good job we're having a Wedding Breakfast instead of a dinner. Your fortune-telling was right again, Winnie. It really is a gift!"

Winnie smiled with gratitude, her frizzy silver halo of hair quivering as she spoke into the telephone. "I just hope everything's under control, young man. I'll see you after the ceremony on Saturday 11 o'clock sharp." I shivered on the young man in the club's behalf.

Mary squeezed my hand as we sat together on the couch watching the elders of her family deal with the realities of life in February 1972.

As two twenty-year-olds, romantically committed to spending the rest of our lives together, we had let the proper grownups do nearly all the organising for our imminent wedding.

Sure, we'd been saving madly for the last year or so. Ever since my mum had advised us, with the wisdom of age and experience that as we were only eighteen, we should wait awhile before entering that rose-tinted state of matrimony we couldn't wait to embrace.

We didn't think of ourselves as naive young kids. We felt we could do anything. And with the optimism of youth, all we had to do was get on with it.

Sitting in Dad's van outside Mary's house in the west end of the city, I had been just a tad taken aback when Mary grabbed me by the back of the head and gave me a great big smacker of a kiss, pulled back, then looked at me with her gorgeous, big, loving eyes, and said, "I think you should marry me!"

So… that was a big decision I didn't have to make! And I hadn't even had to do the down on bended knee bit. Result!

Bye bye, Dennis and Gordon, and any other crappy drumming ex-boyfriends!

I did, however, have to do the traditional 'asking permission to marry your beautiful daughter' bit. But only because Mary knew her dad would really appreciate it. And, of course, I'd do anything for the girl. I was so much in love. Even if it meant putting on my one and only suit and braving the first time I'd ever been alone with Mr Heaney.

What if he says 'no'? Is eloping an option? I wondered.

Once Mary and I had been going out together for a while, I kind of got to know Mary's father. He was the bespectacled guy watching the TV and shouting at the news as I waited for Mary to come downstairs.

Sometimes Mrs Heaney would insist Mary and I sit and have some tea and biscuits, especially on Sunday afternoons.

Putting down his Sunday mail, he felt a rant coming on. "Stupid Tory government. Don't know how to handle the unions. I should know. Been a shop steward for umpteen years… Both sides have to negotiate. Not call each other names on the TV! We'll end up with black outs, I tell you!"

Having worked, or at least been behind the counter, in newsagents since I was eight years old, my vision of the daily news came from a different perspective. I got the news upside down. Literally. Upside down headlines were my norm.

The newspapers were piled up on the main counter. By far the biggest seller was the Labour-supporting *Daily Record*, so it sat next to the till. The *Scottish Daily Express*, giving full support to the new Tory government, was number two, and got a space to itself while the newish *Sun* and the rest of the bunch overlapped each other.

One perk of the newsagent's life is a chance to read any or all of the newspapers every day. Between customers that is. Of course, you do have to learn how to fold them perfectly before putting them back on display… It's not everybody who has the chance to compare *The Morning Star's* slant on Ted Heath's fun and games with the unions with *The Glasgow Herald's* more considered opinions. A quick flick through the tabloids usually confirmed their political leanings. So, I maybe came to a more balanced view than most folk who feel obliged to stay loyal to one particular title.

However, I hadn't lived the life of my future father–in–law. So, I was maybe a bit naive to challenge him on his total support for the unions, as the country rumbled towards power cuts and the three-day week.

"I'm sorry, Mr Heaney. It's very difficult to build a new business that's open to the public if the lights are going to keep going off!" I felt my point was reasonable.

"And you blame the unions, don't you? Not the bloody Tories and the Bank of England for letting inflation force the workers to demand decent cost of living wage rises?" Mr Heaney peered at me through his thick lenses.

"Erm. Well, I'm sure the government should be in charge of how the country is run. I mean, they did win the election. I'm not sure it's right that the miners and electricity workers should make all our lives harder just so *they* can get more money." I felt my knees weakening as his glare grew ever narrower.

"So, you're going out with a Tory then?" He peeled his eyes off me and transferred his glower to his daughter who was sitting on the couch beside me. Jaffa cake halfway to her mouth.

Mary, bemused, looked from her dad then to me. "I don't know. We've not really talked politics. Are you a Tory then, John?" She bit off a piece of the Jaffa cake… delectably.

Mrs Heaney butted in. "You shouldn't talk about politics or religion. It always ends in an upset. Does anyone want more tea?" She lifted her china teapot as she spoke.

I felt myself on the defensive. "No, I don't think I'm a Tory, but I'm not so keen on some of the things the unions get up to either. I can usually see both sides. So maybe I should vote Liberal?"

"Well, that's a waste of a vote for sure." Mr Heaney was dismissive.

"What about the Scottish Nationalists then?" Mary supped her tea. "James and Joyce have actually become party members."

Mr Heaney almost snorted. "Damned silly buggers. They're just a bunch of tartan Tories, wearing kilts and sucking up to big land owners. James'll be doing it to get more clients."

Then Mr Heaney softened his glare and looked at me. "Labour represents fairness and justice for all. Not just those who've got the wit and skill to make a few bob. Never mind the chinless wonders that have neither wit *nor* skill. Just the luck to be born into 'old money.' I've noticed you're a grafter, John, and Mary tells me your new shop is picking up nicely. You'll probably do alright for yourself. Because you have the wit, and the willingness to use it. But don't let any future success turn you into a Tory. 'Cos they're just *not* fair!"

With that, he sat back and re-opened his paper. I'll have had my lecture then…

"Would you like some more biscuits, John?" Mrs Heaney smiled while Mary suppressed a giggle.

"That'll teach me to keep my opinions to myself," I said to Mary as she walked me out to the van.

I had gotten to know Mr Heaney better over time and realised there was more to him than a ranting trade unionist. He was a skilled engineer who'd apparently travelled around Europe and North Africa before the war as part of his training to become a missionary priest, a career path which obviously hadn't been fully pursued, considering he was married to Winnie with four adult offspring, Mary being the baby of the family.

The scary day came soon after Mary's proposal. Mary managed to pick a time when her dad was in while her rather eccentric mum was down Byres Road tormenting the boutique shopkeepers with strange requests, like did they have an old-fashioned lavatory chain she could wear as a necklace. But it *would* have to go with her fur coat…

Mary ushered me into the living room, a wooden pedal operated church organ in the corner where an upright piano might normally live. An old-fashioned, horse-hair, three-piece suite reflected the age differences between Mary's parents and my own mum and dad, who were a good twenty years younger. Blue artificial flowers lingered along the window sill next to the formal dining table. The usual sounds of a kettle bubbling from the kitchen next door were missing along with Winnie.

"Dad? I think John would like a wee word with you." I sorted my tie and tried to smile at my potential father-in-law, while Mary closed the door and scampered upstairs to her room.

The older man was standing by the fireplace, woolly cardigan covering his pot belly. Big buttons straining. Looking behind me at the closed door and the sound of his daughter's movements in her room immediately above us.

Hmmm. I can hear her walking across the room. Oh God, they can hear us…

"Well, John. What can I do for you? This is all very mysterious."

Shoulders back.

Breathe in.

Blurt.

"Mary and I have decided we want to get married."

Breathe out…

"And I'd like to ask you for your permission, Mr Heaney."

Breathe in…

Smile obsequiously.

"Do you now?" His eyes narrowed as he started rummaging in his cardigan pockets, then he pulled out his pipe and packet of tobacco.

Turning away from me, he opened the tobacco packet and placed it on the mantelpiece. Pulled out some Condor ready rubbed and stuffed it into the pipe held in the cup of his left hand, as he turned back to face me.

My smile was now fixed. My back felt damp.

"I see." He focused on tamping down the tobacco. Putting the pipe in his mouth, before going back into his cardigan pocket and pulling out a box of Swan Vestas matches.

He opened the box and pulled out a match.

I felt my shoulders beginning to droop.

He struck the match. It flared into life.

A strange puffing, almost popping sound as he drew the air through the smouldering tobacco and along the pipe stem, before exhaling an enormous billow of smoke. His head almost disappeared behind the grey cloud.

A short coughing spasm later and he was ready to speak.

"So, you and our Mary want to set up home together, eh?" he finally replied to my stuttering opening sentence.

He took another puff. Was that a twinkle I could detect through the cloud?

"I'm sorry, you do mean my Mary?" I dared.

He took another puff, and his eyes narrowed.

"Well… I could ask you if you regard yourself as good enough for my youngest daughter. I could ask you about your career prospects. I know you managed an R.S. McColl's shop and now you're in business with your father. I could ask you if you're going to make our Mary happy?"

I gulped. And said nothing.

"But I won't ask those questions, John. You're quite right to say *your* Mary. But now she'll belong to you *and* us. I'd be honoured to welcome you into our family." Mr Heaney's twinkle had grown into a wide smile as he extended his arm and we shook hands to formally seal the occasion.

He opened the glass door of the display cabinet where the precious whisky was kept for very special moments.

"I think this calls for a wee dram."

I relaxed enough to sit down on the couch, while he performed the ritual of setting out the whisky glasses and pouring the golden liquid from his prized crystal decanter.

I suspect he was glad to have an excuse for an afternoon dram as he handed me a generous measure and raised his glass to toast the moment.

"May you both have a very happy and loving marriage. You most definitely have my blessing."

Phew! Now it's official! Where's my Mary?

Chapter 18

The Wedding

"C'mon people, we're going to be late for my wedding!" I was almost jumping up and down on the pavement as Dad patiently stood still while Mum struggled trying to get the pin to hold the thicker than expected stem of the white carnation onto his lapel.

"There, that should do it." Mum stood back triumphantly to admire her work.

"D'you think I make a good Mother of the Groom?" She smiled posing in her flowery peach trouser suit, while hoping the neighbours would see her whole family, Mum, Dad, and their five sons dressed to the hilt for her number one's big day.

Dad, Mum's husband Jackie of twenty-four years, straightened his shoulders and grinned back proudly. "You're fine. It's my buttonhole everyone will be admiring…"

"Oops, sorry," Alan muttered squeezing between our parents as he tried to get into the back seat of the big Zephyr Estate.

"Aw no!" Dad said as he noticed his carnation was suddenly hanging upside down again. He looked balefully at Mum as he climbed into the driver's seat.

At Last! I thought as the whole family was finally squeezed into the two bench seats of Dad's pride and joy. My four wee brothers squashed in the back. Thomas, just seventeen was very nervous at having to play the role of Best Man. Even though Mary's brother-in-law James, an ebullient and avuncular lawyer who loved the sound of his own voice, would play the part of the Master of Ceremonies. All Thomas would have to do was to simply read out the telegrams and congratulatory cards.

Alan, mischievous as ever, was trying to film the journey between the back of Dad's and my head. Five years younger than me, Alan's film-making techniques would result in great views of Dad's comb over.

Squashed in beside Tom and Alan were the weans. Phil, ten, and Andy, who as a generous seven-year-old, had presented Mary and me with a proudly made Airfix model Spitfire aeroplane as our wedding present. Then logically asked if he could keep it in his new room now that I was leaving home?

Phew… And so I was.

Still, Mary and I were moving into our marvellous one-bedroom tenement flat in Dennistoun just a mile or so from the smashing family house I'd lived in for the previous ten years.

The apple wasn't falling far from the tree… Not yet.

Riddrie,is an area largely populated by Glasgow's aspiring working classes in nice semi-detached or four-in-a-block sought after council houses.

Our street, Riddrie Knowes, was a small area of privately-owned houses that my mum recalled walking through when she was a young teenager in the thirties.

"I remember those two bushes sticking up over our garden wall, and wondering what kind of people lived in such a big house," she proudly proclaimed once we'd moved into what had previously been a doctor's house and surgery.

The big selling point for Dad was the enormous basement garage and extra storage under the house. It would let him take advantage of bulk buying for the shop in Ruchazie in what could be called Greater Easterhouse where we'd lived through the fifties until we moved to Riddrie in the early sixties.

As we passed over the lately completed first section of the motorway from Castle Street to Great Western Road, I felt excitement welling up as we got closer to the time and place that would change my life. According to the vows I was about to pledge, it would be forever. An awfy long time when you're twenty!

At last we left the wide dual carriageway of Great Western Road, sometimes known by its more pompous alias 'The Boulevard.' Skys grey and heavy, with a good deal more snow than we'd had in the east of the city. It gave the prim bungalows a pretty white trim as they led the way to the modernist chapel perched like an unlikely concrete crown in the midst of traditional suburbia.

The photographer captured a couple of poses of Thomas and me, and Mum and Dad with the weans standing at the chapel entrance, then we walked in past our family and friends sitting in the pews in all their finery.

Standing nervously in front of the altar waiting for my bride-to-be to arrive I was approached by Father Kamya who had come all the way from Rome to perform the ceremony.

Mary's mum and dad had met Little Joe, who originated from Kategondo in Uganda, at a White Fathers gathering in Glasgow about ten years previously. As Mr Heaney had almost joined the priesthood in his youth, he still kept close ties with the people he'd come to know and befriend during that period in his life.

So, when Joe was presented as a church student in need of some support to continue his studies, Mr Heaney generously offered to help out when it was necessary.

Subsequently, a rare friendship had grown between the now Father Joe Kamya and Mary's whole family.

I was now reaping one of the benefits of that kindly relationship built over years. Here was this lovely African man, who sported a most glorious giggle, giving me friendly words of encouragement while I was waiting for my bride to arrive… fashionably late. I did think it was all rather exotic, but I was going with the flow.

There was a bit of a hustle and bustle behind Thomas and me as Mary's mum and Big Aunt Peggy sat down in their rightful places on the front seats.

"She's arrived, John." Father Kamya's eyes gleamed as he looked behind me. "She's beautiful."

The church organist, who had been playing a bland, almost soporific medley, burst into Mendelssohn's "Wedding March," and I turned to see Mary resplendent in the white velvet gown complete with a lace hood lovingly hand-stitched by Big Aunt Peggy, who wasn't nearly as scary as Mary made out.

Holding on to a beaming Mr Heaney's arm, Mary smiled at me and all our friends and family as she walked down the short aisle.

Suddenly she was at my side and we were actually going to get married!

Father Kamya said some of the words of the standard marriage vows. I repeated my side and Mary repeated hers. I did notice he hadn't included the 'love honour and obey' line, which Mary and I had joked about. I suspected Big Aunt Peggy's influence…

"You may kiss the bride!"

So I did. And it was wonderful.

Then we went behind the altar to a little anteroom and signed the marriage certificate (where Mary signed with her new married name, to the later consternation of her mum who was informed by the local priest that that meant we weren't legally married. "You've been living in sin!" she cried when we came back from honeymoon.)

The congregation were waiting patiently for our re-entrance. We stood at the top of the three altar steps, and Mary whispered in my ear "Go on! You said you would."

"I hope I don't regret this," I whispered back, before lifting my new bride off her feet and over my shoulder in a kind of amateur fireman's lift.

Then, carrying Mary, clutching her bouquet and laughing with delight, I ran down the steps and along the thankfully short aisle, my face grinning like a Cheshire cat while the congregation erupted in whoops and applause.

That's how to make an exit!

All we had to do now was live happily ever after!

Chapter 19

The Reception

We stepped out of the elegant Austin Princess, the Coop Funeral Service's version of a Rolls Royce Silver Ghost.

A couple of weeks before the wedding, I had finally realised that one of the few things I personally would have to pay for was the wedding car. In their usual efficient way, Mr and Mrs Heaney had ordered what they thought was a suitable vehicle for the occasion.

However, when I saw that my bride-to-be was to travel in an 'ordinary saloon car,' even though it was a Mercedes Benz, it just didn't feel right.

"Mary will have her wedding dress on. She shouldn't have to climb out of a car. She should step out like Royalty or a film star. Don't they have a Rolls Royce?"

Maybe I'd seen too many movies…

My interjection in the planning of the details took the Heaney family by surprise. There were looks from Mary's mum to Big Aunt Peggy while Mary, who had obviously been in on the decision, tried to pooh-pooh my objections.

"John, I've been climbing up into the cabin of your dad's van. I've hung on to your back on that tiny scooter and I now sit in your mini-van with the rust holes in the floor. I've got no problem *lowering* myself to climb out of a Mercedes Benz!"

I don't know why, perhaps it was my only opportunity to stamp a wee bit of my lowly authority, but I fought my corner and lo and behold Mary was now stepping out, not climbing out, of the rather grand, if a little aged, Austin Princess.

The snow had been cleared from the steps of the St Mungo's Centenary Club on Great Western Road which, as a former pupil of the city centre school, I was apparently entitled to take advantage of its facilities. The magnificent Victorian building had originally been built in the 1870s for Mr James Marshall who ran the 'Saracen Iron Foundry,' a huge enterprise in Glasgow which had employed thousands.

It was very impressive with a frontage of marbled Corinthian columns and an entrance hall that could've been on a Hollywood set. A sweeping grand staircase with carved balustrades made an excellent backdrop for the obligatory wedding photos. And it avoided us standing in the snow in some park between the chapel and the reception.

Out of the corner of my eye I caught sight of Mrs Heaney pontificating to the poor young man who had explained the power-cut situation on the phone.

"Excuse me, ladies and gentlemen," a sonorous voice boomed out. It was my new brother-in-law James Gillespie, enjoying his role of Master of Ceremonies. James had a very loud clear voice which he could use very effectively in a court room. It worked here. "As you are all no doubt aware, there will be planned power cuts throughout the day. To take advantage of the time that we do have access to electricity, the management have asked me to ensure that everyone takes their seats as soon as possible. This will make certain we can all enjoy the benefits of the hot wedding breakfast!"

I was in a bit of a daze. I'd never really been the centre of attention before. I knew that Mary was the real centre, but I just kept a grin on my face and let the organisers organise.

The room was magnificent. The sun decided to shine through the large south facing windows, and when the inevitable power cuts did come, we hardly noticed because we'd had our meal and the speeches were in full flow.

Or at least they were in full flow until James announced in his booming voice, "And now we'll hear a few words of wisdom from the groom!"

I looked at Mary, who smiled at me encouragingly.

A sudden dawning…

I didn't know I had to make a speech!

I'd only ever been at one wedding in my life when I was a fourteen-year-old usher and hadn't paid any attention to the formalities (apart from making sure the bride's guests sat on the left…)

“Have you not written a speech, John?” Mary whispered, trying not to laugh at her new husband’s suppressed panic.

“Nobody told me!” I muttered in reply.

I stood up nervously and racked my brains.

I didn’t have a clue.

I remembered seeing a movie…

“My wife and I,” I looked at Mary. Fear in my eyes. Mirth in hers.

A big round of applause.

Relief… for a couple of moments.

What do I say? What do I say?

Mary relented. “Just thank people for coming and gifts and things.”

Ah. I can do that.

Nope.

I can’t.

I had complete stage fright.

I stood there mumbling “Erm… Umm…”

Trying to form sentences in my head before muttering them out in painful inadequacies.

Seventy pairs of eyes willing me to say something, preferably witty and entertaining. But after what felt like a lifetime of Umms and Erms, they would have been happy with a loud burp!

The cringing was pretty absolute.

With Mary’s prompts, I managed to painfully stutter a few thank you’s for coming and mentioned both sets of parents and Thomas and James, and Terry, the bridesmaid. I even managed to thank Father Kamya, sitting, benignly on the other side of my new wife.

Eventually, it was over…

Sympathetic applause.

Sweat running down my back, I sat down.

Mary kissed me supportively then said, “You forgot to thank Big Aunt Peggy for making my dress.”

The sweat turned into a river. *Oh no! Oh no!*

Thankfully, the rest of the speeches were absolutely fine. Another glass of Mateus Rose and I relaxed long enough to enjoy my dad’s gaffes. Especially when he recalled the first time both parents had met, and Mary’s mum, Winnie, on looking at my mum and dad’s wedding photo, looked from the photo to my mum and said the immortal words, “Aren’t the years cruel!”

The guests laughed. Mum suppressed a glare. She would see Dad later…

After the meal was over and the staff were clearing the room, Mary and I went up to Big Aunt Peggy who was sitting regally in a high-backed chair in a side room.

Looking like a time-travelled Queen Victoria in swathes of black lace, she looked up at us and smiled at Mary. “You’re looking lovely, my dear. The dress fits perfectly.”

Mary gave a twirl of appreciation, hugged me, and said, “John wanted to talk to you, Aunt Peggy.”

Her eyes darkened as she looked up at me. “You’re looking good too, John. I enjoyed your speech.” Was that irony behind that steely gaze?

The effects of the Mateus Rose evaporated, and I was back to being a sweat monster as I felt the fabric of my starched formal shirt sticking to my back.

“, well, Aunt Peggy, that’s what I wanted to see you about… ummm… ermm… I’m so sorry I didn’t thank you publicly for the fantastic job you’ve made of Mary’s dress!” *Crawl crawl…*

“If it wasn’t such an important day for Mary, I’d give you what’s for, young man!“ she said icily.

I gulped… More sweat.

Then her face cracked into a big wide grin. “Gotcha! I love to see young men sweat… It was a pleasure, dear boy. I’ve been stitching things up since before the war and it's nice to be appreciated. Don't you worry about it, just enjoy your day."

I nodded feebly, grinned inanely, and looked at Mary.

"See, I told you she likes you, John," Mary whispered as we made our way back to the main room to take our places for the first dance…

Chapter 20

Flight to our New Life.

Looking out of the plane's windows, I recognised the familiar inclines of the Campsie Fells sitting like a protective layer overlooking our home city of Glasgow.

Now covered in snow, the little 'mini mountain' that is Dumgoyne was sitting up like an oversized snowball at the western end of the Campsies. It marked the point where our plane banked and turned left over the large houses and bungalows of Bearsden and Milngavie, their pretty white-covered rooftops criss-crossed by dark ribbons of tarmac.

The plane's engines' note changed as it bounced into a ribbon of turbulence. Mary gripped my left arm even more tightly. I was beginning to worry about my blood circulation, as her slender, but remarkably strong fingers clenched desperately.

"Oh no! We're going to die! We're going to die today! 'S not fair. I've had a wonderful wedding and a wonderful honeymoon, and I was so looking forward to my new married life. And here we are going to die today!" Mary sobbed uncontrollably into my shoulder as the poor passenger on her left tried to look as though he wasn't at all freaked by Mary's demented sotto voce lament.

I held her tightly as the plane wobbled its way down with the slightest of bumps on the well-cleared runway and comfortably slowed to a stop.

Mary straightened, shook her dark curls, and gave me a brilliant smile.

I looked at her quizzically.

"No problem. You just don't realise… It's my prayers that have kept this machine in the air for the last two and a half hours!"

Then she turned to the elderly gentleman sitting in the aisle seat who'd tried to pretend he hadn't noticed Mary's distress and gave him a smacker on his cheek and another beaming smile. “Sorry about that. I really prefer terra firma.”

His face now fully flushed, he stuttered. “It’s… that’s… fine. Have a nice life.”

Here we go… here we go…

Xxxxxxxxxxxxxxxxxxxxxxxxxxxxxxxxxxxxxxxxxxxxxxxxxxxxxxxxx

“There they are!” I heard my mum’s voice before I spotted her in the welcoming crowd just outside the Arrivals doors in Glasgow Airport.

And there *they* were. Mum and Dad with big wide smiles as we hugged and jabbered with a lot of unasked questions as is right and proper for a returning honeymoon couple…

As we were pushing the trolley, Dad was making conversation. “How was the flight?”

Mary narrowed her eyes. I couldn’t help it. “We survived thanks to the skill of the pilot and Mary’s prayers.” That earned me a dig in the ribs.

Ensconced in the familiar estate car, which only the week before had got me to the church just in time, Mum looked back at us from the front seat.

“Well then… how was the hotel? It looked great in the brochure.”

Mary replied, “It was wonderful. Brand new. Enormous lobby with music every night. I won the disco contest the night we arrived. I think all that wedding wine loosened me up.”

Mum looked over at me… but didn’t say a thing. I looked back… and didn’t blink…

There was a harrumph from Dad at the wheel and Mary giggled and carried on. “Magaluf is a new resort so some parts haven’t been finished yet. And it is February, so it was quiet. But we had a trip into Palma which is a beautiful city. We walked all over and managed to find the most marvellous candle maker’s shop. It was like a rainbow of all different sizes of candles hanging from hooks in the ceiling. We filled a whole suitcase with them. The power cuts won't affect us too much for a while. Of course you can have some too. Are they still scarce?"

Mum laughed. "Well, it might have felt a lot longer, but you've only been gone a week, you know." Mary and I looked at one another and grinned.

Mum glanced at Dad and seemed to square her shoulders.

"There's been a wee problem in the flat."

The flat was our new pride and joy. A slice of Victorian architecture enclosed in a hundred-year-old grey sandstone tenement.

Mary's mother had surprised us just a few weeks before the wedding by announcing over the tea and Jaffa cakes that she had managed to find us a suitable flat for two pounds a week rent in our preferred district of Dennistoun. Being a West Ender, it was a part of Glasgow she knew nothing about. And by the angle of her nose, an area she didn't really think was entirely suitable for her youngest daughter…

To her credit, she didn't actually say that.

Mary and I had looked at a few flats for sale, but on my slim earnings in a new business and just enough money to pay for the wedding ring, buying any kind of property was completely out of our reach. We *were* only twenty.

I don't remember worrying about finding somewhere to live. Being a naive eternal optimist I reckoned something would turn up…And it did!

"So, what's the problem?" I asked Mum as we joined the traffic squeezing over the new Kingston Bridge. Mary looked concerned.

"Well, Rhona, your sister, and I were hoovering the carpet and putting away some of the wedding gifts yesterday. We lit a fire to warm the place up for you coming home. Then there was a terrible noise." Mum paused for effect.

Uh huh. Did it blow up? Did it collapse?

"Oh, for God's sake, Marie, don't spin it out," Dad blurted out in annoyance.

"I'm telling them. You keep your eyes on the road!" Mum retorted.

"And this noise?" Mary ventured hesitantly.

"The damned soot collapsed down the chimney and burst into your brand-new living room! We tried to slow it down with the rug but it kept on coming and coming! It was never-ending ! The whole room was in a soot cloud! I couldn't see your curtains!" Tears were in Mum's eyes.

Our shoulders slumped. We'd spent the month before the wedding painting and decorating our new abode. The main feature was the high-ceilinged bay-windowed lounge, which I now pictured in a layer of thick black soot. We'd spent all our savings on the nylon turquoise carpet and white pretend leather suite. The rented white telly put the finishing touch to our new seventies paradise.

"Is it that bad?" I dared to ask.

"Well, we've taken five Hoover bags down to the bins and both your sisters, Joyce and Rhona, are still there, doing their best. It's a lot better than it was..."

Mary said, "That's a terrible lot of work you've had to do. I can't thank you enough. I don't start back to work till Monday. We'll get it sorted!"

We arrived in the street where we were about to start married life.

Heaving the candle-weighted case up the two flights of stone stairs, I met an apparition coming down. Mary's eldest sister, Joyce, the headmistress of a west end private school, was stumbling downstairs looking like an escapee from a Lionel Bart movie, her auburn hair caked with soot. The black streaks across her cheeks completed the vision of a chimney sweep extra out of Oliver.

"You tell your new wife this is one she definitely owes me!" she growled as she passed by me banging her bag of soot off the one-time clean walls of the staircase.

Not a happy lassie. Why was she here if she hadn't volunteered?

"Ah, Mrs Dickson, how nice to see you. Please forgive this temporary lapse in my appearance. We're all mucking in for our baby sister." I heard Joyce enunciating in a different tone to my mum at the bottom of the stairs.

I looked back down and puzzled. Then Mary caught up with me. "Don't mind Joyce. She's only here because Rhona's here. She's not really the volunteering sort..."

I didn't get it. Confused sibling rivalry? Women? I'll think about it later.

I stopped Mary on the landing. "Whoa, girl. One more tradition!" I lifted her up in my arms, kissed her gently, and carried her over the threshold. "Time to get them glad rags off… You've got a bit of scrubbing to do!"

Chapter 21

'The Last Time I Moved House'

The next morning Mary and I tackled the dregs of the soot that had re-settled after Mum and Mary's sisters had cleared up. We were relieved at how limited the damage was. The aquamarine and cream walls and matching fitted carpet weren't quite as vibrant as they had been. But we'd just have to work at it. Mum's verbal picture had prepared us for a much worse scene.

Unpacking our suitcases and the last of our wedding gifts, I found myself telling Mary about the last time I'd moved house ten years earlier, when I was very much just a boy.

"Mum and Dad always gave us plenty of responsibilities. I mean I was only nineteen last year when we opened The Buy In. But the day we moved to Riddrie was just a wee bit traumatic when I think about it..."

I grew up through the fifties in that land of milk and honey that was Ruchazie, on the periphery in the east end of Glasgow. Built on green belt, Mum and Dad were overjoyed when they were allocated a two-bedroom ground-floor flat in the new council run 'housing scheme.'

We had a big corner garden, wrapped around the full extent of the flat. It even had a balcony, though for some reason it was called a veranda. There was a small tree-bordered field on the other side of the road, home for a handful of dairy cows loitering by the tumbledown fence and bushes, contentedly chewing their cuds while watching us recent arrivals playing games galore on the car-free street: the dividing line between new suburbia and the truly rural.

We were still able to play most of the street games our parents had enjoyed as children. We'd play Kick the Can, a variation of Hide'n'seek, Beds, or peever, with chalked-out, numbered squares, where we'd hop on one foot while we kicked an old shoe polish tin (the peever) into the target squares. Quite a skill!

Proper footballs were scarce. But the girls always seemed to have solid rubber balls for 'stoatin' against the walls while they chanted various songs or rhymes. These hard balls were often purloined and were ideal for the tougher boys' game of Dodge the Ball. It's all in the name of the game...

The new houses had been constructed as part of the post-war slum clearance. They were loosely based on the old tenement structures and managed, in the early years, to keep many of the elements of tenement life that folk were fond of. There was a community spirit, or at least us kids had plenty of spirit as we played at wee make-believe shops or chased each other up and over the new-fangled 'dykes' that housed the communal bins, still called middens.

During school holidays or weekends, we were completely unsupervised from when we ran out the door in the morning. We'd maybe pop home for a 'jeely piece' at lunchtime. Then straight back out again until our bellies told us it was dinner time.

Our mums and dads loved us and looked after us but they definitely didn't molly coddle us.

We lived in Ruchazie until 1962 when I was in my last year of primary school. One of our big highlights of the week was the Saturday morning trip to the matinees at the ABC Cinema in Riddrie, at the bottom of Cumbernauld Road.

From the age of about eight or nine, I'd been entrusted with looking after first one, then both of my two wee brothers, Thomas and Alan, two and a half and five years younger than me respectively. Mum would give us a sixpenny piece each and we'd walk up to the bus stop on the main road, a few blocks up the hill.

We'd jump on the blue Alexander's double decker, along with loads of other excited weans. We'd clamber and push our way upstairs to grab the best bench seats we could, pay our fares to the generally good natured conductress, and be transported the couple of miles to our destination. That palace of juvenile fantasy and fun: the ABC Cinema Minors Club. There, in a frenzy of childish enthusiasm, we'd boo and hiss at every black-hatted baddie, then yell encouragement to the Roy Rogers or Errol Flynn hero. Wave to the pals who seemed to have a birthday every other month, and so were invited on stage for yet another badge and lollipop. Occasionally we'd settle down and enjoy a Tom and Jerry cartoon treat. Happy Days...

Our parents really did presume we'd look after ourselves (and our wee brothers). And they expected us to think for ourselves. So we did... Although sometimes they did take it a bit too far...

By 1962 my mum and dad reckoned we needed a new house. We were moving up! They'd decided to buy what we thought was a huge building in an obscure street called Riddrie Knowes.

Once the details had been finalised, we went *en famille* in Dad's Ford Thames van down to what was to become our new home. All six of us. Mum, Dad, me, Thomas, Alan, and our new wee baby brother Phil. We had definitely out grown the two-bedroomed flat.

We ran amuck in the rattlingly empty house. Chasing each other up and down the stairs *inside* the house. Amazed at the basement garage that ran *underneath* the building like the biggest den in the world. Coming to terms with the concept that there was more than one door into our new home. In fact, there were three if you counted the 'French windows' at one end of the living room.

So, we were suitably thrilled as we drove back to our flat in Ruchazie.

Mum and Dad didn't really explain the practical arrangements for the day we moved house. Or 'flitting' as us Glasgow folk call it.

We had been to the new house. We'd seen where it was. We knew how to get about...

So, come the big day I was simply told to gather my two wee brothers after school and bring them down to the new house. No problem!

I remember vaguely trying to map out in my head how to get there. But being the optimist that I am, I wasn't particularly fazed. Just energized and looking forward to moving into a room with just one brother!

So, at four o'clock on a thankfully dry October day, I gathered my siblings in the playground and started the quite complicated trek to our new life.

We'd never walked to Riddrie. We'd always gone by bus with lots of other kids. But we weren't going to follow the bus route. The house wasn't as far as the cinema.

We walked from High Ruchazie through Low Ruchazie with myriads of school kids all making their way home. Down beyond the boundaries of the scheme to the bridge over the Molandiner canal (now the route of the M8). Past the Corporation bus garage and on down Gartcraig Road past the 'four in a block' and posh semi-detached council houses

There was a sameness about the houses on either side of the road, and I didn't remember it being such a long road.

"How far is it now, John?" Thomas was tiring.

This was unfamiliar territory. Then, at the bottom of Gartcraig Road we saw the street sign *Riddrie Knowes* and my bubbling anxieties subsided. My two wee brothers trusted me implicitly. I could never get them lost! I was their Big Brother!

We walked along the road. Different houses here. Bungalows high off the street. A mixture of different-shaped houses on the other side. I didn't remember all these different types of houses…

Where's our new house? It should be here. I looked at every building as we passed, unwilling to ask for help from my tiring wee brothers, especially as Thomas, was beginning to wilt. The younger Alan always had much more energy than anyone else.

It was beginning to get dark. We got to the end of the Knowes and we hadn't found our new house. My tummy was bursting bubbles, *What if we can't find it?* I tried not to show my near panic.

We walked on another few yards. The traffic was much heavier. This was a main road! Nothing was familiar. Then I spied the brash red illuminations of the ABC Cinema way down at the bottom of the hill. Thank God! Something I recognised.

"Are we going to the pictures?" Alan was always hopeful.

"Not today, but we'll be able to walk there from now on." *If I can find our flipping house,* I thought.

We turned back and worked our way back along the Knowes.

Two minutes later we saw an enormous van pulling away from the front of what we then instantly recognised as our new home. *The bubbles floated down…*

As we rushed up the stairs and into the house with yelps of joy and relief, any and all anxieties were banished as Mum and Dad gathered us up and hugged and danced with us up and down our new abode. We were simply home from school. We had come to no harm. We were just a wee bit later than expected…

"Well, I know what you mean, John." Mary lifted the whistling kettle off the 'new' second-hand gas cooker.

"I don't think I'd like to trust Joyce's kids to figure out how to get to a new house by themselves. Though, my mum and dad must have thought along the same lines: I was only five years old when I started primary school in Garnethill, off Sauchihall Street. I remember Mum coming with me for the first few days. Getting on the Corporation bus outside the house on the Boulevard. When we got to our stop just beside the Bundy Club where you and I first met, she'd walk me up to the school so I knew where it was. But after that, I was on my own. My big sister would walk me to the bus stop in the morning and someone would be waiting for me when I came home."

"Well. All that child neglect doesn't seem to have done us any harm eh? Maybe it helped to build our confidence up to the point where I can take my new wife all the way to Mallorca before I'm even twenty-one!"

"Well, you certainly managed that. Now all we have to do is manage to live life like a couple of adults." Mary supped her tea as we sat at the round white table which neatly fitted into the one-time inset bed-alcove in the kitchen.

"Don't be daft. Do you know there's nothing to stop us buying a nice bottle of wine with our dinner? Who's gonna say ye can't do that, eh?"

"So that's your idea of being grown up is it, Mr Dickson?" Mary grinned.

"It's time I started making our dinner. You've never actually tasted anything I've cooked have you? And we can't live on fish suppers like last night, can we?"

I hadn't really thought much about cooking and looking after ourselves. My mum could cook a bit and obviously had to with a hungry husband and five sons. But she cooked dutifully rather than joyfully. So, Mary didn't really have a lot to compete with.

"Well, I did buy you Mrs Beaton's cookbook for Christmas. I hope you've been studying it."

"Just you go down to the off-sales and see if you can find one of those nice bottles of wine you were talking about. I think I might surprise you!"

Chapter 22

The Way to a Man's Heart...

"Hello, darling, I'm home." I role-played as I closed the door behind me, clutching the first bottle of wine I'd bought from a shop. Neirsteiner Domtal with a very colourful label wrapped round the dark green slender bottle. The label had definitely been the selling point.

"Did you get asked for ID then?" Mary looked very pretty in her short skirt and frilly apron stirring something in a pot on the cooker. Bending down to check the oven she was the picture of sixties chic. My heart melted as my hunger pangs grew.

"Don't be daft. With this moustache and sideburns? I've never been ID'd in my life. Ever since we first chanced going into the Milton of Campsie pub when we went camping. We were only fifteen. I must have an old face. Eh?"

"Well, you're definitely old enough for me. Just sit down and I'll serve you your dinner, sir. Perhaps you could open our wine?"

Pretending to be sophisticated, I wrestled with the thin corkscrew that had come as part of a wedding gift.

Another first, I thought as I pushed the point of the T-shaped corkscrew into the centre of the cork. I've seen the waiters doing this in the Sorrento. Our favourite restaurant we'd decided. Even though we'd only been there twice, the head waiter, Umberto had remembered our drinks order from our previous visit.

"A vodka and pineapple for the lady and a whisky and American dry for you, sir? And would you like the Tornados Rossini again?"

We'd been pretty impressed as it had been months since our first visit to celebrate Mary's twentieth birthday.

Mary busied herself taking stuff out of the oven while I twirled and pushed the remarkably inefficient corkscrew.

It seemed to finally get to the bottom of the cork, so I placed the bottle between my legs, pulled hard, and half the cork came out. The rest was still determinately stuck in the neck of the bottle.

One more attempt and it completely disintegrated and crumbled down into the wine. A scum of broken cork was visible with one big lump mocking me.

"Eh… we have a problem," I admitted to Mary who by this time was ladling out the homemade soup she'd made earlier. It smelled lovely.

"Don't worry." Mary smiled as she brought the soup to the table. "Just strain the wine into that measuring jug. It'll be fine. We can pretend we're back in that little taverna on the corner in Mallorca".

Sitting at our table in our new house and about to eat our first home cooked meal, I felt cosy. *This is just right.* Mary had even put a single rose in a slender vase in the centre of the table.

Ach. Life is good.

The soup was delicious. Almost as good as my Gran's…

"So, who on earth taught you to make soup as good as this?"

"Well, actually, Dad is the real cook in our house; he showed me years ago."

"So, what's coming next then?"

"Chicken a' la Mary."

As my new wife fussed over the final presentation, I sat and poured myself a glass of our strained wine. I realised Mary had never had a chance to cook a meal, that I'd eaten. I mentally crossed my fingers.

Mary brought the casserole to the table. A chicken dish covered in a blue cheese sauce like a picture out of a posh cookbook.

Potatoes and vegetables were in separate serving dishes. Very colourful. Not the usual mince and tatties piled on the plate that Mum dutifully put together.

"Well, this looks great." I helped myself to a generous plateful.

"I hope you like it. Joyce and I went to a cordon bleu cookery course a couple of years ago. I'm determined we're going to eat well." Mary smiled and looked nicely pleased with herself.

"That's a bonus," I said as I cut into the chicken…

Ooft! I sat back.

A horrible smell wafted up from the open chicken breast.

Surely that's not coming from the blue cheese? Maybe I'm not going to like cordon bleu?

I tentatively forked a piece of chicken and brought it to my mouth.

"Oh no! Don't eat that!" Mary gasped as she grabbed the fork out of my hand.

"What?" *Well that's a relief*

Mary's eye's filled with tears. "I don't know what's happened but it's definitely not right. The chicken is rank. The butcher's must have sold me an old fowl that's past its best. Thinks I'm a stupid young girl! Oh God, I could have poisoned you!"

I didn't know what to say as she picked up the noxious meal and threw it in the bin. "That'll have to go right down to the midden or it'll stink out the flat. I'm so annoyed at myself! I was looking forward to surprising you with my cooking skills. My Granny told me to always keep a surprise for your man. And look at the mess I've made of it!"

"Mary, Mary." I gave her a hug. "It's just one plateful. The soup was magic! I'll bet tomorrow's grub will be really tasty."

Mary gave me a wan smile as I brushed the tears from her face.

"Well, you can always have a glass of that wine I managed to ruin." I tried. "See, I don't even have a skill I've been holding back!"

"Aye, well. I think I will." Mary shook herself.

"And I think you should get another bottle; that I'll open this time. An' while you're out there, I'll have a sausage supper… just for a change… Wait till that butcher sees me in the morning! 'Cos we're having Tournedos Rossini tomorrow night and he better come up trumps!"

Chapter 23

Harsh Reality.

"What on earth is going on?" Mary asked me as the distant banging noise penetrated my sleeping subconscious.

"I haven't a clue. God! It's three o' clock in the morning!" I forced my eyes open as Mary pushed me out from the warmth of our bed into the cold and darkness of our winter bedroom.

I fumbled for the bedside light as the thumping continued. Pulling last night's shirt on, I felt my way down the narrow hallway until I managed to find the light switch, which for some historical reason was halfway down the wall. My bare toes had already stubbed against one of the empty suitcases waiting to go back to Dad's garage.

Trying to button up my shirt I opened the heavy front door to the unnerving silhouette of two very large policemen almost blocking out the landing light behind them.

"Sorry to disturb you at this time of night, sir. Are you John Dickson?" The larger of the two figures spoke in a surprisingly pleasant Highland lilt.

"Well, yes I am. That's my name on the door. We just moved in last week. What's going on? Is there something wrong?" *Of course there's something wrong, John; otherwise, you'd still be in your lovely, cosy bed.*

The next door on the landing opened and a rather disturbing apparition appeared. A ghostly white face surrounded by a halo of bright pink rollers leaned into the gloom of the landing.

"You alright, John? That's a helluva racket you plods are making. Some of us have to get the weans up for school in the morning. An' my man didnae come home frae the pub till near eleven o clock. Ah mean Ah might no' look like Ah need it but Ah'm trying tae get some beauty sleep!"

"I'm sorry, Rosie. I don't know what's the problem is yet. I just opened the door. Away back to sleep." I'd met Rosie a couple of times when we were decorating. Mary reckoned she was simply 'dead nosy.'

"It's alright, madam. We're sorry to disturb you. There shouldn't be any more noise." The Highland policeman's voice soothed Rosie back into her flat.

Once I'd managed to get the policemen into the living room, it transpired that there had been a burglary at the shop. The alarm had gone off as it was supposed to but because our house telephone had yet to be installed by the Post Office, the only way to contact us was the old-fashioned knock on the door…

"Oh dear, John. I hope this isn't going to be a regular problem." Mary had gathered herself and joined us as the policemen explained that they couldn't see any obvious external damage but something must have triggered the alarm.

"I'm afraid as the key holder, you'll have to attend as soon as possible. The alarm bell is still ringing out. Two of our colleagues are standing guard outside the premises until you get there."

"That's what I get for being organised," I said. "I just changed the key holder's address two days ago from my mum and dad's house to here! Otherwise, Dad would have got the call."

"Sorry to be the bearers of bad tidings, but that's a policeman's lot." The highlander philosophised. The other chap hadn't said a word. He'd been too busy writing everything down.

As the policemen left, I heard Rosie's door click shut. *There'll be questions to be answered tomorrow, I fear.*

"What a great start to married life. We've only been home for four days. Do you want me to come with you?" Mary looked at me helpfully.

"No, Sweetheart. You have to get to your work in the west end for nine. I'll manage," I said manfully. "I gave the cops Dad's number. The station will call him, and he'll probably be there by the time I get dressed and get that ruddy van going."

Ten minutes later I was standing in the slush, van bonnet open while the sleet obscured my vision as I tried to dry off the distributor cap.

As I'd expected the minivan wasn't keen on starting in such damp weather. Neither was I…

Luckily, the machine rattled into life on the third attempt and I made my way through the deserted Dennistoun streets and onto the main road. The shop was just a mile away but the sleet had worsened as I got closer.

The flashing blue lights of the police car parked outside made a dismal scene through the falling sleet and snow.

The red light above the shop facia was sporadic and I could hear the alarm bells ringing. The neighbours will love me, I thought.

Dad's car was sitting side on so they could talk through open windows. On my approach, there was a flurry of car doors opening. We huddled round the big padlock which was still firmly in place halfway down the steel roller shutter. Both window shutters also looked undisturbed. The bright police torch illuminated the thickening flurries which were now turning into big soft snowflakes, freezing my fingers as I fumbled with the keys.

"We had a look around the back," one of the officers shouted over the racket of the alarm. "It's hard to be sure but it looks like there could be slates missing from your roof. We couldn't climb onto the lower flat-roofed back shop without ladders. But a nimbler bloke than me could've clambered up the stove pipes. Then it would be easy to pull slates off the main roof."

"We talked about that possibility, didn't we, John?" I could hardly hear Dad's voice as I now fumbled with the bottom lock on the shutter.

"What with Christmas and the wedding it was on our 'to do' list. But you can't make a flat rear roof not be flat! Stupid design for a row of shops!" Dad, who had been the victim of many burglary attempts on his Ruchazie shop, had previously made the same point… A few times…

"Shoost!" One of the policemen held his hand up, just as I was about to raise the shutter.

"Can you hear anything above that racket?" I said worriedly. Could the burglar or burglars still be in the shop?

"Not sure now. You?" He looked at his partner who shrugged and shook his head.

“Right. Just to be safe, we’ll enter the premises first. Wait till we give the all clear then come in. Where are the light switches?”

“Harrumph, they’re in a cupboard behind the news counter to your left. Another stupid design!” Dad was on a roll.

I pulled the shutter up. It clattered as it rolled into place. There was one more key to unlock in the wooden framed glass door to gain access. I peered into the shop as the policemen shone their torches through the glass.

Nothing seemed to be moving as I pushed the door open and stood back to let the cops do their job.

Their torch lights moved all over the shop and then rested on the high ceiling above the back shelves. A ragged hole was visible and I could see snow fluttering through the torch beams. The broken ceiling alarm wires trailed over the shelves. *Bloody Hell. It’s gonna be a long night…*

“Can you come in and turn the alarm off, Mr Dickson,” a silhouette shouted.

The alarm key was just inside the door, one of the improvements we had made when we took over the shop six months earlier.

I turned the key.

Silence.

Dad moved past me into the shop. “Do you want me to… Whoa!”

He was cut off as a blur came rushing towards us from the shadows.” Out of my f*****g way!”

Dad was pushed aside and staggered into the Irn Bru rack.

The cops swivelled round. Their moving beams blinding me, as the dervish stumbled over Dad’s foot and I instinctively held both arms wide.

I was punched in the chest by a small hard fist as the burglar tried to push past me. But there was too much of me and not enough of him.

I fell backwards into the soaking slush-covered pavement. But my assailant fell on top of me, lashing out and trying to use my thighs as starting blocks.

I clung on.

Lots of shouting and torches waving then the cops grabbed his jacket and heaved him off me.

I clambered to my feet.

I was soaking…

My chest hurt…

We're still going to have to fix the slates on the roof!

The snow's getting heavier!

'S'not Fair… This time last week I was on honeymoon!

They dragged him back into the shop while I saw that Dad was alright. He was fine, if a little angry. Then I walked round behind the counter with the aid of a torch and turned on the lights.

The scene looked so different from the desperate monochrome of the struggle moments before: the boxes of chocolates and brightly coloured rows of sweetie jars behind the other counter. The gondola in the middle of the floor full of groceries. The back wall shelves groaning with toys and Airfix models. Apart, that is, from the section of shelves now empty as the burglar must have used them as a ladder to clamber down from the fifteen-foot-high ceiling.

He must have found it too hard to climb back up…

The two policemen were still dealing with the burglar. His back was to me and I could see the handcuffs glistening on his wrists.

By his slight build, he looked like a young teenager as he answered questions as one cop held on to the handcuffs, while the other wrote in his notebook.

One of the policemen turned to me.

"A good job you were there, Mr Dickson. He might well have got away with it. Have you seen the bag of cigarettes he had inside his jacket?"

Just then the burglar turned and looked at me with pleading eyes.

"My God! Ronnie Johnson! What the Hell are you doing here?"

"What's your mother going to say? She due to open the shop in a couple of hours!"

Chapter 24

A Hard Day.

"Right. C'mon, John. Time you went home. Go and get a bath and a kip. It's half past one now. We'll manage; I'll hang on till you get back."

Thomas had been with us since the shop officially opened at six-thirty when he was due to open with Theresa, the burglar's mum.

That was a night I didn't want to repeat in a hurry!

Once the police had finally left with their underage captive, Dad and I had to scramble up wobbly ladders to the 'stupid flat roof' in the thickening snow. We hauled up a tarpaulin we'd unearthed from a deep corner of Dad's garage, then did our best to spread it over the crudely hacked-out hole in the roof before amateurishly replacing the heavy old-fashioned slates as a temporary repair.

It was freezing on that roof! It didn't help that Dad was trying to 'do the job properly' which I thought was pointless. We'd have to get it professionally repaired later that day anyway!

Eventually, we gave up. There was enough cover to keep the sleet out for a few hours. We went back down to the shop for shelter and to take stock of the situation.

"I think you'll have to sack his mum, even if she is a prison officer's wife. You can't just shrug off a family member actually burgling the shop and putting us through all this hassle!" Dad was not a happy chappie.

I don't want to sack anyone… Maybe Dad'll do it?

Then there had been the very awkward scene as Theresa knocked on the front door a few minutes before opening time.

She was wearing a very quizzical look as I turned the key and let her in. Theresa, originally from Inverness, along with her two sons had moved into the prison officer's quarters just a couple of weeks before we opened the shop. Her husband, Eddie, had been transferred from a high-security prison up north and the timing couldn't have been better for us.

She had managed a newsagent's shop for years in Aberdeen. As a forty-something mother of two, she had a lovely way with her, and all the customers really liked her. She and Thomas often worked together in the mornings, and they liked to have a bit of fun with our somewhat elderly clientele.

"C'moan now. All you coffin dodgers stand in line! I don't know why you have to be here first thing in the morning. It's no' as if ye've got any deadlines or anything… Apart from the undertakers' maybe?"

Remarkably, nearly all the pensioners seemed to enjoy the banter and Thomas and Theresa had become a bit of a morning double act.

"How come you and your dad are here? Is something wrong with Thomas? I thought he was on with me this morning." Theresa seemed to know nothing about the burglary or her son's involvement.

"No, Theresa, nothing wrong with Thomas. I can see him crossing the road just now."

"Oh my goodness! Look at that mess. What on Earth has been going on?" Theresa had spotted the clutter of toys and plaster still on the floor beneath the patched-up hole in the roof.

I looked at Dad and felt myself sagging.

Being a boss at the age of twenty just isn't natural. Especially when dealing with people who were twice my age. I'd had retail management training in R.S. McColl's. But that training didn't cover this situation. There I'd have called security and passed the buck to them. But Dad wasn't going to let me dodge this responsibility.

Thomas came in carrying some of the newspaper bundles that had just been dumped on the pavement outside.

"I slept in! I've only been up ten minutes. Mum said there'd been a burglary. You should have got me up, Dad! What happened? Is there anything missing?" Thomas always was a morning person, very bouncy and ready to do battle with the regulars who were beginning to congregate just outside.

Dad stepped in. "Theresa, John needs to talk to you. I'll help Thomas with the papers. "He turned to me. "Take Theresa into the back shop, eh?"

Oh God! I've going to have to do the dirty work…

Thomas looked from me to Dad and then Theresa. "Eh? What's going on then?" He looked puzzled as he opened the door to the first of our customers.

"C'mon, Thomas. We'll talk about it when the shop quietens down." Dad started sorting the newspapers onto the counter.

I closed the door to the back shop behind us. Theresa took her coat off and hung it in the cupboard while looking perplexed as she waited for me to begin. "What's up, John? What's there to talk about? We've got a real mess to clear up."

I breathed deep. "I don't know how you don't seem to know, Theresa. But we actually caught the burglar inside the shop." Her mouth opened. "It was your Johnnie, Theresa. He couldn't climb back up to get out."

Theresa started trembling. Her colour drained. "Is this a joke? My Johnnie? He would never do a thing like that. Johnnie's a good boy, and anyway his father would kill him if he got into trouble. Sorry, John. There's got to be some kind of mistake."

It made no sense that she didn't know. "Have the police not contacted you? They took him into custody. I saw him in the police car. That was after he knocked me down…"

Her eyes widened. It was sinking in. "I wasn't home last night. I stayed with my mum in King's Park. Remember she fell out of bed last week? She's not got a phone… It took me two buses to get here. Was it really my Johnnie? I'll need to go home, John… Sorry…" She pulled her coat back out of the cupboard and started putting it on, her face now ashen.

"Ok, Theresa. That's what to do. Call us later once you've got a clearer picture." Inwardly I sighed with relief. I hadn't had to sack her… yet!

As Theresa bustled past the queue and out the front door, Thomas and Dad looked at me questioningly. I shrugged and went behind the counter. "I'll serve, Dad. You go home and get some breakfast. I'll call Babs and see if she can cover for Theresa. Then I'll pop along and we can chat".

At the kitchen table, Mum and Dad were debating what to do about Theresa. Mum was always on the side of fairness. “His mum hasn't committed a crime. As John says, she obviously doesn't know anything about it. I mean, she would hardly put her son up to burgling the shop, not care that he'd been caught. Then come in to do her shift! I've got to know Theresa a bit. There's something we don't know. They're a good family. And prison officer's kids tend to keep out of trouble…”

Dad was more dogmatic. “We can't afford to take any chances. He was caught red handed! She's the thief's mother!”

I interjected. “I'm not sure what to do. Let's wait till we hear from Theresa… or the police. In the meantime, I gotta get back. The roofer said he'd be there about now. Thanks for the toast, Mum.”

I was tired and stressed as I went back to the shop to continue tackling the mess and supervise the roof repair. *I'd so much rather be back on honeymoon…*

“Hello, John. Can I come in and talk to you?” Theresa sounded nervous on the phone. It was the next day and things were just about back to normal, apart from fending off the myriads of questions about the burglary from customers.

Twenty minutes later Theresa and I faced each other sitting on the high stools we used in the back shop.

“We know now why Johnnie did it, John.” Theresa had tears in her eyes. I wondered what was coming.

“You know how he goes to Gartcraig Secondary.” I didn't really, but the local comprehensive was where most of the local kids went.

“Well, Johnnie's the new kid on the block and he's been having a bit of a hard time. His Aberdeen accent and ginger hair haven't exactly helped him to merge in. Apparently, he's been getting bullied. We knew nothing about it till the police told us yesterday. The poor wean's been keeping it all to himself.” She pulled a packet of paper hankies out of her bag and ripped it open. I was confused; where was this leading?

Theresa composed herself. “The police got it out of him that two boys from fifth year had threatened him!”

“Threatened him with what, Theresa?”

She sobbed as she wiped her eyes. “They told him their dads were in the jail and if he didn’t do what they told him they were going to murder his father. My Eddie!” She gulped back the tears. “The poor boy’s been terrified. He thought he was protecting his father!”

I sat back and asked, “So, what did the police say? Have they charged him?”

“They said it’s up to the Procurators Fiscal. They let him come home last night. They’ve started investigating the two boys. And right enough, their dads are in the jail! Oh my God. I don’t know what to do!”

“I’m sure, now it’s all out in the open the police and the prison officers and the governor will make sure your Eddie’s safe. And Johnnie’s headmaster should deal with the two bullies. I suspect you and Eddie will be having a word in that quarter.”

Theresa’s shoulders firmed up. “You’re bloody right we will. My Eddie doesn’t say much, but when he does…” She blew her nose.

“But, John. I want to say. Johnnie told me to tell you he’s awfy sorry for knocking you down. I’ll get him to come in and apologise himself. But he’s no’ going back to that school till we’ve had more than a word with his headmaster.”

“I think that’s wise. Away home and see to your family. We’ll cover you for a couple of days… I’ll tell your customers you’ll be back soon.”

Theresa stood up. Then put her arms around me. “Och, you’re a good lad, John. There’s many a boss would have sacked me for whit Johnnie did. Ah’ve got tae thank you.”

Aye well. If it had been Dad who had talked to her yesterday…

Chapter 25

Mary's Day and Rhona's Fray.

"Are you alright, sir? Your eyes will adjust in a minute or two. Just sit back and relax." Mary smiled down at her patient who was grimacing as he tried to cope with his custom-made new contact lenses.

The fashionably dressed young man, who Mary reckoned looked like a trainee insurance salesman, blinked heavily another couple of times then lent forward on the consulting chair as a big grin stretched across his face.

"My God, they really do work. It's like wearing really strong specs… without wearing really strong specs! Now I can see how properly gorgeous you are. What are you doin' the night? It's Friday. D'you fancy going to the Electric Garden? I've got a couple 'o free tickets. My mate's a bouncer there."

Mary, still smiling, though a little less widely, stepped back just a little. "If your vision is so much improved you should have noticed this." She held her left hand up and pointed at the gold band proudly worn on her wedding finger.

"Well, I did actually see it. But you're not wearing an engagement ring, so I thought you maybe wore it to put the wrong sort o' guys off the scent. And I know I'm no' the wrong sort o' guy!" He flecked his shoulders back. "I've got prospects. Especially now I won't be wearing those heavy glasses on ma face." He was very enthusiastic.

"Sorry to disappoint you, Mr… McLetchie." Mary looked down at the customer card. "I can assure you this ring is the real thing. And not that it's any of your business, but my husband and I reckoned a living room carpet was a lot more useful that a shiny ring."

"You gotta give me some credit for trying… Mary?" He looked at her name badge as he stood up.

"Well, it's very flattering, And good luck in the Electric Garden. In the meantime, can I take you over to the cash desk? I'm afraid it's time to settle up."

Mary brought her customer, still wearing his big grin as well as his new contacts, out of the consulting room into the bright front shop.

Mr MacAllister, the optician, was a slim, elegantly suited man in his forties, his salt and pepper hair just curling over his collar. As always, he sported a fresh flower in his buttonhole. After showing a smartly dressed middle-aged lady out of the door, he turned to Mary and her customer.

"I trust everything is all right with your new contacts. You did well with the test lenses you had for a day after your last visit. You should be all right now."

"Oh yes, I'm fine. Couldn't be better. These are far clearer than those test lenses! Now I can see exactly how good looking your girls are. That blond lassie in the back is a stunner tae!"

The optician looked a little flustered as he replied. "Well, yes, Mary and Lynne are both lovely young women. And very good at their jobs. We're very fortunate to have them attending to our clients. Thank you." He then shook hands with his latest satisfied customer before retiring to his back office.

"Aye, he must be rakin' it in wi' these charges. I hope you girls get your share, eh?"

"We're ok. It's almost four-thirty, we'll be finished soon. You have a good weekend. Enjoy your new vision." Mary held the front door open as the young man hurried away to explore his new opportunities.

"You handled that well, Mary. I heard every word. I'd have told him where to get off." Lynne, my cousin on Dad's side, had joined Mr MacAllister and Mary as the new, easier to wear contact lenses had become more and more popular. Business was booming.

Lynne was shorter than Mary, and a couple of years younger. She had a fresh bubbly personality and a mane of natural blond hair.

It wasn't surprising the west end opticians in Hyndland Road was all the rage among bespectacled young men… at least those who could afford the prices.

The optician came out from the back office. Holding an open bottle of champagne and three glasses on a tray.

"Here we go then, girls. Last Friday of the month. And it has been a very successful month. Lynne's done well taking over your full-time hours, Mary. And married life seems to be agreeing with you. Especially now you're only working three days a week".

Mary and Lynne gave each other the thumbs up.

"So why don't you close the front door and have a glass of bubbly. That'll set us all up for the weekend."

Mary and Lynne clinked glasses. "And your poor John's got another hour to work in that shop of his." Lynne sipped her champagne and grinned mischievously.

Mary nodded. "I can't say life's not pretty good at the moment. And tonight we're going for dinner at my sister Rhona's. She and Graham live not too far from here. So, I'm doing a bit of shopping then meeting John there. Rhona's flat's lovely. She's always had a bit of artistic flair. All beige carpets and splashes of ochres. She's working as a window dresser in Lewis's, while Graham's finishing university. I think they'll do well once he's qualified. Anyway, that's me off. See you on Monday. Bye, Mr McAllister." With a quick wave, Mary wafted out to the busy street and headed towards the new Wine Cellar. A nice bottle of Blue Nun would go down well with dinner. Rhona will have already organised candles and flowers on the table. Mary was enjoying feeling quite grown up

Mary's next sister up had married her teenage heartthrob, Graham, just after Mary and I had started going out together. I was actually at their wedding and was introduced as the bridesmaid's new boyfriend… I knew nobody else. So I was *that* guy sitting with the weans at the furthest table in the corner, while my wife to be (though she hadn't asked me yet) was enjoying the limelight at the top table. *And* she was able to hear the full depth of Graham's speech. It apparently far outshone my later attempt by miles… Now if I'd listened, instead of keeping the kids amused by playing shove ha'penny, I might have brought the house down when my turn came…

I was finishing up in The Buy In when the phone rang. It was Rhona. I had no chance to say hello as she blurted out: "Don't come tonight! I've set the house on fire!" Then she hung up.

Chilling!

Hmmm. She must have thought Mary was me.

I knew Mary would be on her way there after shopping and maybe going for a coffee. So, I had to disobey Rhona's order. Although it did sound as if dinner wasn't likely.

I rushed across the motorway, overtaking on the inside, zoomed down Woodlands Road, weaved my way up to University Avenue, and just caught the lights at Byres Road. A nifty left then right and I was on the corner of Lawrence Street just as Mary arrived at the same spot. We were confronted by the sight of Rhona brandishing a frying pan at a brave fire-fighter who was failing to gain entry to her ground-floor tenement flat.

She was in full flow. "I've told you already! I threw the burning chip pan through the kitchen window! I know I should have covered it with a tea towel first. But the window was closer. It's out now! It's in the back court! And I'm not having you lot tramping your dirty big tackety boots all over my brand-new carpets!

She took a breath, lifted her head, and looked around the street. "Who called 999 anyway? It certainly wasn't me!" Her piercing blue eyes dared anyone to answer.

Graham arrived just behind us. He gave us a strained nod, walked past, and quietly took charge. He recognised his wife was already traumatised by having to throw her flaming chip pan out of the window. (It was a present from Big Aunt Peggy!) Ruining her brand-new beige carpets might send her over the edge… He was destined to become a master of negotiation and compromise.

I pulled up in the middle of the street, stepped out, and stood on the pavement with Mary. We looked around. Blue lights bouncing off the tenement walls. Blurred faces peering between curtained front windows. Teatime traffic fighting through the gridlock. Late commuters gathering. Students stopping in their tracks to look. What's going on?

Firemen winding hoses. Loud shouts across the road. "Have you shut the pump down, Donald? We'll no' be here for long."

But there was still an impasse while Rhona stood her ground. Graham hadn't quite managed to hold back the full force of the fire brigade… yet.

“If Rhona’s says no, it’s not going to happen,” Mary whispered in my ear as I stood watching the end drama unfold. Lots of gesticulations and even more frying pan waving until we were greeted by the sight of one particular fireman, shrugging his shoulders, handing his axe to his colleague, then sitting on the front step and pulling his tackety boots off.

There was a round of applause from the street as he stood up, bowed to the gathering, gave a rude gesture to his fire-fighting colleagues, then followed Rhona into her immaculate flat so he could complete his after-fire documents.

I noticed Graham’s shoulders relaxing.

Nobody had been hurt. There was really only smoke damage and a ruined roast chicken Maryland left too long in the oven. As well as a lack of chips, sorry, French Fries, of course.

As I thought… Dinner’s not going to happen anytime soon.

The street cleared remarkably quickly. I even found a parking spot.

“I vote we eat somewhere else tonight.” Graham was still in charge, though Rhona had the look of a victor. Even if she did have a neat little bandage on her wrist as we headed out to the Spaghetti House on Gibson Street.

“A nice bottle of Chianti should finish this day off nicely,” Mary declared.

Chapter 26
Key of the Door

We settled in to a pleasant routine in our new life as a married couple. Once the novelty of actually not living with our parents wore off, the day-to-day realities of housekeeping and daily chores loomed larger. Mary complained that the traditional tenement sink in the kitchen was a bit on the low side. It was probably 'in with the bricks' and must have been designed when the inhabitants were a good deal shorter. The rim of the square porcelain sink was mid-thigh height. When Mary bent over to fish the dishes out, her long legs ensured she ended up with a very sore back.

She had a solution. "If that sink stays, we need to have a plan B. You can wash the dishes every night!" She smiled sweetly.

Having had absolutely no history of DIY (Mum would 'get a man in' for any work around the house), I was at a loss how to solve the problem.

I'd already made a faux pas in our first couple of weeks of married bliss. Once it dawned on us that it wasn't done for a married couple to bring piles of washing to either set of parents, we'd have to deal with our laundry ourselves

Mary had come to terms with using the local laundromat. She became friendly with the lady who worked there and organised weekly 'service washes.' This worked well around her part-time hours in the opticians. We seemed to have plenty of clean clothes. But it was costing us…

There was no way I had spare cash to buy such a luxury as a washing machine. We'd just about scraped up enough to purchase a second-hand gas cooker and a free-standing kitchen unit. It would be a while before we could enhance our kitchen experience by installing excesses such as wall cupboards…

Looking for a screwdriver to wire a plug (I could do that – one of the few practical skills Dad taught me) in one of the many hardware stores in Duke Street, I notice an old-fashioned wooden washboard for sale. I picked it up. *That's what that wee sink's designed for! These things are not just for Lonnie Donegan's skiffle band. These are for washing clothes! That'll save a few bob.*

Pleased with myself, I hurried home to give Mary her new present, convinced she'd be happy to maximise the efficiency of our inherited technology. And so save money on those unnecessary laundry charges. I knew it didn't immediately solve the dish washing problem, but we could come back to that. In fact, we could even save enough over time to buy a new sink *and* a proper washing machine… I was a man with a plan!

"If you think I'm going to turn into a back-broken skivvy by kneeling down and scrubbing your dirty clothes in that ridiculous Victorian sink, you're very much mistaken! If you don't want to pay laundry charges, buy us a washing machine! At the same time as you get us a new bloody sink that belongs in the 20th Century! Geddit?" She dropped the brand-new washboard into the bin, turned round, and marched into the bedroom and slammed the door.

We obviously think differently with regards to finances!

The best I could manage was to get a man in that Mum knew to replace the sink. Mary was overjoyed with her new shiny stainless-steel kitchen toy. No more back-breaking dishwashing sessions. And no need to implement plan B… We'd just have to thole the laundromat charges for a while longer…

xxxxxxxxxxxxxxxxxxxxxxxxxxxxxxxxxxxxxxxxxxxxxxxxxxxxxx

"Should I bring my guitar?" Joe Slyder was sprawled on our 'let's pretend its leather' white settee.

Mary was sitting at the other side of the fireplace from me, bent over the coffee table, concentrating on her list. So I answered, "Of course you should bring your guitar! This is our first ever party outside anybody's mum and dad's house. AND its Mary's twenty-first. We gotta have music. Get Wee Robbie to bring his as well and we can have a jam. I bet some of those folk on Mary's list can sing. Though maybe not as well as Mary…"

Mary looked up. "I'm sure lots of them can sing better than me. But I'll maybe chuck in a bit of opera to up the ante?"

Joe laughed. "I don't know how well that would go down. But hey! It's your party, you can sing opera if you want to!"

After the disastrous debut of my show business career a few years earlier, Joe had persevered. He had real talent and was proficient when playing either the guitar or blues piano. So, he and another excellent guitarist, Wee Robbie, had formed a pub and club band.

Wee Robbie, as his name implies, was a little shorter than average. But with his long dark blond hair and a gravelly voice not dissimilar to Rod Stewart's, he could belt out the hits. Robbie came from the west end of Glasgow. That is the Maryhill west end... He was a bit of a rough diamond and had aspirations to live the rock 'n' roll lifestyle...

Not having access to the trappings and indulgencies of bands such as the Beatles or the Stones, Robbie made do with an old Glasgow favourite... Lanliq Fortified Wine. A predecessor of Buckfast 'Tonic Wine' the favourite tipple of a certain section of west of Scotland society, who seem to like to get drunk and angry as speedily and efficiently as possible.

I once heard Robbie announce halfway through a gig in a Bridgeton pub, "I'll be back in a minute." He'd been enjoying a wee 'swally' of four or five pints of lager topped up by a hidden half-bottle of Lanliq. The rest of the band kept the beat going while he strolled past the crowd and out the front door. A couple of minutes later he strutted back in, went up to the bar for a fresh pint, and re-joined the band centre stage.

With a flick of his hair and a roared guffaw, "Nothing to beat a wee Hughie halfway through a song, eh? Hit it, boys! Let's get back tae 'Maggie May'!"

The band changed names too many times to remember, but Mary and I would often turn up at their gigs where we came across a very eclectic crowd. One night while they were playing in the Amphora in Sauchiehall Street, we got talking to three American hippy types. Very long scraggly beards, headbands, and beads.

Noticing the American accents, I asked as we squeezed into the almost full table, "Hi, guys, welcome to Glasgow. Here on holiday?"

The biggest of them, with slightly scary, wide, blue eyes replied, "Hell, Man, we're AWOL. We ain't going back to that cesspit Vietnam! I spent a year there. ******* blew my mind. We're hanging out here for a bit. Then we're off to Canada. That's the plan man…"

Mary and I were quite taken aback, never having met anyone who'd actually been in Vietnam. The long running war was on our TV screens most nights and was part of the backdrop of our lives.

The band started playing "Nights in White Satin" while we got to know our new American visitors.

Mary asked over the sound of the music, "Are all three of you draft dodgers?"

Scraggy beard introduced himself as Mark, with Jason and Daniel shaking our hands as their names were mentioned. "Excuse me, ma'am, none of us here dodged the draft. We got our papers and we did our duty. But we just decided we don't wanna go back. So we're AWOL, that means absent without leave. We're soldiers, ma'am, only we're not going to fight that dirty war no more!"

His companions nodded in agreement. Jason, more slightly built and sporting a drooping Zapata moustache, leaned over the table. "We were home for Christmas after our first year. Gave us time to think. This war's all wrong. It's nothin' to do with us! I saw things I never want to talk about. There's no way in Hell I'm going back there." He lifted his glass and gulped a goodly portion of his beer.

Mary turned to Daniel. "How long are you all going to be in Scotland?"

Daniel, sporting a week's stubble under a mop of dark tight curls, answered. "Ma'am. We're not sure. We're living with some very nice folks we met on a protest in London. We're kind of camped out in a big apartment near the university. Someone is trying to organise travel for us to Canada. A coupla weeks, I guess." He smiled

Mary looked at me with big bright eyes. I knew what she was thinking…

She turned to Mark who seemed to be the de facto leader. "If you guys are still here next Saturday, you're welcome to come along to our party. It's actually my twenty-first. Most of the band will be there, so there'll be lots of music. You'll get a proper Scottish welcome. What do you say?"

The three army outlaws looked at each other. It was a no-brainer. A pretty girl inviting them to a party in a foreign land with a band included. Way better than Vietnam!

Mark answered for all three. “That’s so far out! We’d love to come. It’s always good to meet new people. And you guys seem really nice. Jason here plays a mean guitar so we might manage to sing for our supper.”

After another couple of drinks and more music from the band, we parted firm friends.

On the way home, Mary mused, “A sprinkling of Vietnam vets among our usual bunch should liven up the party.”

Chapter 27
21st Party Time

It was the morning of the party and excitement was in the air.

My younger brothers, Alan, Phil and Andy, were recruited to help prepare the flat for the big event.

"We gotta have lots of balloons!" Nine-year-old Andy insisted. "It's not a real party if there's no balloons!"

Phil wasn't so sure. "It's a grown up's party. They don't have balloons, dafty. They have games and music, don't they, Mary?"

"Oh, we can have balloons if you want Andy. Here are a few packs John brought down from the shop. You guys can blow them up and put them all over the flat."

I'd organised the day off and had decided it was easier to just do what I was told. Mary had a long list and was happily delegating tasks to her willing helpers.

Joe had turned up early, a very unusual occurrence. He tended to sleep in pretty late on a Saturday, especially if he was playing the night before. We'd missed that gig while Mary completed her list.

"You're the music man, Joe. Can you organise the LPs and the singles beside my new record player in the living room?"

Mary was referring to my birthday present to her, a modest stereo record player with separate speakers. So modest the LPs overhung the turntable. Still, it was great to be able to play our own music for the first time since leaving our family homes. One of the albums we both enjoyed, *The Rock Machine Turns You On,* had been playing since we got out of bed and Mary had unwrapped her present.

Dancing around the flat to the likes of "It Can't be So Bad" by Moby Grape and Taj Mahal's "Statesboro Blues" was a great way to start Mary's special birthday.

By late afternoon the flat was filling up. Mary's mum and dad, along with Big Aunt Peggy, made a rare appearance. We were used to catching up with them on our traditional Sunday afternoon visits in their house, where they were enjoying the fact that the last of their offspring didn't need her room anymore… Mr Heaney had taken up painting and turned Mary's room into an artist's studio. He arrived bearing one of his productions, a brightly coloured semi-abstract still life of the blue plastic flowers and other objects I recognised from their house, including the lavatory chain Mrs Heaney liked to wear with her fur coat…

"Oh thanks, Dad. That's lovely. We'll give it pride of place won't we, John?" Mary smiled grimly at me over her father's back as she gave him a hug.

Aunt Peggy unbuttoned her coat, handed it to me, and sat down in *my* chair. "It's nice to see you've both settled in. The place looks quite clean, doesn't it, Winnie?" She sounded slightly surprised.

Her sister answered, "I never thought Mary would take to housework at all! It shows we *can* be wrong sometimes." Mary looked over at me, so I had to intervene.

"Actually, the fact is, I do all the housework. You know how Mary likes to lie in most mornings," I lied, pulling my most innocent face.

Mr Heaney looked at me as if I'd turned into an alien. "*You* do the housework? You mean the washing and the kitchen and the toilet?" he asked incredulously. "But that's women's work!"

"John's just winding you up, people. Of course I do the housework, especially now I'm only working part time. Although John's very good with the Hoover and he does take his turn washing the dishes, now that we have a decent sink!"

Mr Heaney looked a bit less incredulous. *We couldn't have men doing women's work. Where would that end?*

The doorbell rang and my mum and dad arrived with Thomas. That broke the slight awkwardness as they all re-acquainted themselves. It was the first time they'd been together since the wedding.

Thomas handed Mary a sizable well-wrapped package with a grin. "We think you'll like this."

"This is great," said Mary. "Better than Christmas!" as she unwrapped the parcel. "It's a Teasmade! Thanks a lot."

Big Peggy looked suspicious. "Don't you use those things so you can stay in bed in the morning?" Mary looked flustered as her mum and dad looked at each other.

I stepped in. "It's so you can get up even earlier! 'Cos the tea's made!" My wee joke had gone too far...

Mary had planned the day so that the older relatives would 'partake of some afternoon tea and all the trimmings,' with the hope that once the younger generation arrived, the noise levels would rise and they would feel they'd better go home...

That almost worked. But where did Joyce and James fit in? Mary's oldest sister was over ten years her senior and had married James, the MC at the wedding, when he was twelve years older than her. In fact, James was only slightly younger than my dad. It was a grey area. Maybe that's why they decided to arrive a wee while after the parents et al., just as the tea and biscuits were halfway finished.

James with his outsize mane of silver hair liked to make an entrance. He boomed, "Hello, all you people! Happy birthday, Mary! I demand a hug from my beautiful sister-in-law!" He promptly nearly squeezed the life out of her while Joyce kept a fixed grin on her face.

Their three kids, Tamsin, Toby, and baby Trinity were surrounded with a panoply of baby equipment. Joyce rummaged in one of her many bags and triumphantly emerged with an envelope and a small package. She gave it to her eldest daughter, seven-year-old Tamsin, resplendent in silver taffeta. "Give this to your Aunty Mary, darling."

Tamsin, pale face seriously concentrating, handed both items to Mary, who bent down and gave her niece a big hug and a kiss on her cheek. "Thank you very much, Tamsin the Terrific!" The little girl's eyes lit up as she grinned widely. Aunty Mary was well loved.

Mary opened the card and read out the birthday wishes then peeled the layers of tissue paper from the small box and prised it open.

"Thank you very much, sis," she said as she lifted out a small pewter Celtic cross. "This is very nice."

Joyce looked slightly haughty. "Yes. One of James's clients is directly descended from an ancient Celtic king! He hand-makes these trinkets. You'll see it's engraved on the back with Mary and 21."

Mary turned it over. "It's very unusual. Thanks again. Do you want some tea? I think there are some biscuits left."

Joyce rummaged back in her bags. "Don't be silly, girl! Open one of these." She handed me two bottles of red wine.

Yes, Ma'am! And how on earth do you prove you're directly descended from an ancient Celtic king?

Mary's plan of the oldies leaving early didn't really happen as some of our younger crowd started to arrive.

Wee Robbie battered his way through the doorway heaving a fair-sized amplifier. "For **** **** man why do you have to live two flights up, eh? Where's the booze?" He dumped the heavy box and his guitar case then strode along the narrow lobby towards the kitchen, shouting back, "Happy Birthday, Mary, by the way!"

"Who on earth is that fellow?" James asked loudly, looking from me to Mary.

Dad did his best to answer, "I think he's got something to do with the band. They play that bebop music. It's far too loud for me!"

I had a thought. "Dad. Why don't you sing your party piece? Maybe Mr Heaney can join you? Before the loud music starts?"

Dad feigned shyness as I lifted my acoustic guitar from the wall and hung it round my neck. I had been at parties in both parents' houses and had heard Mr Heaney sing classical Irish ballads, while my Dad's favourite was "Ghost Riders in the Sky" although he called it "Yippee Yi Yay" and sung it with barely a line of lyrics. He preferred the "Dum de Dum" version. Of course, that meant anyone could join in...

A strong strum of E Minor set the scene and Dad was away…

A Dum de Dum de Dum de de. A dum de Dum de de.

Mr Heaney caught the pitch perfectly and joined in just in time with:

When all at once a mighty herd of red eyed cows he saw...

A Dum de Dum de Dum de Dum

Closely followed by:

Yippie yi aaaay
Yippie yi ohhhh,
The Ghost Riders in the sky!

By this time everyone had joined in the chorus so we had to sing it twice!

The kids came running back from the kitchen and were jumping up and down, while Mary rolled her eyes in amusement. Then she started dancing with the kids…

Grins and laughter and applause all round at the ridiculousness of the performance, while both dads shook hands and patted each other on the back.

The doorbell rang again and within a short while the house was crammed full of people.

Cousins and friends and friends of friends. Band members and ex school chums. Jim and Paul with their girlfriends.

And then the Americans arrived. They were exotic creatures to us Glasgow folk. They'd seen the world and all its ills and spoke a language that we kind of understood.

Joe and Wee Robbie set themselves up in the bay window with the lights of the tenements across the road as a backdrop.

They'd even brought a microphone.

"After we all sing "Twenty-One Today," Mary promised us she'd sing a song or two. So… Are You Ready, People?" Wee Robbie roused the crowd.

They then proceeded to perform a heavy rock version of "Twenty-One Today" that had my dad groaning in despair. Too much bebop!

When it all died down, Mary took the mike and whispered in Joe's ear. Then she paused, looked towards me and sang in a sweet clear voice:

The first time ever I saw your face,
I thought the sun rose in your eyes,

And the moon and the stars were the gifts you gave,
To the night and the empty skies, my love,
To the night and the empty skies.

The room hushed. It was spellbinding. When she finished, the room erupted. And I felt pretty good…

The party continued with music and dancing and lots of chat. Everyone was having a good time. We'd been careful to let our neighbours know we were having the do and invited them to join us. The only ones who did were Rose and her husband. I caught sight of them quietly sitting blethering in a corner with a couple of my cousins.

"Give us 'Ten Guitars'!" someone shouted from the back of the room. Joe and Robbie duly obliged…

As these things happen, the kitchen became busier as some people took a break from the music. Mum and Dad had taken the younger kids home, and Mary's parents and Big Peggy had long gone. This meant the oldest person in the house was my brother-in-law James.

I wandered through to the kitchen just as voices were rising…

"Listen, man! You know shit all! You ain't been there. You got no right to tell us what to do!" Mark, our American guest looked angry.

James, face bright red, put on his full courtroom voice. "From a purely legal standpoint, you have no right to disobey your country's laws. If we all cherry picked the laws we agreed with, and ignored those we don't like, anarchy would ensue! I'm afraid if you were in the First World War, you'd be shot as deserters! Thankfully, it's not my problem. But I'd find it very difficult to defend you…"

Jason was first: "Who the hell are you to judge us? We're not deserters. We're simply AWOL. *We'll* decide if we're going back. Not some jumped up English lawyer!"

James was startled. "Excuse me. I'm most definitely NOT English. I'm a very proud Scot. It's your loss if you can't differentiate."

Just then Wee Robbie swaggered in. "Whit's goin' on in here? An Argy Bargy? Och, Ah really love a belter of an' argument... Wait 'till Ah huv a wee swally an' I'll join in. Ye don't get a chance to drink proper when yer playin' 'Ten Guitars' as they say. Y'awright guys?"

At this interjection, James and the Americans looked at each other. Jason spoke up. "Hey, man, does anyone understand this guy?"

James replied, "I'm actually from just outside Glasgow and I haven't a clue what the young man just said. I think he mentioned an argument. And we shouldn't really argue on my young sister-in-law's birthday. Tell you what. I've got some decent malt whisky in this flask. Anyone like a dram of the good stuff?"

After we'd all appreciated James's *quality liquor,* as Daniel called it, I spoke to Mark: "Sorry about that, my friend. Thanks for keeping your temper. We could have had an international incident there."

Mark shrugged. "No worries man. Some people know sweet nothin'. But we wouldn't jeopardise the peace of your home, man. Not after you and your lovely wife have offered us such hospitality. And we've met such really nice people." He looked down at my cousin Lynne who was standing extremely close by.

"Let's go back into the music..." I had heard Joe and Jason breaking into the Woodstock classic "Don't let the Bastards Get You Down!"

We definitely weren't.

Chapter 28
Motoring Joys

The party had ended as a great success, with promises to get together more often with some of my cousins, and even an invite to catch up with our new American friends somewhere mysterious in Canada.

Mary and I turned our thoughts to having a summer break. On a budget. “Now we’ve got the minivan we could even drive to Paris! You keep saying it’s really cheap on petrol. It would be an adventure.” Mary was doing her best to convince me.

Life with the minivan was fine. It was small, yet nippy. I became an expert packer, so that it carried a surprisingly big load from the Cash and Carry or wholesalers. And with a carpet in the back, I could transport friends and wee brothers wherever was needed. But the best thing was: it was mine! Well… it was really the shop’s. But there was no way Dad was ever going to drive it…

I also developed another area of expertise because of my minivan experiences:

It had one or two weak points. Early on I noticed a draught blowing up my right trouser leg. I eventually lifted the rubber floor mat to discover there was a substantial rusty hole in the floor about the size of a saucer. You could see right through to the tarmac. So, we christened the car ‘*The Flintmobile’* after Fred and Wilma’s caveman footmobile. Yabadabdoo!!

Its other main weak point was the number of punctures it seemed to harvest. I’m not sure if it was because the wheels were so small they had more contact with the ground than normal sized wheels. Or perhaps it had something to do with my tendency to shop around for bargain tyres… Who knows?

The spare wheel lived in a void under the rear floor, just behind the driver’s seat. The car jack lived under the seat. They had to be handy… Punctures never happened on a nice sunny day in a car park. No. They usually happened in the rain, on a busy main road or at a junction. Horns blared! Lights flashed. You had to be quick!

I became very quick!

After nearly a year of changing wheels in a hurry, I had acquired a spider wrench, the proper wheel nut removing tool the garage uses. I was in my usual tyre repairers when I spied the old rusty spider lying against a wall.

Mike the mechanic, whom I'd become quite pally with, saw me looking at it as I waited on him repairing yet another puncture, using a nice new shiny one.

"You can have it if you want. Boss went daft and ordered new ones. Maybe he won the pools! My blisters have fair gone down though. Help yourself."

So I did.

It made quite a difference.

My pinnacle of tyre changing prowess happened one day when Mary was with me on one of our rare mutual mid-week days off.

Driving down Cumbernauld Road I slowed down and stopped as the lights changed to red at the junction with Edinburgh Road.

The front offside tyre blew as soon as I stopped. I felt the van dip as the tyre's pressure dropped to zero. A familiar experience.

Mary sighed. "This is embarrassing. There's a queue behind us... Again!"

I went into my routine.

I pulled the handbrake tight.

Throwing open my door, I jumped out as I flicked my chair forward.

I reached down and grabbed the spare wheel and the jack and chucked them beside the flat front wheel.

Waved to the cars behind me. "Sorry..."

Mary handed me the spider from behind my chair.

Rammed the jack into its socket and wound the car up.

Engaged the spider and whirled the first wheel nut loose. *That was satisfying!*

The other three nuts were off in a jiffy.

I heaved the old wheel off and rammed the fresh one on.

Screwed the wheel nuts back on with four equally satisfying whirls of the spider.

Let down the jack and threw everything into the back behind my seat.

Jumped back into my seat. As the lights changed to green… I pulled away.

“Do you realise you changed that wheel between the lights changing from red to green?” Mary sounded astounded.

“Did I really? Shows you how many punctures ol’ *Flintmobile’s* had. We should be fine on our drive to Paris then, eh? So long as there’re plenty of pit stops!”

Mary thought aloud, “I wonder how the *Flintmobile* will cope driving on the other side of the road…”

Chapter 29
Paris or Bust

"You're some navigator, sweetheart." I was impressed by Mary's ability to guide us across London on our way to Dover.

No need for us to use any North or South circular roads. Right through the centre of the city. Driving as near to a crow flying as we could manage. Apart from minor diversions to take in Buckingham Palace and Big Ben, etc., along with a wee whirl round Trafalgar Square. In a remarkably good time, we were on the M20 and the minivan was motoring well.

We'd had no problems all the way south. We'd stopped off in Stratford-on-Avon and ambled along the river in brilliant sunshine. I bought Mary a quirky handmade necklace made out of a chain of curled horseshoe nails. They were crafted by a hippy-looking girl perched on the banks of the river.

A few miles south of London, with the ferry terminal less than an hour away, I was overtaking on the outside lane. There was a convoy of big lorries on the inside lane and a couple of panel vans in the middle lane. I was probably doing just over seventy when…

Bang!

The front offside tyre blew yet again, and the steering wheel wobbled dramatically as the van slipped left towards the traffic in the middle lane.

"Oh my God!" Mary shouted as I wrestled with the wheel.

I could see a red car coming very close behind me as I braked and heaved the minivan between the two vans to my left. The red car whooshed past.

With inches to spare, I made it into the middle lane, still struggling with the steering and holding back from jamming on the brakes. Then I veered across the lane and just managed to tuck myself in behind an enormous articulated truck.

The loudest klaxon I'd ever heard blasted from behind us, raising my adrenalin to sky high levels, as I forced the mini-van off the carriageway and rattled onto the hard shoulder…

"Oh, for God's sake that was scary!" I admitted as I let a gigantic breath escape from my lungs.

I looked at Mary who was in a state of shock. Just sitting there, ashen white and trembling.

"It's all right, Mary. We're fine. Just a wee adventure. You sit there and I'll change the wheel. It might take a bit longer than last time…"

Mary was visibly calming down as she supped from the can of juice I gave her. I opened my door and was almost blown off my feet by the sound of yet another klaxon blast as one more massive truck rumbled past.

I closed my door and realised I was only inches from the edge of the hard shoulder. The bloody door would have been whipped off its hinges and me with it!

"Be careful, John! I still want to get to Paris you know…" Mary was coming round. "Drive the van in a bit. It's pretty dangerous out there." *Good advice.*

A new tyre and a couple of hours later we reached the ferry port. Thankfully it was a different ship from the last one I was on when I could've been declared stateless.

Re-telling the sorry saga I said, "If those Special Branch guys hadn't let me back, we might never have met up that night in George Square… You might still be a single spinster instead of living this life of luxury whizzing from country to country in the superb comfort of the Flintmobile!"

Mary grinned at me and curtsied, "I thank you, kind sir"

Manoeuvring out of Calais highlighted a shortcoming of the minivan that I hadn't fully appreciated. Being a rather basic model, it lacked a number of refinements we take for granted these days. Such as a near-side wing mirror! Driving on the left in the UK, it wasn't such a major problem. I still had my wing mirror and the normal rearview mirror where I could peer through the two back door windows. Travelling south of Calais, Mary had to develop a useful skill of sliding back her window, sticking her head out and double checking if there was anything coming up on our left.

However, driving on the right-hand side of the French roads is difficult enough…

"I want to overtake this tractor," I shouted as Mary slid her window forward.

"Wait for it! Car coming!" she'd shout back while gesticulating for me to hold back. A big Citroen hurtled by us and the tractor, followed by a fleet of 2CVs and Renaults. We were stuck at 25 mph. Then a seemingly never-ending stream of traffic would come the opposite way. Very frustrating…

"I'm going to get a sty in my eye hanging my head outside. I feel like a pet dog. Woof, Woof!" Mary laughed as we waited for a break.

Finally, nothing coming the other way.

"Go for it… Now!" Mary exhorted.

Pulling on to the left-hand side of the road I was astonished to see the tractor pulling over too… The cause of the slow speed was revealed as a tiny vintage car in front of the tractor holding us all back.

For a brief moment, there was only the one old car on the right side of the road while, as far back as I could see every other car was on the wrong side of the road. All trying to overtake the vintage car and each other.

The road to Paris was a harbinger of the terrors to come once we finally reached the city.

As we drove in from the north, Mary's superb navigating skills finally abandoned her. We were on some kind of overpass near le Gard Du Nord, Mary had had enough. "Take this ramp off the motorway. Let's go down to street level. Find a cafe and study the map. I need a pee." *Good idea…*

Once the van climbed down off the overpass, we found ourselves in seedy looking back streets. This wasn't tourist land. Decaying tenements and shuttered windows. But there was a cafe. A couple of tables outside and lights on inside. Welcoming.

We parked the van, got out and really stretched our weary bones. Mary twisting her head to loosen up the tensions caused by hours of doggy impersonations hanging out of the window.

We entered the cafe. Dusty but roomy. Zinc counter with a handful of locals smoking and sipping espressos. A couple at the bar muttering to the bar man.

I found a table we could spread the map over while Mary tried out her schoolgirl French: “Bonjour, monsieur. Deux cafés et deux pain de jambon et fromages s’il vous plait. Aussi ou sont les toilettes?”

“Merci, Mademoiselle. Je vais l’amener à la table. Voila la toilette.” He smiled and pointed towards a large closed door across from the entrance. He obviously thought Mary was far too young to be ‘m’dam.’ She was pleased.

I spread the map out and tried to figure out where the hell we were; Mary opened the door and went through.

As the barman laid our order on top of the map, I noticed one of the locals opening the toilet door and going through. Vaguely concerned as we didn’t have a clue what this area of Paris was like, I watched the door. Mary’s tall, slim figure was quite striking, even in her crumpled travelling clothes which incorporated her usual short miniskirt.

I was surprised to see the local guy come flying back out the room a moment later with a startled expression on his face.

“Mon Dieu!” he exclaimed as he marched right out the front door.

What’s going on?

Mary, giggling, came out of the room just as I was getting worried enough to go in and find her.

Her face was red. She was embarrassed! Completely out of character.

“I think I made a bit of a boo boo!” she explained.

“Behind that door, there’s the strangest combination of facilities I’ve ever seen.”

"Uh-huh?"

She continued as she supped from her coffee. "In to the right, there's a phone booth, with the phone in the corner. Right?"

I nodded and listened.

"In the far corner there's a kind of cubicle. But it hasn't got a pan or anything. Just a hole in the floor! And what looks like two places either side of the hole to place your feet! I reckoned that must be for guys. Pretty crude I thought."

What's coming?

"So, I wondered what I should use. And I noticed a kind of wally basin hanging on the wall. With water running and a puddle at the bottom. That must be for me! So, I pulled my tights and knickers down and tried to kind of perch on it. It wasn't easy. Not at all comfortable, I can tell you. French design is rubbish!"

Oh no! I can see what's coming…

I felt my own face reddening.

"So, I'm straddled there, finding it difficult to balance. Just doing my business. I was bursting by the way… And then the door opens and this French guy just stares at me! So, I froze there and stared right back. Thank God he went straight back out."

I couldn't help but giggle at Mary's innocence. There was no reason on earth why she should have ever come across a male urinal in her sheltered Glasgow life. I found myself explaining the plumbing facts of life.

"I'll not make that mistake again! Does that mean I was supposed to use that hole in the ground? Yuck!"

"Right, Mary Can I go now?" I shouted as we dared to leave the safety of the kerb outside our hotel and join the melee of bashed vehicles whizzing along what we thought was a modest back street.

"Go! Go! Now!" Mary gesticulated as I pulled into the miniscule gap in the traffic.

Horns blasting all round us, I tried to blend into the mayhem. Sweat bursting over my eyes. Heart racing as I tried to keep my nerve and make it to the next set of traffic lights.

"What the hell…" I shouted as a battered 2CV flew out of a side street and almost spun into position right in front of me.

I gave up. Pulling into the nearest gap by the kerb, I stopped the van, prized my white knuckled fingers off the steering wheel, and switched the engine off. I took a very deep breath…

Mary stared at me. "You know we must have travelled at least a hundred yards. It's quite a bit longer to the Louvre…"

I turned my head and narrowed my eyes. "I don't have enough French genes to drive in this madness… In fact, I don't think I've got any French genes… I can't cope!"

We only lasted a few days in Paris. We abandoned the van and managed to make good use of the Metro to catch some of the more obvious tourist sites.

After the most expensive couple of drinks we'd ever heard of in a cafe on the Champs Elysees, we decided we were going to run out of cash way too quickly. We checked out of our very modest pensione and headed back to Blighty. We'd aim for the Isle of Wight where Mary had spent many happy family holidays.

And where she definitely knew how to use the loo…

Chapter 30
Canadian Connections and Shocks at Home

"Don't worry. We'll manage," Mary said as she hugged my mum. "It'll be an adventure. An' me and the boys'll have fun. I'm going to practise my cooking and baking skills on them, while you're away... So they'd better behave or I might make them eat Brussels sprouts and meringue!" She looked down at wee Andy who had his fingers down his throat in mock horror.

The airport at Prestwick lived up to its role of a gateway to another world. Queues of excited travellers, mostly couples, all surrounded by bunches of friends and relatives eager to share in the thrill of intercontinental travel.

Mary and I had just come back from our first anniversary's 'second honeymoon.' A cheeky wee four days to Ibiza, away from the sleet and snow of Glasgow in February. As the plane hard-landed on the runway that seemed to extend right over the sea, Mary almost burst my left arm. There were shouts of, "Oh my God!" from many passengers, and it seemed an awful long time before we rumbled to a stop.

The intercom speakers crackled to life: "This is your Captain speaking. Sorry about that folks. They seemed to have lowered Ibiza by a couple of feet since yesterday!" A ripple of nervous chuckles followed and Mary finally loosened her grip and my arm pinned and needled its way back to life.

A couple of liberal Cuba libres for Mary before the return flight definitely saved my arm from permanent mutilation.

"Ok, John, I'm fine now. Totally sober. Ready for the next challenge. I mean, how many twenty-one-year-old wives get to look after their four brothers-in-law, while their husband's parents fly off to Canada?"

I knew that Mary was well aware how much the trip to Canada meant to Mum. They'd had many kitchen conversations over the last few months. And the chance to step into Mum's matriarchal shoes would be fun.

....

Mum had been 'pen pals' with a number of her Canadian cousins for decades. A few months after our wedding, she'd decided that the invitations to visit their country were overwhelming, and now doable. All because her eldest son and brand new daughter-in-law were capable of looking after the business, and the rest of the family. For a whole three weeks!

Plans had been made.

Mum and Dad had joined the obligatory Canadian Air charter club, an essential precursor to accessing a charter airline in the seventies. For some bureaucratic reason the discounted fares could only be purchased by club members.

There was a cumbersome process of regular payments to prove you were a long-term club member. Nothing like today's simplified online booking systems. The only alternative was to fly via scheduled airlines such as BOAC or Air Canada, which were way beyond the purse strings of most folk.

It had been Mum's ambition to visit Canada since she was a little girl growing up in the full force of the great depression in the thirties. She was the second oldest of five sisters, living in severe poverty in the east end of Glasgow.

Their kitchen had a small square of lino. Floor boards were scrubbed and bleached till they were almost white. The one gas fire in the house had no back plate to enhance the heat. Being cold was normal. Frosted windows every winter morning. No bed linen, old coats covering the sisters huddling in the bed. Scrabbling not to be the girl on the edge, lumbered with the short sleeve…

According to Mum they were in a constant state of the giggles. Oblivious to their deprivation, they loved playing street games, when dozens of kids would form circles and chant songs:

One, two, three, O'Leary,
I saw Wallace Beery,

Sitting oan his bumbaleree,
Kissing Shirley Temple.

Alternatively, they'd play at 'wee shops' using different coloured stones as their 'shop stock.' Or organised games such as 'peever' or 'kick the can,' a version of hide and seek.

They were happy, but I remember Mum telling me about them only having one soup spoon in the house. The rest of the cutlery had long been pawned. Of course, her dad, my Granda John, would get first use of the spoon… It's hard to imagine in these days of smart TV's, mobile phones and laptops.

They made the best of the very little they had in their corner of Glasgow's ubiquitous poverty. One hint of a brighter, bigger world was the occasional parcel from Canada. Maybe once a year a box would arrive and they'd all gather round the kitchen table.

They'd stare at the exotic maple leaf stamps and the address panel. "*From Hamilton, Ontario, Canada.*"

Gaga would untie the string and carefully roll it and put it away in a drawer. She'd do the same with the outer brown wrapping paper, folding it and laying it beside the string for future use.

Breaths held as she opened the box. Shining expectant eyes.

"Look! Look!"

A pair of long suede gloves for Betty, the eldest. "Look at me! I'm going to the theatre."

A bracelet and matching necklace for my mum. Red and shiny crystals. "They were the brightest things I'd ever seen."

A fancy headband and earrings for Josie, daughter number three. The blonde cheeky one. "I might get myself a boyfriend with these. What do you think?"

Sadie, the serious fourth daughter was given a silk scarf. "I won't be so cold now when it's snowing."

Margaret, the youngest, was overjoyed when she was given a pretty crinoline doll, whose eyes closed when she laid it down. "It's just like a real baby."

Gaga lifted out tinned ham, jars of jam, and a whole layer of fresh apples.

She looked across at Granda Joe, then handed him a big tin of tobacco. "Ach, they shouldn't have gone to that trouble… Ah'm jist away tae fill ma pipe."

Then Gaga read out the accompanying note from her eldest sister Rose:

Dear Marie (My mum was named after her mum)

I hope you're all well. Times have been tough here over the last couple of years. Although maybe not as tough as we hear it is in Scotland. The steel works aren't doing as well as they used to. However, our family gets bigger and bigger. Our sister Jeanie has so many children, now she's up to nine; she's run out of names. We're proud to now have a Mona, and a Lisa, as well as some of the apostles; Peter, Paul, and John. The way she's going she's maybe aiming for the full dozen!

The summer is very hot. Winters are a lot harder, when the snow can be up to ten feet deep. Then it's hard for the men to get to work. But we manage.

Give my love to all your girls, and say hello to Joe. One day I'll get over there and meet them all personally.

Lots of love

Your sister

Rose

Gaga brushed a tear as she placed the tinned ham and jars of preserves on her bare pantry shelves. Then she wrapped the hand-knitted shawl she'd been given around her shoulders.

"Some days are good days. Today's one of them…"

My mum was fascinated by the idea of very hot summers and snowy winters. Once she had left school and had her first job, she started writing letters to some of her cousins. And realised just how big an extended family she had over there… Her mum told her their story:

Around 1910, the eldest daughter, Rose Campbell, had left her home in Kirkintilloch to try her luck in domestic service in New York. She managed to find work alright, striking it lucky by being employed as a nanny by one of the silent movie era's biggest stars: Douglas Fairbanks. She looked after his baby son, Douglas Fairbanks Jnr, who became a major movie star in his own right, marrying Joan Crawford and later recognised and honoured as an American navy war hero.

This early success sparked a veritable splurge of Atlantic crossings over the next few years resulting in three of the Campbell sisters and one brother finding work, then love, in the steel town of Hamilton, Ontario. In fact, all four Campbell siblings married four Nolan siblings who'd originated from Ireland. Then they all had very big families, as was the fashion... Consequently, Mum was related to a sizable portion of Hamilton's population.

And that's who they were going out to visit. Umpteen cousins that Mum had kept in touch with as well as the elderly matriarch, Aunt Rose. Lots of family gatherings, and Dad would entertain them with his "Yippee Yi Yay" song and maybe even an occasional "April Shower."

In the meantime, Mary and I were enjoying being in charge of the whole set up back home.

I split my days. In the morning I'd go up to Dad's shop (in the Zephyr of course...) and check the previous day's takings, etc. I'd pop into Mum and Dad's house for a bite of lunch. Then work a half shift in The Buy In.

Mary commented, "Oh, you are a busy bee, my man. Quite the Area Manager. Looking after two shops for three weeks. Enjoying it? Is it very stressful?"

"No, I wouldn't say it's stressful. I am pretty busy, but Dad's got it organised so that the shop just ticks over. This is about the quietest time of the year. Maybe I'm daft, but from an early age I seemed to crave responsibility... And if you ask for it, sure as fate it'll come your way..."

Thomas took this chance to up his game by being the *de facto* manager of The Buy In. It all seemed to come together. It was a good exercise in stretching our abilities. Plus, my wee brothers got to enjoy Mary's nascent cooking and baking skills.

Everything was fine until I decided to take a proper day off. Both shops closed early on Sundays and the misery of the rain and sleet through the week had suddenly changed. We'd woken up on the Saturday morning to a winter wonderland of snow-covered gardens, trees laden with inches of deep snow glistening in the glare of real sunshine, and a cloudless blue sky. What a difference!

Andy and Phil banged on the bedroom door. "Can we go to the Campsies? Dad took us last year wi' the sledges an' it was brilliant!"

I was standing at the window looking out on the transformed Riddrie Knowes. I'd love to go sledging, but I had a pretty full day ahead, including a trip to the Cash and Carry. In fact, I might have difficulty driving. The snow looked pretty deep on the road outside.

Mary opened the door to let the boys in as a plan formed. "Tell you what," I said, "if the snow lies overnight, Thomas and I could both take tomorrow off and we could all go. How does that sound?"

Mary grinned at her two youngest brothers-in-law who were jumping up and down. "Ok, guys. Let's go organise our winter picnic and dig out some warm clothes."

I went ahead and did my duties, slithering about on icy side streets. Loading juices and sweets for both shops into the back of the Zephyr. After a pretty full day, I came back to an excited household.

"Hey, John, we had a great snow fight with the Burnetts next door, and Alan helped us to build a snowman." Phil's cheeks were bright red as he helped himself to some of Mary's homemade steak pie. "This is great, Mary. I better no' say it's better than Mum's, but she is pretty far away… She won't hear me!"

Laughter all round as we talked about the next day's fun. Mary interrupted, "Have you noticed how much colder it's become in the last couple of hours? I popped through to the living room and there's frost on top of the snow. We'll need extra layers tomorrow. The TV weather said it was to go well below freezing, but nice clear skies. Woolly bunnets all round."

Sunday morning arrived just as bright as the day before, but there was even frost on the inside of the bedroom windows. It was going to be a cold one.

Corn flakes downed. Filled rolls bagged. Warm clothes for everyone. Two old wooden and steel sledges, one new-fangled plastic moulded one, and a couple of Mum's baking trays, chucked into the back of the car along with extra jackets, and we were on our way.

An hour later, we joined the crowds of other Glaswegians who'd had the same idea. The car park off the Fintry road overlooking the villages of Campsie Glen and Lennoxtown was overflowing. Families dragging sledges through the icy heather, halfway up the snow-covered hill. Racing each other down through the gullies. Screams of delight as sledges tumble. Impromptu snow fights add to the fun. Hands warm on hot flasks as fingertips numb. Lots of laughter as Alan goes flying. Lands spread-eagled and ends up lying on the hard-packed snow and continues to slide as far as he could go. Right down to the edge of the road. Stops just in time to avoid a car laying him low.

Afternoon twilight crept up on us as the sledges and tin trays were bundled into car boots. Joining the convoy of happy rosy-cheeked folk driving home for Sunday tea with the darkening Campsies casting their shadows on the villages below.

"It's freezing in here!" Thomas exclaimed, as we traipsed through the kitchen into the darkened hallway. Mary stopping to turn the dials on the cooker. "Dinner in about half an hour, guys."

A few minutes later, Alan came back down from upstairs. "I can't get the shower to work, an' I'm boggln'." He'd used his chin as a brake a few times on the hill, and the snow had got dirtier as the day wore on. "An' I can only get cold water in the bathroom sink. I'm freezing' as it is!"

There seemed to be a hot water problem, but Mary boiled a couple of kettles and we all managed to clean ourselves up enough to sit and enjoy her homemade broth, and the good old-fashioned mince and tatties she'd prepared the day before.

Next day was a school day, so much coaxing needed to get Phil and Andy to bed. The day's excitement hadn't slowed their capacity for knocking lumps out of each other as they were shooed upstairs.

After a couple of games of cards, Thomas announced he was off to bed, "Some of us have to open a shop first thing, while temporary area managers seem to be neither here nor there…" I threw a cushion at his departing back.

The rest of us followed him upstairs soon after.

Mary and I had been enjoying sleeping in Mum and Dad's bedroom, with its old-fashioned mahogany headboard and sheets and blankets. We couldn't decide whether we preferred them to our up-to-the-minute 'Continental Quilt.' Either way we were very cosy. The house had warmed up eventually once the heavy metal storage heaters did their duty. Sleepy time…

"What's that sound?" Mary shook my shoulder. I woke up and peered at the clock. "It's five o'bloody-clock! What sound?" I had been having a really good dream about whizzing down the Campsies on skis, jumping over those skimming sledges, and then zooming down beside the river that seemed to be flowing faster and faster. And noisier and noisier…

"Has Alan left the bath tap on or something? I can hear gushing water," I said as I pulled the bed sheets back. Mary was shaking her head as she sat up in bed. There was a glimmer of light trickling through the curtains from the streetlamps outside. I felt my way to the door. The bathroom was round the L-shaped hallway past Alan's room on the left. The hall light wouldn't work, so I tried the bedroom light. It was the same. "Try the bedside lamps, Mary." She reached over and a small puddle of light appeared on her side of the bed. It wasn't much but at least a little light spilled into the hallway, which had no window. I could still hear water gurgling somewhere.

I peered through the semi-darkness as I stepped onto the hall carpet.

Splash!

It was wet!

Very wet...

Oh, Bloody Hell!

My bare feet sloshed through cold wet carpet as I edged my way round to the bathroom.

As I pushed the door open and felt for the light cord, I caught sight of an unnerving vision. The frosted window let just enough distorted street lighting through to reflect on the stream of water running down the central light fitting and splashing onto the linoleum, which had turned into a small rectangular pond.

I decided not to pull on the light switch cord…

Mary splashed behind me. “The water in the pipe must have frozen, and then burst through. Now we’ve heated the house it’s flowing freely. What are you going to do?”

My shoulders slumped. “I’d figured out the burst pipe angle,” I said. “We’ll need to get the boys up, their rooms might be flooded too. Then try and turn the water off. I think the stop cock is in the kitchen somewhere. Any idea if there’s a torch anywhere?” *This was going to be a bad Monday!*

We opened the boys’ doors. “Everybody up. We‘re being flooded. All hands on deck!”

Andy and Phil jumped out of bed right away. Excited voices: “Wow! Our carpet’s soaking. I can make waves!”

In the meantime, I could hear the water still gushing out of the burst pipe into the loft above our heads.

“Has anybody got a torch?” I shouted.

“Just turn the light on, John.” Alan pushed past me into the bathroom, his bare feet creating a small tidal wave. “See?”

He pulled on the light cord.

The ceiling light burst into life, illuminating the scary sight. The dripping water started to fizz as it ran over the warming bulb.

Not Good!

Alan’s eyes opened wide.

He started jumping up and down.

“The floor’s electrified!” he shouted, as Thomas came up behind the crowd of us gathered round the bathroom doorway, mesmerised by Alan’s electric dancing.

“Turn the bloody light off! Ya nutters!” Thomas stretched past me to grab the light cord.

"Give us a shot!" Phil and Andy squeezed into the bathroom to join Alan in his surreal pursuit.

"Ach, it's just a tingle." Phil was splashing his younger brother with the electrified floodwater.

All three of them were now dancing a kind of watery highland fling.

This can't be happening. I was just dreaming about super sledging down the Campsies…

"I found a torch in Andy's bed." Mary handed it to me. "The tap's probably under the kitchen sink."

The gushing noise was still loud over our heads. I pointed the torch at the ceiling.

"Run for it!"

"Move!" I shouted

The plaster was sodden with an enormous sagging belly right above our heads! I grabbed the two younger boys and heaved them towards Mum and Dad's room, while Thomas and Alan and Mary trotted backwards along the hallway, everyone's eyes fixed on the sagging plaster.

Crack!

"That doesn't sound so good…"

Crash!

A big chunk of ceiling plummeted to the floor, followed by a veritable torrent of water, pouring on top of the heap of broken plaster.

"That was so-o-o close. I was standing right there a second ago." Thomas scratched his shaking head, staring at the sodden pile.

Hurrying down the stairs, peering under the kitchen sink with the wee kiddie's torch. More than one tap to turn. Turn them all off. Bloody difficult… Quick!

"That's it, John! It's slowed to a trickle," Thomas shouted from upstairs.

What a way to start the week…

Five days and a massive clean-up later, we were all waiting eagerly at the airport.

"There they are!" Wee Andy shouted as he spotted Mum and Dad among the crowds streaming through the transit doors.

"Will *I* tell them about the flood, John?" Thomas grinned at me.

"Let's wait till they're back in the house. The burst pipe's fixed and the floor's dried out. Mum will enjoy organising the redecorating," I said, hopefully.

"Aye, till she sees that big hole in her ceiling!"

Mum was wearing her precious fur coat she'd saved up for in anticipation of the freezing Canadian winter. Dad's chunky sheepskin jacket looked positively threadbare beside it.

Hugs and handshakes as we gathered round, vying to push the baggage trolley to the waiting car.

Dad gave me a quizzical look. "Everything ok?"

"The shops are fine," I answered truthfully. "We had a wee problem with a leaky pipe in the house, but it's fixed now. Although you might just want to get a plasterer in..."

Dad and Mum looked at each other as we moved towards the exits.

Phil, skipping on the tiled floor, asked his Mum, "Was Canada really all that cold?"

Mum shivered in memory. "When we stayed with Aunty Betty, we took her dog for a walk round the block in the snow. It was so cold I could feel my fillings freezing... I couldn't get back inside soon enough!"

All squeezed into the car, we made our way back to the Dickson family home, where Mary had laid on a scrumptious buffet of Canadian-themed items. Maple leaf shaped sandwiches, Mounties on gingerbread horses, and a welcome home cake with lumberjacks and a Niagara Falls backdrop.

"I did the Mounties!" Phil was keen to show off to his mum and dad. "I cut out the maple leafs!" Andy was close behind him.

Alan wasn't to be outdone. "Actually, the Canadian theme was my idea! I've decided I'm good at delegating…"

"Of course you are, Alan. The food's lovely. We've missed you all. And yes, we have had a great time!" Mum was still relishing her dream trip.

She and Dad had traipsed upstairs to inspect the damage. "We'll deal with it tomorrow. I think I'm what 's called jet-lagged." Dad puffed his cheeks out and rubbed his eyes. "Let's have a go at Mary's buffet."

Questions, questions. Were the cousins nice? What kind of cars do they drive? Did you see a moose? Do they really have basements in their houses? Is Niagara Falls as big as it looks on the telly?

Sitting in the living room, cup of Glasgow tea and nibbling one of Andy's Maple leaf sandwiches, Mum slumped back in her favourite comfy chair.

"It seems an awful long time. A three-week visiting trip. We met so-o many people I'm related to. And that means you lot are too! You'd be so welcome! I lost the plot as to who was who. I gave up after the first week. I kept saying 'we've probably already met?' Sometimes it worked. I got on really well with my cousin Rosemary. The one I've been writing to for years? Och, she's lovely. Isn't she Jackie?"

Dad, equally slumped in his chair, looked up, stopping himself from dozing off. "Aye. Rosemary's nice. She was born on the very same day as me! Fifteenth of June 1925. Is that not amazing? Now *that* was a *really* good day!"

Chapter 31
City Slickers to Country Bumpkins

New Year's Day 1974. All the Christmas and Hogmanay fun behind us as we luxuriated in the only day in the year that The Buy In was closed… Over a calming mug of tea with lemon slices floating on the top, we had a moment to reflect on where we were, and how we were doing.

"What do you mean you could do with a fresh challenge?" I was startled at Mary's comments. "I thought you were really enjoying our life."

Mary looked pensive. "Yeh, of course I do, but maybe sometimes I feel it's all a bit too easy. You know?"

I looked askance, "Maybe for you, young lady, with your nice cushy part-time number, with plenty of time off to prepare fancy dinners. By the way, I really like them! But I don't really have that luxury."

I did feel a bit peeved as Mary shrugged her shoulders and looked up towards the kitchen ceiling. "That's part of the problem. It is a bit cushy. I know you work pretty hard and maybe don't have time to lift your head. But I've been thinking…"

Uh oh…

Mary and I had been married for nearly two years. We were still enjoying our marvellous flat with the enormous living room that could accommodate a (small) band in the bay window. And it was only ten minutes from where I worked. That meant I could come home for lunch. And if Mary wasn't working one of her three days a week in the opticians, we could enjoy lunch together, in the slightly subsiding kitchen that had space enough for two very comfy chairs either side of the fireplace.

We were close enough to the city centre to be able to go to the cinema and still catch the last bus home. We could meet up with Joe and his band in almost any city centre pub and enjoy the company of the band members and their increasing circle of hangers on.

We could have visitors easily, because we were so central. Alan and Phil and Andy would appear at our door on a Saturday morning and drag us round the corner to the Rollerina, the converted old Dennistoun Palais and get us whilrlin' round them boards.

The shop was doing what it was supposed to. It was never going to be more than a local suburban newsagent, but it paid our humble bills, with Thomas and I managing modest incomes, albeit I got a couple of pounds a week more for shouldering most of the responsibilities. Customers kept coming back, so we must have been doing something right. The only niggle was the fact that The Buy In had been going for more than two years and Thomas was beginning to make noises about when he was going to take over… I'd talked about it to Dad, I felt a bit guilty, but Dad was more dismissive: "Thomas isn't ready to run the shop, he's too busy socialising and making those amateur movies he loves. Besides you've got a wife and bills to pay for. Thomas'll be fine…"

I still felt there was a problem without a solution, but Dad was the boss.

In the meantime, Mary and I had no kids, with plenty of time to look forward to that in due course. We could enjoy each other's company. So we did.

We'd alternate Sunday afternoons between Mary's parents and mine. Newspaper quizzes and games of Scrabble or Monopoly with my wee brothers, alternated with family gossip and arrangements to occasionally look after Joyce's and James's kids. This could be great fun. We were the cool, young auntie and uncle. I played guitar while Mary sang sweet songs or rock 'n' roll. They'd sit open-mouthed, and even try to join in. Then their parents would come home from whatever important lawyerly event they'd been at, and we all would drink Martini and listen to the lawyerly gossip.

Life was quite comfy. What's wrong with that!

Silly thought to have…

"I think we should have more than one business. I reckon I could be a businesswoman instead of a part-time optician's receptionist." Mary looked down from the ceiling and stared at me with those glorious big eyes.

I felt myself melting, but just a bit. "And what is your big business idea?"

Mary looked down. “That’s the problem… I’m not too sure. I think it could maybe have something to do with food? Seeing as how you think I’m not too bad in that department.”

“Not just me, and you know that. But I’m afraid it’s going to be quite a while before The Buy In is going to generate enough funds to take on Reo Stakis and Ye Olde Worlde Inns.”

Mary glared at me. “I’m not suggesting we take on the world, but it would be nice to have a goal. Yes?”

I couldn’t argue with that.

And sometimes life just gives you a helping hand…

A couple of weeks later, Mum spoke first: “I know you’re both happy in that smashing flat. But it is rented. Looking ahead, the right thing to do is to buy your own place.”

Dad nodded as he took a bite out of his gammon steak garnished with pineapple, chips, and chase after peas. A la Stakis Olde Worlde Inn.

We were having a grown-up dinner and talking grown-up talk.

I felt I had to say something. “We’re managing fine. But you know the shop’s not making enough for me to come up with a deposit for a house. And we’re actually very happy where we are. Aren’t we, Mary?” I looked at my wife who had a dreamy look in her eyes.

Mary leaned forward to Mum and Dad and whispered. “Are you talking about doing something about a deposit?”

The upshot was a parental version of a ‘help to buy’ scheme. Not quite a gift, but it could open that door if we wanted it to.

Mary got up and ran round the table and gave Dad a great big hug. He actually looked embarrassed! Mum looked happy.

Looking at me, excitement bursting out of her, she exclaimed, “Now we *can* make plans!”

Bye bye comfort zone…

……………………………………………………………………………

Most people dread moving house.

Mary loves it!

The morning after we'd had our conversation with Mum and Dad, she was on the phone to every estate agent in Scotland.

I think I'll let her get on with it.

Does this mean the party's over?

It wasn't.

It just moved out to the country.

Mary found what she thought was an idyllic two up, two down ex-miner's terraced cottage. Right on the main road that runs from the village of Lennoxtown and up and over the Campsie Fells, those moorland hills that had been on my horizon since our Ruchazie days.

Just along the road from my first camping adventure. I still laughed when I thought of Joe Slyder's sodden 'leather' shoes melting in the campfire. That was only eight years before. Just a daft boy and here I am now, two years married and looking at houses. Wheech!

After viewing the completely refurbished house, with its wood-panelled, fully fitted kitchen diner, and the enormous strip of back garden, Mary had fallen in love with it. I thought it was nice. But it had its drawbacks.

"Look, John." Mary was selling the concept. "No more climbing two flights of stairs after squeezing the van into a parking place. The front door is right on the pavement. There's a cute wee dairy through the wall that sells bacon and eggs and rolls. I won't have to wander all the way down to Duke Street for the basics."

I put my points. "It's ten miles from the shop, so no coming home for lunch. I'll miss that. It'll take you forever to get to Byres Road by buses. How will that work? We'll never see anyone we know 'cos we're so far out in the country. The rooms are far smaller than the flat's. Our couch won't fit. Now if we could only pull our flat out of the tenement and put it in a garden somewhere…" I fantasised.

Mary arranged for my mum to come along and view the cottage and get her opinion. Apart from worrying about the dangers of the front door being on the pavement if Mary and I had any kids in the near future… big hint, Mum loved it.

It's just impossible to win an argument with your wife *and* your mum.

So, the flitting came in the spring…

Chapter 32
Country Fayre... and Buster!

"I think this place is going to open up a whole new world for us!" Mary twirled, arms outstretched in our new back garden. "Look at the hills! Smell the greenery! Taste this country air!"

Her enthusiasm was infectious. I felt a huge smile enveloping my cheeks. I joined in the spirit. Holding hands, we pulled each other round in circles. Whirling in unison. Eyes locked. Loving the moment. Yes! Country air definitely trumps city pollution any day.

Before we got too dizzy, I pulled Mary towards me and gave her a great big hug. "Ok! Let's be happy here. Not that we weren't happy in Dennistoun by the way!"

Mary laughed, "I know… It was a great start. But I'm going to blossom here. Watch this space…"

We pulled apart and surveyed our new landscape. A long narrow strip of coarse grass. Low-level fencing separating our neighbours. A sturdy shed at the top of the garden. Half a dozen steps leading down to the common service access for all the inhabitants of our row of two up, two down cottages.

"Did you notice the 1821 plaque on the gable end?" I asked Mary.

"Aye, I mentioned it to Mr Drummond in the dairy next door. Apparently, the houses were built for the cotton printers' way back in the day. Our house used to be two houses. Two rooms on the ground and the same upstairs. With an outside privy in the back lane. He says one of his older customers was born in our new back bedroom in the 1890s… I'd like to meet her. I bet she'll know who's who in the village."

"I've no doubt you'll get to know who's who. With or without that particular old dear," I said, as we walked back down the garden stairs and faced up to the mountain of yet to be unpacked boxes.

Once we moved in, I felt as if I'd moved to a far-off land, way out of my territory. The wee cottage in sunny Lennoxtown was also in 'Campsie' as the locals confusingly called the village. But not to be mixed up with Milton of Campsie the *next* village along, from where the camping trips started.

Mary loved it, but I wasn't so sure. Having had lots of space in the big, high-ceilinged rooms of our Dennistoun flat, I felt confined and claustrophobic. I kept hitting my shins against the coffee table and felt pinned against the wall when we were eating in the well-designed, but cramped kitchen diner.

I missed the two comfy seats by the old Dennistoun kitchen fireplace.

I had to commute a lot further. No more nipping back home for a quickie lunch. I was away all day working, although I did look forward to coming home to a well-cooked meal and a happy young wife.

Then Mary had what she thought was the clincher idea to help me adjust and enjoy our new country life. With the summer's light suddenly blasting through the pulled back curtains, I woke up on my birthday morning to a strange snuffling noise. The bedroom door opened and I was confronted by the most boisterous golden Labrador puppy I'd ever encountered. He had glorious shiny eyes, enormous padded paws, and he definitely looked like he was grinning from ear to ear.

As he romped around the room with Mary laughing in the doorway, I clambered out of bed and grabbed hold of my birthday present. What was I to do? A dog? A dog? I looked at Mary's happily expectant face and didn't have the heart to say, "No thanks."

"His name's Buster." Mary was excited.

"Well. That's a good name." Buster agreed by wildly wagging his lower body while I couldn't help nuzzling his ears.

Once you give a dog a name, it's not just a dog. It's a family!

I was hooked.

Things settled down to a routine and Buster quickly grew bigger. He'd enjoy our occasional jaunts to the local pub, the Swan, where he was eventually able to put his front paws on to the bar to be rewarded with a cold meat pie from Jock the landlord.

....

"Big Bruv Iain's asked me to help out with the new baby's christening," Mary announced one evening. "I've asked Mr McAllister for a couple of days off. He said ok. That ok with you?"

"Fair enough, if your boss says it's ok. It's ok." *Not that we could do with all your wages…*

So, Mary became involved in helping out at her niece's christening in Glasgow's south side.

A natural organiser, Mary found herself in charge of the cooking and catering for the after party. Iain's wife Maureen was "ever so grateful, Mary. You make it look so easy. And you do put on such a lovely spread."

Sprawling over the couch back home, exhausted, after the damned hard work the christening had turned out to be, Mary was reflective.

"You know. I enjoyed the christening and feeding all the hungry faces. I've been catering at family functions since I was about nine, helping Granny make her steak pies. Maybe I should try and make a business out of that…"

She put her mind to it and looked around.

……………………………………………………………………………………………

A few weeks later Mary met me at the door as I came home from the shop. It was a Friday evening, but there was a tension that was different.

"What's the matter, sweetheart? Champagne not quite up to Mr McAllister's usual standard?"

"That's not the problem." She closed the door behind me. Shoulders stiffened. Head down, not my Mary's usual demeanour.

"I hope you're not mad at me…" She looked up at me through those natural thick eyelashes.

I'd already had a hard week. The longer commute wasn't helping. What now?

"Uh huh?" We were in the living room by now. *Please get on with it. I'm hungry…*

Mary looked anxious. Scared to tell me something?

Should I worry? I said nothing.

She took a deep breath. Stood up straighter. "You know the fruit shop beside the police station? On the Main Road?"

"Uh huh?" *I'm still hungry. And you usually make really good food… And we both enjoy it…*

"Well, I was in there the other day… On my day off…"

"Which one of your days off was that?" I said, instantly regretting the tone.

Mary's head snapped up.

"Whoa! We agreed that I'd go to work part-time after we got married two years ago! What's your point? Do you want me to feel guilty, 'cos I can't help you out in the shop from here? You want to tell me 'you told me so'?"

Well, actually, I do! But if *I do, this scene will get even more difficult… And I could do with my dinner…*

Diplomacy won out. "Look, I'm sorry. You were about to tell me something that's obviously bothering you. I can't know what it is until you say the words! What's the problem?"

Mary sucked in her breath through clenched teeth.

"I've handed in my notice to McAllister's and offered to take over the fruit shop next month!" she blurted out at a speed I couldn't quite take in.

"Pardon? You've handed in your notice? You've been there for over four years. Did he just say, 'Fine then, Mary, bye'? I thought you were important to him and the business?"

Before she had a chance to answer, the other half of the sentence soaked in.

"What do you mean you've offered to take over the fruit shop? Are you mad? Have you any idea how hard it is to operate a good fruit and veg shop? To start with, you have to go to the fruit market in the middle of the night to buy your daily stock. And you can't even drive! How's that going to work?"

My mind was whirling. Am I supposed to do a night shift as well as run The Buy In? This country air's definitely gone to her head…

Mary's eyes were wide open now. A mixture of fear and determination.

"Don't be so daft! The Walkers are giving up the fruit shop because… because… Well actually, it's because he's a crabbit old codger who's fallen out with most of their customers, though they didn't say that. But I was talking to old Mrs Lafferty, you know, who was born upstairs?"

This was getting more surreal by the minute…

Mary was on a roll. "Mrs Lafferty says they've only had it for a couple of years as a fruit shop. But they don't go to the fruit market like you were saying, so nothing's really fresh, and Mr Walker's the 'spittin' image' of his grandfather who was 'always an arrogant fool.' When he had a drapers shop further up the road, he'd never stock the local school uniforms because he thought 'maroon was a stupid colour.'"

By this time, my shoulders were slumping. I was trying not to be angry. Our new world was about to get a lot harder. But I didn't know how yet!

Get on with it, woman!

I felt myself glaring…

Mary took another deep breath. "Remember I said I wanted to be a business woman? Maybe do something with food? Well… My plan is to transform the fruit shop into a traditional Tearoom and Gift Shop. We've got all these folk passing through the village on the way to the Campsies. And yet there's nowhere to even buy a cup of tea."

I was listening intently. *And how are we gonna make this happen?*

Mary smiled almost timorously. "I've even thought of a name… I'm going to call it 'Country Fayre.*'* We'll have cream teas and scones and buns, as well as rolls and bacon and…"

"C'mon, Mary, we really should have talked this over before you made these life-changing commitments. Have you actually done the arithmetic?" *And I was still hungry. It was going to be a long night.*

Mary gave me her most engaging smile and put her arms lovingly round my neck. “I know you’re good at that bit, my clever John. But I’m good with the food… And there’s a nice casserole bubbling in the oven.”

Chapter 33
Buster and a Grave Moment

A lot of sweet talking and convincing later and I was on board with Mary's plan. I'd even convinced myself that if it worked, it could be the start of a new proper business. Possibly even a way to let Thomas take over The Buy In. He'd been making louder and louder noises about when it was 'his turn' to take it over. Mum told me that Dad kept telling him that he wasn't ready yet, and besides, "John's got a mortgage now, and all his household bills. You're still living at home, rent-free. Just be patient…" Thomas turned away, scowling, and said nothing. For now.

But my guilty feelings were growing. Maybe the tearoom could sort out Mary's ambitions. And get Thomas off my back?

Lots of plans and loads of hard work.

We entered the maze that is the 'planning process.' The fruit shop didn't have the proper planning classification to sell food. We needed something called 'Class 3.' So, we had to go to the council offices in Stirling and fill out endless forms… Pay them money… then wait…

"What if they say no?" Mary was worried. Her month's notice was almost up. Mr McAllister had started a new girl. Mary and Lynne, who'd be moving up to Mary's more senior position (and a bigger glass of the Friday champagne), had been training her on the basics.

"What am I going to do? The Walkers have put up signs saying the shop's closing next week. They've told everybody it's being turned into a tearoom and gift shop, and it might not happen because some bureaucrat says no!" She was literally wringing her hands. I'd never seen her so stressed.

"Well, you could always get a wee job with Mr Drummond next door… That'd be handy." I ducked as the rolled-up dishtowel whizzed past my head.

The very next day, after my umpteenth phone call to the planning department, we got the letter we'd been waiting for. All systems were go!

"Yippee!" Mary danced round the coffee table. I tried to join her, and then banged my shins…

We got the keys and got stuck into converting the fruit shop. We had a very limited budget. So it was paint pots all round and sprucing up the existing fittings.

The biggest expenses were a full set of new bistro tables and chairs, and some second-hand kitchen equipment to help feed the hungry faces.

I nearly put myself in hospital gluing the new Formica surface over the ancient chipped wooden counter. The fumes from the tub of glue blurred my vision and almost knocked me out cold.

Mary came into the closed shop with Buster after his evening walk. I held up my very sticky fingers. "God knows what kind of kick those glue sniffers get out of it. My head was spinning. Damned difficult to lay that Formica squarely with the whole shop gyrating at the same time."

Buster waggled his backside, jumped up, and tried to lick my fingers… "No, Buster! You're crazy enough as it is!" Mary said as she pulled him away.

…………………………………………………………………………………

The tearoom opening meant Buster wasn't going to be getting as much exercise as he had been, so arrangements had to be made with one of our well-meaning neighbours, whom Mary had met in the next-door dairy the day after we moved in.

Sarah might have been described by Rabbie Burns as a sonsy lass. Her love of watching telly and 'looking after her mum' (who was one of the bastions of the local rambler's club), had resulted in a more generous figure than she'd sported a few years earlier.

"I don't mind looking after Buster when you're working. Might help get me back in shape. How hard can it be?"

She was about to find out on her first doggie walking episode.

The big day came. A sunny Saturday morning and 'Country Fayre' opened its doors. Free tea and coffee to all comers was a great marketing success.

Every seat was taken by what seemed like every villager.

"This is nice. Just what Campsie needs" and, "Free tea? Yes, please. Well, ok, I do fancy a homemade roll and sausage, and maybe a wee cake?"

Mary and her new crew, hand-picked with the help of Mr Drummond and old Mrs Lafferty's daughter, Lizzie, were all working hard, and Mary was more than pleased at the reactions she was getting from her happy customers.

In the meantime, Buster was having a good day. Sarah had taken him in before Mary went down to the tearoom. Fed and watered him. Then, well wrapped up for her first dog walking exercise, she bundled Buster out into the street.

Buster had never quite got the idea that it wasn't *only* me he had to obey. When he was a new pup, I had taken him to dog training classes and tried to get him to behave like a dog should behave… I listened to the trainer's instructions. Put on my most authoritative voice: "Sit, Buster!" and he should have sat. But sometimes all he would do was wag his tail fiercely, grin widely, then hop, skip and jump round my legs, wrapping my ankles tightly with his lead till *I* had to sit!

However, after a good few weeks, I could *usually* keep him in check and he would even walk to heel (depending on his mood…).

"Buster!" Sarah shouted as she was pulled down the hill, six stone of canine muscle easily out-performing Sarah's somewhat full frame.

Buster had spotted the Swan Inn door opening. He knew all he had to do was lift his paws on to the bar and Jock the landlord would gift him a whole meat pie! Sarah's wee doggie biscuits were really only the hors d'oeuvre.

Sarah gave up trying to pull Buster back. She simply clattered her way down the street trying to keep up. They reached the pub door and, true to form, Buster ran in and raised himself to his full height, big paws on the bar. Drooling grin, wide open. eyes, sparkling in anticipation.

Sarah staggered in behind him, somewhat dishevelled and definitely out of breath.

"Aye aye, you're early." Jock the elderly landlord smiled as he reached into the yellowing glass display case and pulled out a fresh pie.

Buster's grin got even wider. Jock tossed the pie up in the air and Buster promptly jumped up a couple of feet and expertly caught the pie before swallowing it whole. This was his party piece, and when the pub was busy in the evenings, he'd earn a round of applause along with extra packets of crisps from his appreciative audience.

However, it was early in the day. There was only one other customer in the bar. Big Seamus, the local 'landscape gardener' who had taken the day off as he was going to his uncle Patrick's funeral later in the day. Old Paddy had been one of the village's 'characters' and until recently had held court in the Swan of an evening. He would tell tales of 'derring-do' in his young days as a renowned local poacher. Then, with a surprisingly rich baritone voice, he would occasionally and unexpectedly burst into song. The pub's hubbub would quietly die down while the notes reverberated around the room. Uncle Paddy would be sadly missed.

Seamus eyed Sarah up and down. Sometimes sonsy works…

"You must be thirsty running after that beast." He winked and grinned as he patted Buster with his massive hand. "What'll you have?"

Sarah was disconcerted. She'd known Seamus since schooldays, but he was usually surrounded by a bunch of his mates and brothers. The McGilligans were a big Campsie family. And she was seldom in the pub. Her mum didn't approve.

"Ok then. I'll just have the one." Sarah tried not to blush. Jock the landlord looked from Seamus to Sarah and poured the drink. *Aye aye* he thought to himself. *Takings'll be up today.*

A few hours later, back in the tearoom. Mary and company were clearing up after their first busy lunchtime. I arrived just in time to pop in and be regaled with tales of first-day success.

"So you had a good day?"

"Absolutely mobbed. Couldn't have been better!"

"That's great," I said. "Is Buster with Sarah by the way? I'm sure I saw her with that Irish bloke. You know the big gardener? I didn't see the dog."

"I did think she'd pop in with him but I've not seen her since this morning. She's probably taken him back home." Mary grinned. "Maybe Seamus has turned out to be the man of her dreams."

` As we drove up the Main Street towards home, we were held back by a large crowd of murmuring mourners, slowly walking behind the tall black hearse which was inching its way towards the graveyard on the brow of the hill. They must have just come from the chapel along the Main Street.

"Oh, that must be Old 'Uncle Paddy's' funeral," Mary said.

"Uncle Paddy?"

"You know him. The old bloke in the Swan. Sings songs and always had biscuits for Buster." Mary reminded me. "Some of the customers asked if I was going to the funeral… Maybe we should show face… Customer relations?"

I was looking forward to a celebratory glass of wine, but it looked like duty calling.

We patiently and respectfully waited till the last of the many shuffling mourners had turned right into the long driveway which snaked its way up the hill in the centre of the village.

Two minutes later we had parked my van at our front door which faced the other side of the churchyard.

We could just see the mourners and the priest gathering round the new grave. The coffin balanced on the poll bearers' shoulders. We quickly walked up the side path to join the throng.

Just as we were reaching the edge of the crowd, we heard strange shouts and squeals ahead of us. Sarah's shrieking could have been heard the other side of the Campsies: "Oh my God. Grab him, somebody!"

Mary and I looked at each other…

We could see a commotion of arm waving scattering silhouettes as the flashing yellow blur that was Buster waggled its way between the mourners' legs, his lead flailing wildly behind him. Hands clutched uselessly at the flying leather strip. It was futile. Buster knew where he was going… I closed my eyes as he made a scrabbling dive and disappeared under the timber straps and into the newly opened grave…

And started digging…

The crowd froze…

A bedraggled Sarah wheezed to a stop at the edge of the grave. She knelt down, peering into the open grave, and shouted: "No! No! Buster! Please come out!"

"That's me Uncle Patrick's grave, ya stupid woman. Why'd ye let yer idiot dog jump in there before he's had a chance to be bloody well buried." Seamus's intoxicated anger could be heard just as clearly as Sarah's shrieks.

"But it's not *my* dog!"

"Well, ye *told* me it was *your* bloody dog!"

"I was trying to impress you." Sarah wailed pitifully as she knelt down at the grave's edge, watched by the mesmerised mourners who seemed to be in a state of communal shock.

Just then Buster's head popped up. He tried to jump and scramble up and out of the grave. Sarah caught his collar with her right hand and tried to heave him out. Having had a wee bit more than 'just the one,' her judgement was not at its sharpest. She reached out with her left hand and the loose ground crumbled from under her bended knees. A small avalanche started falling into the grave. Buster yelped as he realised his opportunity and used Sarah's tumbling, sobbing, body as a human ladder to jump up and out of the putative tomb.

"Buster, don't!" Sarah yelped then slithered sideways into the grave as though in slow motion.

There was a collective low moan…

As some of the crowd tried to fish the blubbering Sarah out, Buster, shaking himself all over, grinned widely before running breathlessly over to me and Mary.

We stood numb…

Buster woofed loudly as he whirled excitedly around our legs. Our shocked faces tried to express horror, shame, and sympathy

We also failed to retain any vestige of dog owning credibility.

The village faces turned from staring at the debacle by the open grave to staring at our feeble attempts to get Buster, the cause of it all, under control…

“Somehow I don’t think we’ll be quite as busy, tomorrow.” Mary whispered…

Chapter 34
Horses for Courses

My earlier anxieties of being marooned in the far-off lands of the Campsies proved to be unfounded. If anything, our geography became a bit of a draw.

"Who's that at the door?" I shouted downstairs. Mary had got up before me to let Buster out to the back garden. *And you think he'll stay there?*

"It's Phil and Andy! They've cycled all the way from Riddrie. Come on down and be a host to your wee brothers, you lazy sod!" Mary shouted back as I heard the door close.

Ok. Time to get up early on my one day off…

I gathered my wits, pulled on my jeans, and ran downstairs to welcome my two youngest brothers.

"Morning, Munchkins. How long did it take you to get here? It takes me half an hour in the van".

Phil stuck his chin out. "Well, we left the house at eight o clock and it's just quarter past nine. So now we know how lazy you are!"

I answered back: "It's my one day off a week. I'm not going to feel guilty about having a lie in. Just because you guys decided to turn up. Where's Alan by the way? I know Thomas is in the shop."

Andy chimed in, "Alan's playing guitar at his pal, Ewan's. I heard them talking about it last night. Then he was talking about going out to the disco."

Talk of guitar touched a chord (boom boom) and I sat down and picked up my new acoustic instrument that Mary had bought me for Christmas. I was still enchanted by the tone. I sat on the couch and strummed quietly as Mary and the boys made plans.

I heard Mary say: "Well, I've covered myself from tearoom duties today because I've arranged to go horse riding with wee Tamsin and

Toby down at the Riverbank Hotel. They've got stables and they do pony treks for beginners. Do you guys fancy having a shot?"

"That sounds brilliant." Phil and Andy were both grinning from ear to ear.

"I didn't know anything about this," I butted in. "How come I'm not invited?"

Mary had an answer. "You were supposed to be helping Joe and Robbie at some afternoon gig. Remember?"

I did. But it had fallen through. So I had a free day!

"Well, I'll come along too. I've ridden once or twice before. Round and round a paddock. I fancy a wee trek out in the country. I'll keep my legs tightly squeezed and be in full control!"

The doorbell rang for the second time that morning. It was Joyce, dropping off Tamsin and Toby. I recognised the bossiness of her tone. "Right, Mary, Tamsin will be fine but Toby *will do as he is told!* OK, Toby?"

Mary replied, "I'm sure Toby will have a great time, Joyce. Tamsin too. Look we've got John's wee brothers, Phil and Andy. They're coming pony trekking with us. It'll be even more fun. You all set?"

I pulled myself out of my slump on the settee. "How's you, Joyce? I don't suppose you fancy a bit of pony trekking through the forest. See if you can beat the weans?"

"Not for me thanks, John. I've no wish to compete with my children. They know who's boss. Don't they, Toby?" She turned to Mary. "Toby can be such a handful. And now he's started a bloody stuttering affectation. Just to hold us back! Good luck on the horses. Goodbye, John's brothers. I'll be back late afternoon. Don't let them injure themselves too much, sister! Bye bye." I heard her Rover V8's deep gurgling as she started it up just outside on the street.

Once her big sister was gone, Mary got organised. "Right, people. We're walking down to the hotel where the stables are. John, keep Buster on the lead. Mrs Kelly won't want him spooking the ponies. We can leave him with one of the stable hands while we're trekking."

We all did as we were told and set off down walking to the other end of the village. The kids took turns in holding Buster's lead. He was happy to be going out on a walk with a whole bunch of people instead of just me or Mary.

We reached the recently renovated hotel, where they had let out the original stables to Mrs Kelly. A formidable horsewoman who'd recognised the possibilities of building a pony trekking business, alongside her more formal horse riding and training school.

We stood as a group just inside the straw strewn grounds of the hotel. Buster's lead was still being passed from child to child.

Mrs Kelly, sitting high on a large horse, clip-clopped effortlessly towards us, horsewhip tucked under her arm.

She looked down: "Mrs Dickson, I presume. Here for the two-hour pony trek? I thought there were just three of you?"

Mary spoke up. "That's right. I did book for three. But we've just had these two lads turn up at our door and my husband, John, here reckons he'd like a go. Will you manage?"

Mrs Kelly looked bemused for a minute then called over to one of the stable girls mucking out the stalls and saddling the ponies, ready for the outing. "Patricia! Do we have six horses available? Two of them suitable for children." She looked down at me while she waited for an answer. "Do you ride, Mr Dickson?"

I felt uncomfortable looking up at her. The late morning sun was behind her, so her head was in silhouette. "I've had a couple of goes, I'm no Lester Piggott. But I'll be fine."

"In that case, you can ride Rusty. She's big, like you, but she's fairly placid." *Like me?*

Patricia, the stable maid, came over and had a confab with her boss. Mrs Kelly looked down at us all again.

"Right. We have a problem. We have six horses available. Including two Shetland ponies, for the two youngest children. However, we are a saddle short. So one of the adults will have to ride bareback, or miss the trek." She looked from me to Mary who spoke up. "There's no way I'm riding bareback. I definitely need stirrups."

Oh, what the hell. Why not?

"I'll have a go. I've seen it in the movies. Could be fun."

Patricia and a bunch of stable girls brought all six horses out to the yard. Buster was getting excited at the idea of playing with these big animals, but Mrs Kelly nipped that idea in the bud. She called down to one of the younger stable girls. "Helen, can you take the dog and tie him to Lassie's kennel door. There's food and water there. He'll be fine watching the comings and goings for a couple of hours. "

A flurry of excited kids and long-suffering horses later and we were off. The two Shetland ponies carrying Tamsin and Toby were being hand-led by two girls. Phil and Andy were allowed to ride their medium-sized ponies while Mary was showing off her trotting skills.

I was feeling good. All there was between me and Rusty was my jeans and a horse blanket. No stirrups. Just the strength of my thigh muscles and my sense of balance. It was far more comfortable than my previous attempts. I didn't have to try and sit up and down for the 'rising trots.'

Rusty and I were as one.

Or so I thought…

I looked behind me. Four happy faces under four riding caps, gently bouncing along the bridleway.

Patricia, on a lovely black and white pony, led the way. We were all going at walking pace. It was quite pleasant, the sun was shining, birds were twittering, butterflies and horse flies dancing in the air.

But half an hour later I was getting bored. I called to Patricia.

"Are we going to be riding at this speed for the whole two hours?"

She turned and hesitated. "Well, if you like, you and Mrs Dickson can ride on just a bit. Follow the path through the forest till it reaches a low summit where there's a clearing. Just trot around there until we catch up."

Yay! Freedom!

"Fancy a race, Mary?"

"I'm racing no one. I don't mind trotting a bit faster. On you go if you think you can handle it."

Can I handle it? Rusty and I are as one!

I gave them all a nonchalant wave as I edged past Patricia. I could see Rusty's ears twitching as we moved out of the queue.

"Right, Mary, let me see you do your stuff."

Mary, ramrod straight, nose in the air, trotted past me on Whiskey, her dark brown pony. Rising and falling as she'd been taught years before when she'd entertained the notion of becoming a show jumper. It only lasted the one summer. The mucking out eventually persuaded her otherwise.

As Whiskey and Mary passed us, Rusty snorted. I could feel his muscles twitching as I held on to the reins. *He wants a proper ride.*

I pulled back on the reins, pressed my knees in, and heeled him just a tad.

And we were off!

We weren't galloping, but we were cantering faster than I'd ever experienced.

Yippee Yi Yay!

I could feel the big animal bounding along between my legs. I was hunched forward, holding her mane as well as the reins.

This is brilliant!

The trees rushed past and we belted out of the woods. I saw the clearing. *Time to slow down now, Rusty.*

My knuckles gripping the reins as I tried to pull his head back. Then I remembered someone talking about tugging then loosening the reins.

Uh oh! C'mon, Rusty. Obey…Please?

We kept on going. Rusty was enjoying herself.

We were heading straight across the clearing and I was beginning to get worried when I saw another rider coming the other way. I recognised Mrs Anderson, Buster's vet. *Of course she'll ride horses.* I tried to wave back as if I knew what I was doing. But I was scared to let go. We hurtled right past her. She caught the fear in my eyes, so she wheeled round behind us, raced up alongside me, then expertly pulled on Rusty's right rein, forcing both horses to ride in an ever-decreasing circle.

As we slowed, I felt my knees trembling and weakening. I started to slowly slither off the side of the horse as the blanket moved underneath me.

"Whoa there." The vet, with remarkable strength, managed to stop my roll and heave me back on to Rusty's back while she brought both horses to a halt.

We stopped. Knees shaking, I managed to pull myself upright.

"Been riding long, Mr Dickson?" the vet asked with a knowing look.

"'Bout an hour," I replied accurately, if a bit breathlessly.

"No, I meant…"

"I know. I know. I'm very much a beginner. I think this is my third time on a horse. It was exciting for a while there. Thanks for being the cavalry. Buster will be pleased you saved me."

She smiled, just as Mary and the kids came out of the woods and into the clearing.

"Wow, John! You were really flying!" Phil shouted. "You should be on the telly. On the Grand National!"

Andy joined in. "That's right. Mum could place a bet on you and we'd be millionaires!"

Patricia took control. "Ok, folks. We're going round the clearing then we're heading back to the hotel." She looked at me. "Do you want to ride on further, Mr Dickson?"

She mustn't have seen me being rescued. I can keep my dignity for a wee while longer…

"Not at all, I'll keep the kids company." I played safe "You all having a good time, kids?"

"It's ok, just a bit slow," Tamsin muttered.

"Well, we can fix that. Could you get your girls to run back while they're holding the ponies, Patricia?"

Patricia looked a bit uncomfortable. "If you say so, Mr Dickson."

Mrs Anderson, the vet gave us a cheery wave. "I'm going to do a wee circular hack. I might see you all down at the stables. Take care." She nodded to me.

We arrived back where we'd started. I was pretty happy to dismount until I tried to stand up and found I was now bowlegged! My inside thighs were throbbing…

Phil and Andy had jumped off their ponies and were racing Toby and Tamsin to untie Buster who was straining at his leash, his rear end waggling furiously. Toby managed to be first to hold Buster's lead.

Mary and I were gathering our stuff together and paying a normal-sized Mrs Kelly, now she was off her horse…

Mrs Anderson arrived beside us and started to dismount from her horse. *Ah, my rescuer,* I thought. I'll tell Mary about my drama later.

Suddenly Buster started barking loudly, and Toby, startled, let go of his lead.

Buster, recognising the vet as the person who usually stuck needles into him, started running in circles round the bunch, barking loudly as if to warn us all that there was a nasty jaggy person in our midst!

The vet's horse whinnied and snorted, *What's all the noise about?*

"Get the dog out of here NOW!" Mrs Kelly meant business. Mary grabbed for Buster's lead, while I instinctively watched the horse, holding my arms out to keep the kids back.

The big animal suddenly reigned up on his hind legs just as the vet was halfway off, her left foot still in its stirrup. She tried to pull on the reins but the horse twisted away from her and she started tumbling…

She's going to land really badly on her back!

I jumped forward and just managed to grab hold of her inches from the old cobbles. Her foot was still trapped in the stirrup as her horse rose ever higher. Eyes rolling wildly.

"Oof! Gotcha!" I got my hands under her armpits and tried to keep us both away from the flailing hooves.

In the meantime, Mrs Kelly had run to the other side of the horse and yanked the rein in her very professional manner. The horse's front hooves clattered onto the cobbles as the vet managed to free her foot.

Mrs Kelly was stroking the horse's neck as our vet clambered to her feet. A little dishevelled and not too much dignity lost.

"Touché, Mr Dickson. One good turn?"

Chapter 35
Mary Caters & the Bank Job

I got used to my commute between Campsie and Glasgow. It was actually a wee time to myself as I travelled the back roads through the village of Torrance and over the Forth and Clyde Canal. Skirting by Wallace's Well, the memorial positioned on an awkward bend on a back road from Lenzie. Built on the very spot the great Scottish hero of Braveheart fame was arrested all those centuries ago…

In nice sunny days, it was easy to just mull on the day-to-day tasks. On the way to work I'd be thinking about mundane things such as meeting the Cadbury's rep for a regular order. Or planning the outlines of the next week's timetable.

Other times I'd be thinking of more pressing concerns…

The tearoom had settled down to a rhythm that wasn't quite fulfilling its promise. It had to generate more income.

It turned out Lennoxtown wasn't exactly a tourist Mecca. They tended to whizz by on their way over the Campsie Fells to Fintry and beyond. While the tearoom was building up a reasonable regular custom from locals and the occasional rep or van driver passing through, it wasn't really paying its way.

Mary had been talking along the same lines the previous night: "We could always do some outside catering. You know, sandwiches and platters of salads for local businesses. Easy stuff." Famous last words.

So, she placed an ad in the following week's Local Herald:

Mary Caters

We're Full of Ideas

To make your Function Special

From a Buffet to a Banquet

Call us for a Quote

Amazingly we had our first enquiry the day after the paper came out. We were just getting up, when the phone rang beside the bed.

"Is that Mary Catering? This is Mr McAllister of the Bank in Kirkintilloch."

I handed the phone to Mary. "The Bank Manager's looking for you. What have you done?" Mary looked puzzled as she listened to the caller.

Then she smiled.

"I'd love to come along for a chat. A new branch opening, you say? All your best customers? I'll see you at two o'clock sharp." She put the phone down with a yelp.

I was confused. "What's going on?"

Mary smugged, "That was only the Area Manager of the Bank. They're opening a new branch in Kirkintilloch town centre and they want 'Mary Caters' to quote for the catering. And… they like to support new local businesses! That's us, folks! I have an appointment at two today!"

"Well done, you," I said. "And if they're inviting all their good customers, it's a great chance to show off your skills." *This sounds great!*

I had a thought: "Can you actually do this?"

Mary grinned. "No idea! But we'll have a go, eh?"

Mary racked her brains to come up with an idea that might appeal to a banker… It was to be a finger buffet so puns were the plan.

After a bit of chit chat in the manager's office, Mary described some of her options. "Well, I thought your guests might like a wee chuckle so the plan is to have little handmade flags in your corporate colours over each tray of tasty bites. Keeping the bank theme, we'll have long thin sandwiches flagged *'Teller's Fingers,'* some *'Egg Mayo with Interest,'* and the obvious *'Vault au Vents,'* etc."

The bank manager liked the concept and told Mary that if we could also supply alcoholic and soft drinks for their guests, Mary Caters could have the job!

"Of course we can. We'll provide your guests with a fine selection of wines and spirits," Mary promised. Mr McAllister smiled and they shook hands on the deal.

……………………………………………………………………………

"Are we allowed to supply liquor without a licence?" I asked James, our brother-in-law and in-house lawyer.

"So long as the bank's customers are getting the drinks for free, it's effectively a wholesale order, so no licence is necessary." James's legal knowledge demolished a potential deal breaker.

A quick learning curve later and a little help from our friends and family and we were all set.

Mary had recruited her brother Iain to help run the drinks side of the event. He'd worked in a number of bars over the years, although his main job was as a 'time and motion' consultant, helping major firms improve their productivity. The role required an ability to motivate people into changing their habits and become more efficient. The trick was to achieve the efficiencies without antagonising the workforce. Iain was very good at making a wee joke and getting them on his side.

When the day arrived, we were unloading the heaps of spirits and bottles of beer and wines which I'd sourced on a sale or return basis from my usual cash and carry. Iain asked, "So what's the deal with how the bank pays for the drinks?"

I explained that a bank staff member and I would check the stock in, and then again when the function was finished. Then they'd be billed for whatever had been consumed. Simple arithmetic.

Iain piled the last crate of beer into the back office we had been allocated as a store. He looked at me. "That means the more the customers drink the more the bank pays, the more money you and Mary make?"

I concurred: "That's the gist of it."

Iain looked thoughtful as he started setting up the bar.

Once we'd checked the stock in, I left Mary and her team to get on with it as I had to go to work in the shop. I'd be back later in time to help with the packing up.

"Bye, Mary. Have fun. It's all looking grand. See you all later." And I was off.

The opening was due to start at one and finish around five. As the great and the good of Kirkintilloch gathered in the shiny new branch, there was a lot of voices proclaiming admiration at the bank-themed buffet. A few chuckles at the puns, and a general air of jolliness. It's not often one gets something for nothing from the bank!

Iain had the help of Sarah, our sonsy-faced neighbour, who was anxious to prove that she really could be useful after the debacle of Buster and old Paddy's grave. She'd jumped at the chance to maybe meet some of the bank's better-off customers. They'd set up the well-stocked bar in the manager's office, just off the public area.

The first couple of guests trickled through, nibbling their teller's fingers, and approached the bar.

"Well, Peter, business seems to be on the up, seeing as you've just opened your second dealership." Iain had been introduced to Mr Rintoul, the branch manager, when they'd first arrived.

His smartly suited companion replied, "Fingers on the pulse, Frank. Onwards and upwards. This is all very nice, Frank. Very modern." He scanned the office which he knew he'd be seeing again in private. He was very much aware he was one of the new branch's best customers. His eyes lit on one of the whiskies on display.

"Is that Antiquary whisky you've got there? One of my favourites. Could I have a dram, please?"

Iain gave him the full winning smile: "Would you like a large one, sir?"

The guest's eyes brightened. "Very kind of you! That would be excellent." He turned to the manager. "What about you, Frank? Go on. Not every day you open a shiny new branch…"

The manager hesitated. "Ok, Iain, isn't it? Just a small G&T then, please?"

Iain scooped in some ice cubes, before absent-mindedly pouring a rather large gin topped up with a modicum of tonic.

Sarah, following Iain's lead, turned to the smaller, slightly more rotund chap who was suddenly standing quite close to Mr Morrison. "What can I get you, sir?" she asked with a big smile.

"I'll have the same as my brother, please. He knows his whiskies. And his cars. And what's your name, my pretty one? You've got lovely eyes… I'm Tony, by the way. This is a nice set-up." He looked around as Sarah, her cheeks flushing at the compliment, almost over-filled the glass.

"You don't want ice, do you? I don't think there's much room." She tossed her head like a model in a TV shampoo advert, but her heavily lacquered bob stayed firmly stuck to her scalp.

Tony raised his glass in thanks. "Here's to beautiful eyes. I really like my women to have a fuller figure." He stood back admiringly. "And you tick all my boxes! How'd you like a wee run in the Merc out to the Country Club tonight? They do a marvellous chateaubriand."

Taken aback by this unexpected suggestion, (the last chap who'd shown an interest in her had ended up heaving her out of an empty grave), the flustered Sarah decided to go for it. Wasn't one of the reasons she was helping out just in case she could meet a better class of man? And here she was! Her very first customer asking for a date! In a Merc! And the Country Club! She felt a warm glow rising up to her already flushed cheeks. "That sounds very nice, Tony," she said demurely. "I'll see you later then." She had another go at tossing her hair… It still stayed stuck.

Overhearing the conversation, Peter turned to his more diminutive brother and shook his head, then looked at Sarah. "You be careful with him, young lady; Tony likes to play the smoothie, but he's all soft and gooey on the inside." He swallowed the last of his Antiquary. "That was lovely. Any chance of another?" Iain glanced at his co-worker but said nothing.

Of course, the guests quickly got wind of the generosity of the bar and it was soon thronging. The general air of jolliness grew into a merry hubbub as the alcohol flowed.

As the now packed manager's office spilled into the front area, Mary pressed through, where she spotted her brother and her neighbour competing in sweat production as they tried to keep up with demand.

She finally squeezed in behind the manager's desk, which was doubling as the bar counter. "How come it's so busy in here? It's mid-afternoon. And they're all getting rather merry," she whispered to Iain as she scanned the flushed faces.

"Yes, well. We're being very nice to them," he whispered back as he poured a large whisky with his right hand while simultaneously re-charging a slightly dishevelled head-mistress's vodka and lime with his left. "The merrier they are the merrier you and John'll be." Iain gave her a wink.

Mary's mouth fell open as the penny dropped. "But what if the bank manager sees you pouring lots of large ones?"

"That's not a problem, it's not *his* money. He's almost keeping up with his customers anyway. See him over there having a great laugh with that Town Counsellor? That's his third large G&T."

Mary looked around at all the happy faces and shrugged her shoulders. "When we're all packed away, I bags one of those big Antiquaries. We've worked our socks off in there."

Sarah sidled up to Mary, nudged her in the ribs and whispered. "I've got myself a date!" Her cheeks were red with excitement.

Mary was taken aback. "Really? Who's the lucky man?"

"That chap over there. The guy with the ginger hair. His name's Tony Morrison. His brother's got the car showrooms. I've been particularly generous with his whiskies. He told me he drives a Mercedes and is going to take me to the Country Club for dinner tonight! A bit better than a pie and a pint in the Swan, eh?" Sarah gave her best impression of a flirty smile in the direction of the dumpy chap leaning against the wall, whose over-stretched suit looked like it used to fit him before he'd put on a stone or two. He waved back to Sarah, and then noticed Mary standing elegantly beside his new date. He looked her up and down and gave her a drunken leer that Sidney James would have been proud of.

"Good for you, Sarah… I think…" Mary shivered as she turned away. "I better get back to the grub. This lot are as hungry as they're thirsty."

Sarah poured yet another large whisky. But her bottom lip trembled. She'd seen the leer.

I got back from the shop just as the last stragglers were bouncing out the door. I'd noticed a number of the local great and the good teetering along the High Street.

I came through the door as our GP, Dr Fitzsimons, was shaking the bank manager's hand vigorously. "That's one of the best free lunches I've ever had. Make sure you give young Mary there any catering jobs going. Lovely people! Lovely people!"

He swallowed the dregs of his umpteenth whisky. And was about to hand his glass to the manager when he stopped and turned as he heard a female voice from the bar/office: "What the Hell do you mean? Go back to your place? How daft do you think I am? I saw that dirty look you gave to Mary! You're just disgusting! Away and bile yer heid!"

I was just about to see if I could help, when I had to step back, as the less successful Morrison brother came flying through to the public area. He flailed his arms before crumpling to the floor. Sarah was stronger than she looked... She stood in the doorway, wiped her hands, then folded her arms in a way that reminded me of the late Les Dawson. "And...your brother told me you're married with two kiddies! You should be ashamed of yerself!"

He clambered to his feet, hanging on to the counter. "Ah just fancied ye hen. Don't make a song and dance aboot it. It wiz the whisky talkin'." He drunkenly swivelled his head to face Iain, who was now standing beside Sarah. "Bloody good stuff, by the way, pal!"

Sarah scowled. The bank manager looked uncomfortable as Peter Morrison, one of his best customers, came back through to collect his miscreant brother. "Here we go again, Tony. I knew I shouldn't have brought you along. Sorry, Frank, I'll see you next week as arranged." He looked at our team, as he took the weight of his sagging brother. "Thanks for an entertaining lunch, folks. Next time we have a new car launch, I'll give you a call. I promise Tony here won't be in attendance."

Taking his brother's weight, he managed to shake Mary's then my hand before dragging Tony out the front door which was being held open by Mr Rintoul, who looked rather bemused.

He addressed Sarah. "So sorry about that, young lady. My clients are usually much better behaved. I hope you won't hold it against us." He looked from Mary to me and Iain.

"A wee bit of excitement at the end of the day. Eh, Sarah?" I offered, hopefully.

"That's not right. I was excited at the beginning of the day when that wee scumbag wiz all talk about Mercs and Country Clubs. I thought I wiz onto a good thing. So I'm not so sure I'll be back here, Mr Bank Manager. By the way, is Peter Morrison married yet? He seems nice."

Iain said, "Well, he did mention he would give Mary a call for a new car launch. So you might yet get that opportunity!"

Sarah's eyes lit up at the possibility.

After the remaining stock was checked by one of the bank tellers, we packed up the van and headed for home.

I looked across at Mary. "Well, did you have a good day then? Apart from Sarah's 'episode.' More to the point. Would you do it again?"

Iain, sitting in the middle seat, butted in. Sarah had decided to pop into the Antonine pub, where she used to work. "I think that might depend on whether the bank pays up when they get the bill for all those generous measures…"

Mary mused, "Och, I'm sure they will. They've never had happier clients. Apart from wee fat Tony, of course!"

Time to sample that last bottle of Antiquary, I think…

Chapter 36
The Family BBQ

"Look what I've got!" I called as I struggled my way through the front door.

"What's all the banging?" Mary came across the living room wiping her hands on a tea towel.

"It's another beautiful day. The weather's supposed to last over the weekend. Why don't we get some folk up and we'll have a barbeque. Seeing as how I've just bought one at the Cash and Carry!" I was chuffed with myself as I presented my new shiny piece of kit. A basic portable charcoal BBQ, with two wheels at the front and a shelf under the 'adjustable' grill.

Mary took a step back and took it in. "That's not going to hold a lot of food. I'll cook stuff in the kitchen and top up the great steaks you're gonna make, Mr Barbie!" She grinned and went back to her kitchen duties…

Uh oh. Is this a good idea!

Mary had been enjoying the early build-up of the catering side of the business. What she really enjoyed was 'feeding the hungry faces.' And was happiest when tasked with organising a feast.

After the success of the 'bank job,' the phone rang with opportunities for substantial catering functions, including a fundraiser for one of the major local political parties.

"We'll need you to provide a running buffet for five hundred people. Can you do that?" the local party secretary asked Mary. "Your advert does say 'from a Buffet to a Banquet.' I suppose this is a bit of both!"

Mary, never one to duck a challenge, said: "Of course we can. We'd be delighted."

However, unlike the banks back in those days, political parties don't always keep their word.

Having accepted the booking for five hundred guests, we geared up, organised and staffed the event to cater for five hundred guests.

A lot of work. A lot of time. A lot of money in food and equipment and staff.

But *they* sold less than half their tickets...

"We'll pay for Two hundred and forty-seven people. I'm afraid that's all the tickets we've sold." The secretary was quite brusque as Mary presented her bill at the end of the lacklustre evening, after offering double portions of the excess food to anyone who could manage it.

Mary was furious: "But you booked for five hundred! You're the people who're running the country! If you can't keep your word about a local catering event, why should anybody trust you with their votes? I'm not prepared to accept your half payment. I'm going above your head!"

Mary was stunned. Her new small business couldn't afford to shoulder the loss caused by the incompetence of her high-profile customer.

Suffice to say that even after writing to 10 Downing Street and getting a pass-the-buck reply in a Port Cullis embossed envelope, which of course the postman *had* to knock on the door and personally hand deliver, ("Friends in very high places I see"). We finally had to swallow the bitter pill and accept the miserly payment on offer.

We'd learnt a lesson. Our booking forms became watertight after that. Most folk had to pay up front. As they do for holidays. And we never again catered for any political organisation.

The phrase '*they couldn't organise a piss up in a brewery*' comes to mind...

The word was out. Mary and John were having a 'garden party come barbeque' on the Saturday.

Mary set the rules. "This is an afternoon event. There'll be kids there. So we'll stick to beer and wine. No hard liquor. I don't want anyone getting drunk..."

The word was duly passed. We were expecting quite a few folk. We'd had a couple of parties since we'd moved in, and they'd been great fun. Singing and dancing till the wee sma' hours.

The layout of 'oor wee hoose' made it ideal for an outside party. There was a broad service lane running behind the row of terraced cottages.

Just that week we had dragged our old upright piano out into the lane. We'd inherited it from Mary's Big Aunt Peggy. She who could not be refused! It was actually in a terrible state, and we'd been told it wasn't worth paying to have it re-tuned. Especially once we were gifted a second, far more modern piano from my Aunty May in East Kilbride. It was a well-polished instrument, with an element of sixties style. Lower and smoother, it actually sounded pretty tuneful. While I could plonk out a few basic tunes, Joe Slyder, the originator of my short-lived musical career in LSD had improved his musical talents considerably, and he could easily give Jerry Lee Lewis a run for his money.

The piano in the lane was still just about playable, we hadn't quite figured out what to do with it. Disposing of an unwanted piano can be a bit of a problem. Hence our respective aunts' solutions. Gift them to us! In those days, elderly relatives presumed the next generation would welcome their ancient instruments, as they modernised their living rooms. Especially if you'd shown any sign of musical expertise. "Ah you're great on the guitar, John. I'm sure you'll soon master this awld piano…It's almost tuned!"

The sun shone yet again on the Saturday morning as Mary, ably helped by Sarah and Betty, our neighbour from the house next door, prepared heaps of food for the hungry faces that would arrive in the early afternoon.

My duties were to walk Buster and try and exercise him out (an impossible task) and collect a couple of trestle tables from the tearoom; erect them in the garden along with my new BBQ toy; and buy beer wine, cider and soft drinks.

Joe and Wee Robbie from the band were first to arrive and immediately started playing the outside piano and an acoustic guitar.

Mary and co were clattering trays in the kitchen to the strains of "Johnny Be Good" from just outside the door.

Next to arrive were my mum and dad and all four brothers. Thomas had brought along his pal Enrico, a Riddrie neighbour from a lovely Italian family. Enrico was very expressive and had taken gesticulations to a higher plane.

"Ah Bueno, Mary!" Enrico exclaimed. "You have a wonderful home! And is that live music I hear coming from your garden? Exquisite! I know that tune! That's 'Can't Buy me Love!' Hey, boys, can you play 'Oh Sole Mio?' " That was after he'd hugged all three women working in the kitchen, giving them each a kiss on both cheeks.

"Hey! You can hug me anytime!" Sarah called after him as she buried her hands back in the sink full of lettuce leaves.

"My goodness! What a good-looking young man. I hope my Brian wasn't watching that. I can feel my cheeks flushing!" Betty's colour was indeed a lot brighter than before.

"If he does it again just slap him on the bum. Then he starts waving his arms in the air! It's great to watch," Mary advised with a laugh. "Time we took this grub out to the garden. Ready, girls? Watch yourself climbing those stone steps. They're narrow, and steeper than they look."

While Phil held Buster on a short leash, the girls convoyed platters of food up the steps, Andy and Thomas willingly helping them to the tables while pinching slices of cold meats off the platters.

I was gingerly organising my array of burgers, bacon and sausages (I'd concluded steaks were way above my pay grade…), when Andy thought it was a good idea to toss a raw sausage over towards Buster! — who also thought it was a good idea and immediately did his jumping in the air and catching it in his mouth party piece.

"That's so cool!" Andy shouted as Phil struggled to hang on to the now drooling dog…

It took all my self-control not to skelp my wee brother as he picked up another sausage.

"Stop it, Andy." Phil was panicking. Then Andy's eyes brightened as he ran round the table and waved the sausage in front of Buster's nose before tossing it into the long grass by the garden shed.

The manoeuvre worked… Phil went sprawling on the grass and was dragged a good few feet before letting go of the leash. Much to everyone else's amusement.

Having now tasted two delicious sausages, Buster wanted more. He sneaked round the shed and got himself into position right across the table from me.

He stopped for a second and looked me straight in the eye. Weighed up the pros and cons. Decided the pros were way ahead and jumped up and grabbed a whole string of links before galloping back round the shed and across Betty's little fence. Clambering through her vegetable patch, he high-tailed it down her steps onto the service lane. And away!

"Right, you two!" Mum was on her feet. "Go get the dog back. But I think he can keep the sausages! Do you agree, folks?"

There was a general consensus that the price of the pantomime was a lack of sausages as we watched Phil and Andy racing each other down the lane.

In the meantime, Alan, having brought his own guitar, was sitting with Joe and Robbie, belting out "*Summertime... And the Living is Easy...*" Very appropriate.

"Hello. Hello. Hello. Are we on time?" Joyce's voice came calling out of the kitchen. James followed behind her while Tamsin and Toby ran in front and galloped up the stairs. "Go on, Trinity. You can climb those stairs! You're a big two-year-old now! Did we just see your dog running down the street with the barbeque hanging out of his mouth?"

Eventually, after Buster was dragged back, everything settled down to a very pleasant sunny afternoon. The tables were groaning with Mary's culinary creations while my first attempt at a sausage-free barbeque was ably helped along by Jim and Joe and Robbie.

Mum sidled up to me after I had delegated to Jim and Joe and was having a well-earned beer. "I know Mary said it was just to be wine and beer. But you know I don't like either of them. I feel a wee bit like a criminal! I've got a half bottle of Bacardi in my bag and I've been topping up those glasses of coke I've been having. You don't mind do you, John?"

What was I going to say? Be gone, Mother! Never darken my door again!

Hardly…

"No problem, Mum. Nobody will notice. Everyone's enjoying themselves too much. Have you got a seat? We've brought a few of the catering benches. I think Dad's about to render his "Yippee Yi Yay." Now he's had a beer. That means I'm on duty." I grabbed my guitar. "Ok, Dad, I'm a comin' pardner!"

After Dad had got everyone singing along to "Ghost Rider" I noticed a bit of movement in the shed at the end of the garden. I wandered up to see what was going on.

It was Robbie. "Shusht, John. Ah canny find ma drink. Ah'm just pouring masel anither yin. Ah kin only take so much canned beer. An' thone wine's no' the same as the awld Lanliq, that magical, proper strong wine." He was pouring himself a hefty measure from a vodka bottle then topping it up with diluting orange.

Robbie wasn't my mum. "C'mon, Robbie! Mary made it very clear. Just beer and wine. You're already half-pissed!" I grabbed the vodka bottle from him and half hid it as I walked towards the kitchen, intending to hide it in a cupboard.

Halfway down the narrow garden Betty stopped me. "Is that a sneaky wee vodka I spy? Any chance of a wee shot into this lemonade?" She held out her tumbler.

What could I say? I obediently poured.

I resumed command of the barbeque while Joe helped Robbie down the stairs to restart the live music. It took an effort but they made it. True to form, Robbie burst into a rasping "Maggie May" with a thumping piano backing. You'd even think he was sober.

Everyone was socialising merrily. I noticed Mum and Joyce exchanging stories of motherhood while their broods were running wild up and down the garden. Playing hide and seek and generally having a ball…

Then the shambles began…

"That wean's drunk! He just staggered then sat down!" Betty was standing unsteadily pointing at Toby, Joyce's four-year-old son.

Toby had a glass of orange juice in both hands and was trying to finish the dregs. Joyce scrambled off the catering bench with such force that it fell backwards, carrying Mum with it…

Snatching the glass out of her son's hands Joyce sniffed the remaining contents.

"Bloody Vodka! Who's drinking bloody vodka?" Her head birled hatefully, reminding me of the girl in the Exorcist.

Toby, meanwhile, had managed to climb back on his feet and started walking towards his father who was standing sternly, wine in hand, unusually saying nothing.

As he walked there was a noticeable sideways stagger. Two small steps left. One step right. Then he put his arms out to steady himself. But it made no difference. Two small steps left. One step right. He wasn't getting far, so James walked forward and lifted him putting an end to the mesmerising spectacle. He carried him downstairs muttering about finding an empty bed to let Toby sleep it off.

Thomas and Enrico were rescuing Mum from her undignified position, legs up in the long grass behind the overturned bench.

"My God. You poor lady. Are you all right? Can I refill your glass?" Enrico fussed.

Mary came running out of the kitchen where she and Sarah had been washing dishes. "What the Hell's happened? James said Toby's drunk?"

Betty was standing forlornly in the middle of the gathering crowd. "John gave me vodka. But I've only had the one. Here it's here." She held up her half-finished glass.

Joyce glared at me. "You? John? Vodka? I was told in no uncertain terms that there were to be no spirits here today. Isn't that correct, sister?"

I reacted, "Wow! Wait a minute. It wasn't me! I took that bottle off Robbie. I was enforcing Mary's rules so nobody would get drunk, never mind a kiddie."

Joyce's voice rose. "I want to know who's responsible for getting my son drunk!"

Silence.

Well, apart from Enrico, who was concentrating on keeping his friend's mother happy by asking loudly, "Do you want some more of that

Bacardi in your coke? I see a bottle on the grass beside you. Though there's not much left."

Mum looked embarrassed and perplexed. Dad looked at her. And shook his head… *There'll be words tonight.*

A blond head of hair appeared coming up the steps from the music area outside the kitchen. Wee Robbie raised himself to his full five-foot-three. He pointed his finger at Joyce. "Listen, missus. It wiz probably ma voddy yer wean drank. Ah loast ma drink a while ago an' that's when John caught me pourin' a top up. Awright? Ah'm sorry aboot yer wean. But we aw make mistakes. An' it's never too early tae try a wee drink anyway. It'll dae him good in later life!" Joyce's mouth was hanging open as she tried to decipher Robbie's words. He carried on. "But Ah must object tae your hypocrisy. Ah saw ye pouring' big gins oot that bottle that's stickin' oot yer bag on the grass there." His finger now aimed at the offending Gordon's lid peeking out of Joyce's bag where she'd been sitting, getting quietly sloshed with Mum.

So much for Mary's prohibition…

All eyes now turned to Joyce, who bristled.

"Right. Where's James? It's time we were going!" She bustled around picking up her bag and a shawl now lying on the ground. "Nice to chat, Mrs D." She nodded to Mum who was looking more than a little unsteady.

Mum looked at Dad. "I think we should go too. It's been a great afternoon, John and Mary. Thanks for everything."

Recognising the day had come to a natural, if awkward end, Mary and I went down to the bottom of the stairs to see our guests through the house.

Laughter was still coming from the tables up on the garden as Robbie and Joe and Jim and Alan recounted the afternoon's events. Buster was happily munching his way through the crumbs scattered all over the garden.

We were thanking Betty and Sarah for their help when we looked back up the stairs to see both Mum and Joyce clinging onto each other. They were at the top of the stone steps. Hands reached out to grab them as their knees buckled simultaneously. Shocked expressions on both faces as gravity decided their only route was to tumble down those narrow stone steps, banging bits of bodies against the side walls.

I tried my best to catch them as did Sarah who was nearest. But their momentum, and combined weight, was just too great.

"Ouch. Aouch!" Mum shouted as she banged her head against Joyce's shoulder.

"Bloody Hell! These are the stupidest stairs!" Joyce screamed as she rolled down the last two steps landing badly on the ground on top of the sprawling figure of my mother.

Many hands grabbed many parts of the two bodies as we all did our best to get them to stand upright.

"For God's sake, Marie. You've had too much of that Bacardi! It's as simple as that!" Dad was shaking, scared she'd hurt herself. But apart from a couple of scratches and a bit of shock, Mum was unhurt. But her dignity wasn't

"I feel dreadful," she whispered. "I'm never going to touch alcohol ever again."

Joyce's reaction was a tad different.

Brushing her hair into a plausible shape with her fingers and checking that her limbs were all working she declared, "James! Take me home NOW! I need a proper drink! James?"

There was a bit of an aftermath to the family barbeque. Sarah and Betty fell out over something one of them said in the kitchen. I don't know if Enrico was mentioned. Joyce forgot to take her three children home, including poor wee Toby who woke up the next day with a bit of a hangover. Mum never did take another drop of alcohol. And it was quite some time before I mentioned the idea of another barbeque…

Chapter 37
Sibling Changes

"You know how Dad and you… and Mum as well really, just don't agree I'm up to running The Buy In after four years as 'Assistant Manager'?" I looked up from my newspaper returns. Thomas was standing on the customer side of the counter. I was surprised to see him on his day off. It was mid-afternoon. The shop was deserted.

I looked up. "Sorry? What you on about?" My head was still coping with the number of *Daily Records* we'd been credited with, compared to the number we'd actually returned the week before. Oh! The glamour of a newsagent's life! "Why are you here on a Tuesday? Can you not stay away from this Mecca of fun and frivolity? At least that's what it's like first thing in the morning, according to some of your customers. Have you not stopped bopping pensioners on the head with their rolled-up papers yet?"

"Yep, I can still wallop quite a few of them. They seem to get out of their beds early enough to queue up for it. Along with their morning rolls of course. Can we talk in the back? I've got some news," he said as he bustled his way past.

I motioned to my afternoon colleague, Babs, that she was on her own as we went into the back shop.

I closed the door. "Well then… What's going on?"

"You know how I've been thinking for a while now about how long it's actually going to take for me to take over the running of this place the way Dad originally had in mind?"

Uh oh… Is this going to get difficult again?

Thomas drew a deep breath. "I've decided it's just never going to happen. So, I'm officially handing in my notice… I start a new job a week on Monday." He broke into a big wide grin.

I can't say I wasn't taken aback. I knew Thomas was restless and I had turned into a bit of a glass ceiling. But there'd been no talk of looking for another job. But hey! Good luck to him!

"Well done! ...I think. Buggers my life up of course. But good for you, Thomas. And where is this new job?"

"Well, that's where there's a wee bit of irony. Seeing as how you and Dad don't think I'm good enough to manage this wee suburban newsagent... Because a week on Monday I'm going to be the new manager of the Argyle Street branch of R.S. McColl's!" He said triumphantly.

"Really? That'll be great for you! Well done that man. I'm really pleased for you. I mean, it'll be bloody hard to replace you here, but I'm sure you'll be a lot happier working where there's more chance of promotion. You might even end up being that area manager I wanted to be. Of course, Dad'll say that's you're joining the competition! That was the angle he used to get me to leave."

I shook his hand in congratulations. He nodded his head. "It might take a while to get that kind of promotion, but you never know. Still, I will miss this place."

After Thomas left, I mulled over the big news. In a way it was my fault Thomas felt he had to leave. I still felt guilty... I decided to call Mum. As she answered the phone, I pictured her sitting on the seat of her phone table in the lobby. She always answered with her 'phone voice.' "Hello. This is 770 7915, Marie Dickson speaking. Can I help you?"

"Hi, Mum. it's me, John. Did *you* know Thomas is leaving The Buy In? He's got a job in my old firm. Manager of their Argyle Street branch. I mean, I'm pleased for him, but this place isn't going to be the same."

Mum interrupted. "I know, John. He told me he was going after that post. Between you and me, I think the fact that he's your wee brother has helped him to get the job. Don't tell him I said that, by the way. He's feeling bad enough about leaving as it is."

Is that Mum trying to make me feel better?

"Mum, I feel guilty about Thomas not getting his opportunity to run The Buy In the way Dad talked about years ago. I feel I've been standing in his way. And like you've always said we should 'be fair.' And it's not been fair to Thomas."

"Don't be daft, John. Thomas will be fine. You've got responsibilities that he simply doesn't have. And just remember, I know I've always told you all to be fair to others, but I've *also* emphasised that you, and everyone else, should also be fair to *yourselves*... You've worked very hard at building up that business. In all honesty, in ways that Thomas probably couldn't have. At least not up until now. It wouldn't be fair to *you* to just hand over what you've created and simply walk away, just because your dad voiced a half-baked plan years ago. Let's hope Thomas does well in his new job. Well, it's actually a new career. We'll have a wee celebration the night before he starts. Ok? And by the way, don't dare bring me any Bacardi!"

That sounds like a plan, Mum.

Chapter 38
Flying High?

"Hey. Look at this!" I said excitedly to Mary. "Someone's brought hang gliders to Scotland. And anyone can try it. It's only £14. I'm gonna have a go at that! I've seen some flying over the Campsies. It looks fantastic."

Mary looked at me and her eyes screwed up. "What do you know about flying anything? Never mind hanging from a big kite." She looked sceptical.

"Says here no experience necessary, and you get full training from a qualified instructor. They must know what they're doing," I said optimistically. "It's not too far… Dumbarton somewhere. That's only half an hour away," I said as I picked up the phone.

Working in the shop and helping out at the occasional catering do had helped to keep me fairly fit, and definitely full of the *'Why Not'* mentality that I like to think hasn't been watered down too much over the years.

So, the following weekend we found ourselves a bit bewildered as we drove our big red catering van round the suburbs of Dumbarton looking for an address that turned out to be a three-bed semi in a very innocuous, unadventurous-looking street.

The door opened and I was definitely a bit nonplussed when a fresh-faced chap answered the doorbell. He was a couple of years older than us. Wispy longish hair and what could only be described as 'bum fluff' on his chin. Intense blue eyes peered at us through yellow sunglasses. Wearing a flying jacket style leather jerkin. Or rather almost wearing it, as the thick white plaster covering his left arm, snug in its sling, forced the jacket to hang off to one side…

"Is this The Sky's the Limit?" I asked tentatively.

Mary looked at me. I looked at the chap. "Oh yes! You must be John and Mary. I'm Johnnie. We spoke on the phone. I hope you're raring to go!"

Johnnie walked us past the chintz curtained windows and through a side entrance of the double-doored garage to the left of the house. I felt in a bit of a daze.

Inside the cluttered garage was another surprise. Tethered to a beam on the roof was a large metal triangle made from tubular aluminium. There were straps and leather bits hanging beside this contraption. Beneath it was a wooden milking stool.

Mary was hanging back while Joenie explained that the contraption was called an

'A-Frame' and that's what we'd be using to control the height and direction of the *'Glider.'*

The leathery straps and pouches made up the harness we'd be wearing as we glided up through the thermals…

Having explained that his broken left arm was nothing to do with hang gliding, and that he'd be absolutely able to train us with one good arm, we naively proceeded to be 'trained' in the use of the *'simulator,'* as Johnnie described the lump of metal and twisted straps.

After a couple of hours of dangling two feet off the garage floor, pushing and pulling the metal triangle, Johnnie declared we were almost ready to fly. All we needed to do was read up on the photocopied aeronautical pamphlets he'd given us and come back the next week. By that time his plaster would be off, and if the weather was suitable, we'd be up, up and away!

We argued. All the way home. "I don't believe he walked into any lamppost! The guy's in cloud cuckoo land… and you want to join him!" Mary was scathing.

"But we've paid the money. And anyway, I think I understand how it works now. It's all very logical. It'll be fine. And those other folk who turned up said Johnnie's an ace."

"Or an ass. Did you notice one of them was hiding a broken finger?"

I studied the pamphlets avidly, and being that determined optimist, I began to look forward to soaring through blue skies, dipping and diving over meadows and hills…

The following weekend we drove back to The Sky's the Limit's Global Head office. Johnnie's 'colleague' had let him down and their usual minibus with customised roof rack wouldn't be available.

Being understanding and helpful, Mary and I helped Johnnie load the twenty-foot rolled up hang glider into the back of *our* van. Not having a roof rack, we had to perch the front of the glider on top of our dashboard and let the end stick out the tied together open back doors.

The three of us squeezed into the front seats, with me driving. Mary had only got her provisional licence a few weeks previously, and although Johnnie's plaster was gone, he was still bandaged and his arm was weak. Must have been an angry lamppost...

We drove past the carbuncle of Dumgoyne, a little steep sided mini-mountain, at the end of the Campsies, and headed through the picturesque village of Drymen towards Balmaha, on the eastern shores of Loch Lomond. There we parked the van in the shadow of the Conic Hill, a popular destination for fitter folk looking for a good view of the Loch. Unloaded the long and very much heavier-than-air hang glider which rested on Johnnie's and my shoulders, while Mary followed carrying the A-frame and the straps that would keep me attached. We started a mini trek through the spindly trees covering the slopes of the Hill.

We came to a clearing about two-thirds of the way up where Johnnie scurrled around opening up and spreading the glider. With its triangular frame and multi-coloured striped fabric it looked like an oversized dart.

Eventually all was ready. Standing on the slope of the hill, trussed up in the leather harness with straps biting my inner thighs, holding the heavy, ungainly wing above my head. The slight breeze coming up the rise lifted its nose while I struggled to stop its edges waggling. It was very heavy and difficult to hold in position, as Johnnie reminded me of his, and the manual's, instructions: *As you rise from the ground gently push the A-frame out then gradually bring it back and centre it. Don't push it out too far or the wing will lift too high and the 'craft' will stall.* I had read the words many times and they were racing through my head as I gingerly stepped forward.

One... Two... Three steps. And suddenly the ungainly heavy contraption that I could barely hold upright a millisecond ago was holding *me!* I was in the air! The bushes that had been in front of me were under my feet as I caught a glimpse of a sparkling Loch Lomond and the surrounding glorious scenery.

Almost immediately I lost my cool. The 'training' evaporated. Some internal force made my arms stiffen out in a spasm. The A-frame was pushed to its maximum. The front of the wing lifted almost vertically. The nice, soft, but muscular breeze that was holding me up disappeared as the wing changed shape and lost all its aerodynamic properties. The 'craft' and I plunged straight down.

My rear end hit the rhododendron bush as the glider collapsed around me. The A-frame hit me a glancing blow and I was buried in a mess of bushes and metal and fabric.

I was annoyed.

I had caught a glimpse of my dream.

And I had let myself down *(boom boom!)*.

Mary and Johnnie scrambled down to me.

"Oh my God! How are you? Have you broken anything?" Mary exclaimed as Johnnie examined the state of his precious equipment.

I clambered to stand up. Miraculously I was fine, a few scratches, but nothing to worry about. This falling out of the sky was a doddle!

Johnnie was pulling the glider out of the bushes and spreading it open on the grass.

"That's amazing. It's fine. A wee dent on the A-frame but that's easily sortable… D'you want another go?"

I did, but I looked at Mary. She shrugged. *It's your funeral…*

"OK." I forced my shoulders back. "I like to think I learn from my mistakes," I said pretentiously

Ten minutes later I had the déjà vu moment as the wing lifted me off the ground. Just a wee bit higher. Just enough to do me damage as I hit the ground through a less forgiving bush and managed to use my upper right arm to bend the A-frame into more of a W.

"Mmmm, not so much of a doddle this time," I muttered as Johnnie and Mary struggled to extricate me from the tangle of bent glider and harsh bush.

I managed to stand up, but I could feel, and see, my right arm swelling up dramatically.

Mary took charge.

"Right, you Pillock. So much for your 'simulator' and professional training. Look what you've caused! You and I will carry this stupid contraption down and my John can follow behind. We need to get to a hospital with an X-ray."

A suitably contrite Johnnie did as he was bid, and we hurried down to the van in a surprisingly short time.

The glider was hastily bundled into the back of the van as before, with the front resting on the dash while the end stuck out the back, not quite touching the ground.

"Ok, Mr Sky's the Limit, you're driving. Your lamp-posted arm will just have to make it." Mary didn't mince her words as I squeezed into the middle seat.

Johnnie drove as fast as he could along the narrow twisting roads to the nearest general hospital. My arm was throbbing and Mary was glowering. Johnnie didn't say much.

We arrived at the modern Alexandria Hospital. It was mid-afternoon and the large car park was almost empty.

"There's the Emergency Department over there," I said, pointing towards the other side of the car park.

"I'll just park here," Johnnie muttered as he started reversing into one of many empty spaces about a hundred yards from the building.

"Why here?" Mary wondered, as the van slowly moved backwards towards the kerb.

Suddenly, there was an almighty explosion! The van's windscreen erupted in a cloud of pellets of broken glass which swiftly settled back down all over us and the innards of the van's cabin. Then I realised the stupid plonker had reversed into the kerb and jarred the metal-framed glider forward, straight through the windscreen! The noise reverberated around the empty car park as doctors and nurses came streaming out of the building to see if a bomb had gone off. It was loud enough!

"What an unbelievable imbecile!" Mary hissed at me as we staggered across to the hospital entrance. Johnnie was squeamishly following behind, the van left forlornly like a scrapheap out of place.

I was treated quickly and efficiently. Nothing broken, but it was my turn to wear a sling.

We went back to the van. And tried to brush the grains of broken glass off the seats.

"I'm driving," Mary decided as we piled in.

"Really sorry about the window and that." Johnnie was having a bad day, as Mary kangaroo-hopped the van out of the car park.

"I don't suppose you fancy coming back next weekend?" Johnnie wondered.

Mary and I just exchanged glances…

Chapter 39
A Drive on the Wild Side

It was a quiet Sunday morning a few weeks later, the morning after a merry little party and sing-along. My eighteen-year-old younger brother Alan had stayed over and was hanging around itching to "Do Something!"

Alan had always been full of energy and derring-do. His early years were colourful. When he was just three years old our mum franticly ran out of the house searching for her 'baby' who had disappeared out of our corner garden.

Five minutes later he whizzed past her. One chubby leg through the triangle of an 'eighteen-incher' adult bike. His hands gripping the handlebars and miraculously managing to balance and steer our neighbour's pride and joy, as I ran behind him in a state of wonder and exhilaration!

Until Mum caught up with both of us…

A year or so later… A hot sunny day, and Alan and Mum were sitting in the garden. As Thomas and I were at school, Mum decided to entrust her number three son to go out to the tinkling ice cream van for two ice cream cones. Then she waited in anticipation of saying 'well done' to her youngest son after his first opportunity to show he could take on responsibilities.

She was more than a bit nonplussed when he appeared back in the garden concentrating on licking off the drips of the one and only ice cream cone.

Mum looked at him quizzically. "Well? Did you not get *two* cones, Alan?".

Alan lifted his eyes from his task: "Aye, Mammy. The man gived me two cones. But yours fell on the ground… and a dug ate it!"

No equivocation there then…

As soon as he reached sixteen, he had managed to save up for an elderly moped and had learned to cope with the rudiments of riding the 50cc bike with his 'L' plates proudly displayed.

I must say I encouraged him at the time. I still had fond memories of my first Lambretta, long since departed to scooter heaven.

He loved and enjoyed it for a good few weeks, until he unexpectedly lost a battle with a parked car on a soaking wet road, ending up in hospital with frightening internal injuries. Two operations and six months of convalescence morphed his normal chirpy demeanour into a muted depression, until one day Mum told him that one of his school chums had come out of a visit muttering, "I really miss the old Alan."

That seemed to buck him up, and he focused his time improving his guitar skills and continued his convalescence belting out brilliant versions of classics such as "Summertime" and the Beatles' "Golden Slumbers". That musical therapy seemed to do the trick, and a few months later he was fit enough, physically, and mentally, to return home. It wasn't long until his old energy and derring-do was back in action. He even passed his driving test first time round. (Just like his big brother).

After my unnerving hang gliding experience, I was happy just to sit in our ain wee hoose in Campsie reading the Sunday papers.

"C'mon, let's go to that new Bear Park near Stirling. Looks like fun! I'll drive... You can relax in the van..."

"I agree! C'mon, you. You'll get fat sitting on that couch on such a sunny day." My effervescent wife was on Alan's side.

So, I heaved myself out of my Sunday stupor and handed Alan the keys.

The sun was indeed shining as we gathered some ingredients for a picnic. Buster was pleased as punch to go on a Magical Mystery tour in the back of our rattling old red Bedford van.

Singing along at the tops of our voices, we drowned out the post-sixties pop music tinnily blaring from the van's primitive radio, bouncing along the back roads over the Campsie Fells to the outskirts of Stirling.

"Welcome to Stirling Bear Park'". The overhead sign heralded our arrival. (I believe it's since evolved into Blair Drummond Safari Park.)

"Look! It says you can drive right through where the bears are! They're not in cages like other zoos. Hey, that's cool!" Alan was excited.

"Ah, but look at that other sign." I pointed at a long list of Do's and Don'ts.

"No pets… We can't take Buster in!" At the mention of his name Buster started running round in circles on the carpeted floor of the van. *It must be time for walkies!*

"Look! More rules." Mary started reading them: "No Stopping. No Getting out of your Vehicle. Keep your windows closed at all times. These bears must get pretty close."

"Ach! Rules is rules… we'll be fine." Alan manoeuvred the van behind the small queue of family cars slowly moving into the entrance. "Cover Buster up or we'll no' get in."

"Mmm, not sure about this," I muttered as I managed to coax the dog into lying down while I threw a couple of jackets over him. He looked puzzled. *What about walkies? I smell grass and trees.*

With surprising ease, we paid our way in without any fuss, and found ourselves snaking into the body of the park. We drove into a valley with shallow hills gently rising on either side. A stream meandered through the valley to our right. Very pretty, almost idyllic.

The cars stretched out past the "Do Not Stop" signs on both sides of the single-track road.

"Look there's a bear! Over there under that tree!" Mary pointed towards a large brown bear lazily munching what looked like a small branch, just on the other side of the stream, in the shadow of a small clump of trees.

"There's another one on this side of the road." I pointed. I was impressed by the size of these beasts. *You don't wanna mess with them!*

"I can't see them properly!" exclaimed Alan twisting in his seat, trying to look both ways while keeping the van slowly moving.

"I'm gonna miss them. 'S'not fair! This was my idea!"

Suddenly, petulantly, stupidly, Alan stopped the van and turned off the engine!

Mary and I looked at each other.

"Are ye mad? For God's sake, don't stop here! You'll get us all killed!"

Alan laughed mischievously. "Ach, they're too far away. It was getting boring… And there's nobody behind us."

To our astonishment he rolled down his window…

"What are you doing, Alan? This is supposed to be fun! You're scaring me!" Mary's eyes were widening.

Buster, feeling the fresh air through the rolled-up window, tried to clamber over the back of the seats. *Time for walkies!*

"Here Beary, Beary," Alan ridiculously called to the bear on the other side of the stream.

I felt my skin tingle with instant sweat.

The bear trundled towards our static bright red van. It was about fifty feet away.

The three of us and Buster, stared at it as it raised its head, sniffed, and waded through the shallow stream towards us.

"Shut the bloody window NOW!" I hissed at my wee brother.

"Ach, it'll be fine. He just wants to say hello."

Thump! Thump!

Suddenly the van rocked from side to side.

I was jolted and fell against Mary who was sitting in the middle seat. She screamed as she looked past me and saw another bear right outside my window.

Its head was enormous as it looked right at me. I understood the concept of turning to jelly…

At this point Buster started barking and running back and forth inside the back of the van. *Trying to protect his family's territory.* This didn't ease the tension…

"Ok ok. We'll go." Alan finally conceded as he turned the ignition key.

The engine turned and stuttered but didn't start…

The first bear was about four feet away as Alan, finally realising the extent of his foolhardiness, frantically wound his window up.

We were all shouting at each other as the first bear reached the van. He stopped. He stared at us. Another enormous head inches away from Alan separated only by the thin pane of glass.

There was a triple intake of breath as he grabbed the driver's large wing mirror.

Crack!

He'd effortlessly snapped off the full chunk of equipment and started gnawing at the rubber trim which kept the mirror in place.

Alan turned the key again…

The engine sputtered into life.

The van limped forward.

I began breathing again.

Then it stalled…

Suddenly, there was a clatter and an unexpected draft from the rear of the van.

Our heads turned in unison.

Buster's barking reached a crescendo.

Bear number two had ambled round to the rear of the van and simply pulled the rubber trim off one of the back-door windows and the glass had just fallen out and smashed on the road!

The van was being demolished as we sat there. *I could have been finishing the Sunday papers…*

The bear at the back's hairy right arm reached through the empty window space and into the van, his massive head looking through the remaining rear window.

Stretching full out over the back of the seat, I just managed to grab Buster's collar as he frantically tried to attack the encroaching limb. *I didn't think a dog versus bear fight would have improved our situation…*

The internal shouting, sobbing, and barking was suddenly drowned out by a very loud human roar from about fifty yards away: An open jeep had pulled up on the side of the hill, and a giant of a man stepped out. Dressed in a green park ranger's uniform, he must have been about six-foot-five.

His shout had immediately caught the attention of both bears. I thought: *This guy could take them on! He's in the right job!*

Both bears slowly ambled towards the giant who held out the temptation of what looked like the best of salmon.

"We've just been rescued by the Jolly Green Giant," Alan inanely quipped before finally getting his act together and managing to start the engine.

The relief was tremendous as we slowly caught up with the other cars up ahead.

I tried to stay calm and not knock my wee brother out. At least not until we were out of the bloody park!

Eventually the road looped round and we reached the exit in our bear damaged van.

The open jeep pulled up beside us and the giant ranger tapped on Alan's firmly closed window. He reluctantly lowered it.

"I belief this belongs to you?" he said in a heavy East European accent, as he handed over the buckled and broken wing mirror, along with the now useless torn rear window trims.

"Sometimes it's a good idea to obey ze rules. Yes?"

"Oh, you're dead right, I definitely agree! But not quite as exciting."

Alan always had to have the last word…

Chapter 40
Catering Larks

"That's Dad retiring next month. I wonder what he's going to do with himself." Mary was just off the phone to her mum. "Or rather, I wonder what Mum's going to do with him hanging about all day?"

It was a Tuesday evening just after we'd had our spaghetti Bolognese and watched another episode of the original Star Trek. I rated Spock's logic, Mary preferred Captain Kirk's sense of morality. Great entertainment.

I stopped finger-picking the guitar. "I suspect Big Aunt Peggy'll shift him out of the house. She spends as much time at your mum's as she does in her own flat. I wouldn't fancy being stuck between them when they're putting the world to rights."

"Any functions on this weekend? I've lost the plot." I had tried to decipher Mary's diary before and given up when I couldn't make out the words for all the doodles, which covered every page. Apparently, it happens when she's on the phone.

"I'm surprised you actually turn up anywhere with that mess of a diary of yours!"

Mary made a face. "I'll have you know my system works well. All I need to know is how many? What food? Where is it? And when do you want the hungry faces fed? Then it all falls into place! It's quite a good wee team we've gathered now… Thelma in the kitchen, and Big Jessie out front. And nobody argues with Big Jessie. Not even the Bride's mother! Do you remember the time she picked the Best Man up and bodily threw him out of the wedding for being 'jist too friendly' with her girls?"

Oh, I remembered. I had heard the commotion from the kitchen where I was lumbered doling out the peas and carrots:

Big Jessie's voice silenced the room: "I know you're the Best Man! I can see you're the Best Man! That's why yer sitting in the Best Man's seat at this wedding! But I saw you pinging oor wee Helen's bra strap while she wiz serving' yer best buddy, the groom there… Twice! And

Ah'm no' havin' that! In fact, we're all no' havin' that! Just because she's blond and pretty, and you're bald and ugly, ye think ye can dae what ye like? Well, yer wrong… Up ye get!"

I poked my head through the kitchen hatch and watched the scene unfold: The tables full of guests in all their finery. Mesmerised. Nearly every mouth was wide open. I felt my stomach knotting as the Mighty Jessie heaved him out of his seat. Mary, standing at the kitchen door supervising the flow of food, looked towards me. Her mouth was just as wide as everyone else's.

"Haw! Hen! Ye cannae dae that tae the Best Man!" The groom's father tried to intervene, pushing his chair back and getting to his feet. All five-foot-four of him…

"And dae you think *you're* gonna stop *me*?" Jessie glared down at the diminutive top table guest as she huckled the Best Man out of his chair and frog-marched him through all the tables towards the front door.

"Gie's a break! Will ye?" was all he managed to muster as he struggled with both arms up his back, slip-sliding along the dance floor.

Jessie pulled the door open as she simultaneously shunted him outside into the car park.

It was raining…

Just before she shut the door on him, she declared: "You can stay out in the rain until it's time for yer speech. Then, and only then, if you promise to behave yourself, ye can come back in to entertain your guests… Right?"

As she marched back through the tables slapping her hands, she stopped and looked around.

"Ok, folks, fun's over. Youz can close yer mouths now. The food's on its way. Your Best Man'll be back in time to make his speech. Now that he's got another wee story tae talk about…

……………………………………………………………………

Mary brought the conversation back to my question. "Well, we've no planned functions on this weekend but we've got a nice wee funeral the Co-op called about for tomorrow. I know it's kind of wrong. But when I pick up the phone and I'm handed a fresh funeral, (*is there any other kind?),* I think: Yes! Funerals are so-o much easier to deal with than your fully-fledged weddings. It's so simple. Turn up on time. Everyone sits down. Feed the hungry faces. Everyone eats heartily. No one ever complains. Hand the right person the bill. Tip to Big Jessie to dish out. Leave the mourners to fight over the spoils and the last of the free drink. Pack up. Pop into the Swan for a reward refreshment with the girls. Go home. Job done…"

I replied. "Well, I'm very impressed with your efficiency. Long may it continue? I know I just kind of muddle through."

"Well, there's no muddling through in this business. I devise my action plan and it's in stone!" Mary bowed theatrically then voiced her thoughts about her dad's imminent situation. "Do you think Dad could maybe help out in the shop or even the odd function? You know. Keep him going? He is only sixty-three. It's just because of his tunnel vision that he's been offered early retirement. Have a think. Eh?"

I smiled as enigmatically as I could manage and resumed my quiet guitar picking…

Next morning, Mary assembled her troops at the tearoom. A quick run through of that day's itinerary and they whirled into action.

Thelma finished off the steak pies to Mary's satisfaction, while Jessie organised the picking of the crockery and other kit, packing it into crates and loading the van.

An hour's bustle and they were ready to go.

Squeezed between Jessie and Mary, Thelma mused, "How come you've no' got a mirror, Mary? An' the back door's windows a' blacked oot. Does that no' make it harder tae drive?"

Mary grimaced and looked across at Jessie who knew all about the safari adventure. But her loyalty to Mary stopped her from letting the troops know.

Jessie slapped Thelma across the back of her head. "Never mind yer bloody questions! They steak pies better be spot on. These poor folks we're goin' tae will be grief stricken. They're gonnae need quality food and drink tae help them cope. Never mind yer mirror questions!"

Thelma, rubbing the back of her head, objected, “Whit dae ye mean? Better be spot on? Mary trained me proper! Have ye ever had a complaint? Naw! By the way, you’ve gied me a headache! Where ur we goin’ anyway, Mary?” She turned her back on her colleague.

Mary, changing gear as she pulled away from the tearoom, replied. “We’re going to sunny Twechar by the sea! As they like to say.”

The red van rattled along. The three girls in the front with another two waitresses precariously perched on the very trestle bench that Mum had fallen off at the barbeque. It was quite a skill to hold on to the crates of crockery while pressing your back to the van’s side panels. But Lorraine and Shirley were well practised. Just the occasional catastrophe when Mary braked too suddenly.

They were just waiting to turn right at Queenzieburn when the van spluttered and died.

Mary turned the key…

Phut…

She turned the key again…

Phut you! It seemed to say…

Big Jessie piped up. “Right, girls. It’s exercise time. Out an’ push the van over to the side of the road. Mary, there’s a phone box on that corner. Want to call the Co-op folk? And maybe John?”

Mary, recalling her boasts of efficiency the night before, decided to just call the Co-op. They might have a mechanic. Besides, John was miles away working in The Buy In.

“Hello. Is that you, Julie? Mary Caters here. We’ve got a bit of a problem… Our van’s broken down on the way to the funeral in Twechar. You guys wouldn’t have a spare van knocking about?”

“Oh dear, Mary. I don’t think we’ve got a van. I’ll go and get Mr McIvor. Hold on please.”

Big Jessie was half inside the phone box. “What did she say? I think you should phone John. He can rescue us in that daft Russian van of his…”

Mary was listening to Mr McIvor. “Shoost, Jessie! Well, we’re just outside Queenzieburn, Mr McIvor. Do you think you can help?… You’ll send a vehicle?… Twenty minutes?… Oh. You’re a life saver! That’s great!”

Mary pushed Jessie out of the phone box. “No need to call John. We’re sorted. Mr McIvor’s sending a van. Get the stuff ready to be transferred. It’ll be here soon.”

Five catering staff in black and whites standing by a stricken red van on the edge of the village of Queenzieburn was not a normal occurrence at eleven o’clock on a Wednesday morning. A crowd of locals started gathering. What else is there to do?

Twenty minutes passed. No co-op van.

Twenty-five minutes…

“We’re gonna be late for the bloody funeral!” Jessie wasn’t happy.

One of the locals, who could have passed for Sarah’s twin, Mary thought, spoke to Jessie. “Are you lassies goin’ tae a funeral? Where is it? It’s no’ ma Aunty Sheila’s in Twechar is it? Ah couldnae make the service but Ah’m going tae the purvey. Ye couldnae gie me a lift by any chance?”

Big Jessie looked her up and down, holding back a sneer she replied, “Ah think if we could give *you* a lift we’d be giving *ourselves* a lift first. Don’t you think?”

“Oh, Ah see. Yer broke down then! Ah didnae realise. Ah thought ye were just havin’ a wee rest ye know. Nae problem, Ah’ll just get the bus. It’s due in five minutes anyways. Dae you want tae get the bus tae? It goes right past Twechar Halls.”

Mary and Jessie looked at each other. Jessie said “Ah don’t think that would work, Hen. We’ll see you in there when we’re dishin’ out the steak pie.”

Just then, Thelma shouted from the front seat of the van. “You’ll never believe this!”

“Excuse me, please.” Mary smiled at the crowd as she walked round to the front of the van.

Oh God!

A hearse!

A bloody hearse!

The grinning driver opened his window and doffed his chauffeur's hat. "The boss said you needed transport, Madam. Here I am!

"Ah'm no' goin' in the back o' no hearse, Jessie!

Ouch!"

So much for an Action Plan in stone… John will love this…

A couple of months later with a fully serviced van and a slightly more flexible action plan, Mary introduced her dad to her girls as the latest member of the team. Resplendent in black trousers, white shirt and black bow tie and bottle bottom specs, Mr Heaney stood to attention in the tearoom prior to loading the necessities for the wedding later that day.

Big Jessie spoke up. "Right, Faither. You're welcome tae join us, but if I shout move! It means I'm in a hurry. Ok?"

Mr Heaney replied, "I've no intention of getting in anybody's road, dear lady. Mary tells me you're the power that makes it all work. I bow to your greater knowledge and experience. However, if you want to know anything about precision engineering…" He smiled benignly.

Jessie grinned. "I think we'll get along just fine, Faither. Do you think you can manage that tray of cutlery? It goes in that crate over there. Cheers."

Mr Heaney added another layer of character to Mary Caters. He only went along to the bigger functions where his role was to make sure the customers were happy with the service. His avuncular presence reassured the usually nervous Mother of the Bride who was always worried that their daughter's special day might not be quite perfect.

"Don't worry, my dear, Mary is an excellent cook. And she's trained her staff *very* well. I started teaching her when she was nine you know. And she's a *brilliant* organiser. She takes after her old man. Now let me seat you in your rightful place at the top table."

When not performing as mine host at Mary Caters functions Mr Heaney found his family had other roles for him. James, the solicitor, had him acting as a courier, delivering important documents. Graham, who had invested in a tenement block off Gallowgate in Glasgow, had his father-in-law knocking on doors every Friday, collecting rent from those tenants who were able and willing to pay. The more difficult ones were referred right back to Graham…

I found a job for him come Christmas time when I put him in touch with my old boss, Big Peter. The Kelvin Hall Carnival still needed someone to be there even in the quiet afternoons.

One day I met up with Mr Heaney in the Harlequin pub near the Kelvin Hall. He'd pop in there for a pie and a pint before starting his shift.

I asked, "So how are you enjoying being a Showman, Mr Heaney?"

He gave me a puzzled look.

I explained, "That's what the travelling folk who operate the carnival call themselves. Even Big Peter's a member of the Showman's Guild. Don't worry. It doesn't mean you have to perform a song and dance routine…"

He supped his Guinness. "I don't know if I'd mind doing a bit of the old soft shoe shuffle. I was not a bad dancer by the time I met Mary's mum. Anyway, working here's a lot easier than all these other jobs I seem to have got involved in. Retirement? I've never been so busy in my life! I was delivering James's writs this morning. And your Mary wants me to come along on Saturday for a Christmas dinner dance. Although I must say I'm actually enjoying the variety. After over thirty years peering at minute measurements in Rolls Royce, it's nice to be out and about and meeting different people."

"It'll be quiet at the toy stall though?" I was thinking back to the year I was lumbered there. Bored out my skull.

Mr Heaney thought, "Well, it's very restful, apart from the cacophony of noise of course. But Peter's been very fair, wages wise. He seems to be a nice man. And I'm already into my second book. Although I did have a bit of a crisis yesterday."

"Really? A crisis?"

“Yes. A school party arrived unexpectedly and they all wanted balloons blown up. I got a bit flustered and spilled my glass of water into the till. The money was actually floating! So, I decided to *Stop All Sales*, while I dried out the cash. It took nearly half an hour.”

“So, you mean… essentially, you chased the customers away?”

“Well, yes, I suppose. I know a couple of them were crying. But the money was all wet!” Mr Heaney was on the defensive as he registered my facial reaction. My thoughts went back to all those scoldings Big Peter had dished out at the slightest possibility of losing any money.

“I’ll tell you what, Mr Heaney. Don’t bother telling Big Peter… You might find his sense of fairness has limitations…”

He looked a bit nonplussed. Then I realised: It was my sixteen-year-old’s persona that would have worried. Mr Heaney’s had a life already. He doesn’t have to give a damn. And I didn’t want to put Mary’s dad under any kind of pointless pressure over a few lost balloon sales…

So, I raised my glass. “Never mind all that. Just you enjoy your second book. Here’s to your happy and busy retirement. And may it be full of variety! Cheers!”

Chapter 41
Christmas with the Heaneys

"Traditions! Traditions! Why do we have to have traditions?" I shouted up the stairs to Mary. Buster ran around my legs. I had to be careful to keep them together, or he'd default into figures of eight, and I was standing in our tiny hall. The front door behind me, the living room door to my right. No room to swing a cat, never mind a six stone Labrador.

"Merry Christmas, Buster. That's Sarah knocking on our door. I'll see you later, and take you for an extra walk, when I'm home in time for that nice glass of wine." I opened the door. Snow and sleet covered our neighbour's woolly bonnet. "Happy Christmas, Sarah. Thanks for this. We'll bring you back a pig-in-a-blanket."

"You're so generous, John… But tell Mary Merry Christmas and thanks for the woolly tights. I've got them on. See?" She lifted her coat to display the bright red tights, and then winked mischievously. "C'mon, Buster! You better not jump up on Mum again! She's still recovering from the last time you pressed her against the cooker…" Heaving at his lead, they disappeared into the swirl.

I closed the door on the weather.

"Because our elders and betters like it that way." Mary had stuck her head round the wall at the top of the stairs. A halo of tightly permed curls bouncing round her partly made up face. "That's who we are!" She briefly stared at the mascara brush between her fingers and blinked in annoyance at my interruption. "Christmas is very important to my dad. He was going to be an actual priest for God's sake… Until he met Mum… then had the four of us… But *we're* not going to let him down! *We're* going to enjoy the full Heaney Christmas dinner with all the trimmings. And anyway, *I* did most of the trimmings yesterday, along with the prep for the turkey, while you were flogging selection boxes in The Buy In. And you know we'll be going to your lot for Hogmanay next week, when I'll have to… *enjoy*… all those New Year speeches. *And* help your mum make *my* steak pie."

I like our Hogmanay with the Dickson tradition of the full steak pie dinner after midnight. Followed by raucous speeches interrupted by incessant heckling. And one or two libations…

"So, no relaxing Christmas Day for us then?" I sighed as I succumbed to the inevitable. I'll probably be squeezed between Joyce and Rhona, while our brother-in-law James sits across the Christmas table shouting at his offspring to "Bloody behave or I'll have a word in Santa's bloody ear for next bloody year!" All while scoffing the whitest slices of Mary's succulent turkey roast. Bah humbug didn't come close…

After a hurried bowl of cereal and a whirlwind of van packing, we set off to enjoy the blessings of Christmas dinner with my in-laws.

Travelling from Campsie to the western outskirts of suburban Glasgow through driving sleet is at best tolerable. But when the sleet is falling on black ice it's much more adventurous. Especially if the Christmas Day drivers have mostly had a wee Santa's dram as they've lain out the wean's presents in the early hours of the morning. It dulls the pain of reading instructions on how to assemble that *Chopper* bike or present *Great Uncle Bulgaria* of *Wombles'* fame's best profile in front of the mantelpiece.

"Look at that idiot!" Mary shouted as a two-tone Ford Capri slithered across the road in front of us from left to right just as we were coming into the village of Blanefield. I could see the driver wrestling with the wheel, trying desperately to keep it in control as his whole family waved their arms and shouted at him.

Through the sleet a blue Austin Allegro skittered towards them.

The Capri driver touched the brakes just too firmly, and the tan and black hatchback's rear end danced across the road, pulling the rest of the car with its flabbergasted occupants, fractionally past the now swirling Austin Allegro, as its front wheels bounced off the kerb, causing the car to ricochet backwards across the de-facto ice rink of a road. I feverishly manoeuvred the van through an extraordinary ballet between both vehicles, in a twirling, slow motion pirouette worthy of a standing ovation in London's Covent Garden. Even if I do say so myself…

My knuckles finally relaxed as all three vehicles slithered to an unscheduled stop, none of us facing our chosen way, but allowing three ashen faced drivers to weakly wave to each other in recognition of our astonishing driving skills!

I'm convinced they'd both had Santa's drams. But not me, I didn't have any weans…

"By God! You were lucky there! That could've been a massacre!" Mary said as I gingerly performed the slowest ever three-point turn to point the van back to our original direction.

"What do you mean, lucky??" I exclaimed. *Hmmm…*

Half an hour of very careful driving later we arrived at Mary's family home. I remembered that moment, sitting outside in Dad's van when we became an engaged couple. And all I'd had to do was say "yes."

Arms loaded with presents, we opened the front door and into the cram packed living room.

"Merry Christmas, Aunty Mary and Uncle John!" The three Gillespie kids had obviously been primed. Tamsin, Toby, and Trinity, all sporting red and green Christmas pullovers, were holding carefully wrapped presents, waiting for our arrival.

"Aw, that's so sweet." Mary piled her load of presents on top of my pile as she hunkered down and gathered her nieces and nephew in a big group hug. "And a Merry Christmas to all of you too. What have you got here?" The three children ginned widely as they handed over their gifts.

"Should I open them now?" Mary teased.

Joyce and James sitting up at the table. The ex-church organ at their back. Both wearing benign smiles as their offspring looked forward to Mary's reactions.

Rhona and Graham sitting on the sofa. Three-month-old Ross on Rhona's lap, hungrily sucking at his bottle of milk, chubby fingers clinging to the still warm glass.

Rhona looked up from her feeding. "Go on, Mary, what did they give you?"

Grinning as she ripped the paper off the first present, Mary smiled at Tamsin, fists in her mouth. "An egg timer! That'll come in handy…"

The next present was Toby's: "I-I-I- h-hope y-you I-like it." His stuttering hadn't improved. I looked at James's thunderous face as he glared at his son.

"Why, it's a nut cracker! We like nuts, don't we, John?" Mary looked up at me as I nodded obediently "Yep. I must say… I do like my nuts…"

Rhona smothered a snigger as she handed Ross over to Graham. He'd finished his bottle and needed his back rubbed.

Finally, young Trinity shuffled over with her offering, which turned out to be a set of wooden spoons. "They're *very* useful!" Mary exclaimed as she hugged her giggling niece.

"The children have heard about your new catering businesses. Hence the cookery themes." Joyce smiled as Mary nodded appreciatively. I handed over our presents to the kids who rapidly tore open the T-shirts and toys packed within.

Big Aunt Peggy, ubiquitously dressed in black, pushed open the kitchen door, a tray of roast potatoes gripped tightly in her oven gloves, steam misting her specs. "Right, you lot. Up to the table, now that Joyce has managed to re-cycle the teacher's presents that her class gave her!"

"Oh, Peggy! I told you not to tell them." Winnie shook her head as she followed her sister from the kitchen.

Uncomfortable looks all round. Joyce gulped and looked down. But not a word was said.

All squeezed round the extended table. Every chair used. I sit at the corner on the arm of Mr Heaney's prized recliner. I've been more comfortable. At least I've managed to avoid the 'wee' chair that poor Graham's lumbered with. No amount of cushions will bring him up to size. I nod at him sympathetically as he tries to keep his balance. He shrugs resignedly.

Mrs Heaney and Big Aunt Peggy, ably assisted by Mary and Rhona, lay out the feast.

Golden turkey. Plump and perfect. All the greens, and carrots too. Stuffing piled on plates a-groaning. Gravy boats awash with flavour. Crackers snapping. Children laughing. Mr Heaney's eyes are sparkling.

Mary, on a proper seat, nudges me as Baby Ross grins widely on his mummy's knee. Enjoying all the company.

"I saw that look, Sister." Joyce grinned from the other side of the table. A forkful of turkey poised in front of her mouth.

Mary looked over. "Sorry? Look? What look?"

"That was a broody look, if ever I saw one..." Joyce said, smugly. The turkey sliver made it into her mouth.

"I was just enjoying Ross's happiness. Today's a happy day. It's Christmas. I know it's *your* favourite day, Dad." Mary looked towards her father, who glanced at Winnie, his wife. "Of course I love Christmas. I was at midnight mass last night, although I noticed none of you were there." He looked around the table with a mock scowl. "That new Choirmaster hasn't quite got them working together. Not like when you three girls were on that balcony in my heyday! Now, that was powerful music. So good the BBC filmed us for *Songs of Praise*. Remember?"

"Great days, Daddy." Joyce glinted across at her mum. "I'm just wondering if maybe Mary... and John have got any plans... they'd like to share."

Whit?

Winnie put her knife and fork down. The hubbub died. "Now, Joyce. Just because you've managed to produce three joyous children, and your brother's wife, Maureen, is expecting her second baby any minute, is no reason to presume that Mary is going to be in the family way anytime soon!"

Aunt Peggy felt a need to say something. "You all know, I've never had any children. But I'm happy to have been involved with all you nieces, and of course, Iain and his family. Which might be bigger by the time we finish Christmas dinner!" She burst into a fit of the giggles. I looked at Mary who shrugged then whispered. "I saw a nearly empty bottle of advocate in the kitchen..."

Rhona piped up. "You haven't mentioned Ross, Mum. Is that because he's adopted?" There were tears welling up in her eyes as she hugged her baby tightly. Graham reached up from his wobbly cushions to put his arm around her.

"Don't be silly, Rhona," Winnie pushed her seat back as she moved round to her daughter. "Joyce was inferring that Mary *might* be expecting, or more likely inferring that she *should* be expecting after three years of marriage. I don't know if she is. That's Mary and John's business… But your Ross? He's a very special child. Any silly girl can get pregnant and have a baby. And too many don't really want them. But your Ross was wanted so-o much by you and Graham… You went to so much trouble to be that baby's mum and dad that he's possibly the most loved child I've ever known." With that she hugged Rhona and Ross. Graham smiled at his wife and went back to balancing on his 'wee' chair.

Table cleared and moved back. Dishes washed. Tea and biscuits all round. Mr Heaney sits proudly on the piano stool and primes the foot pump of the old church organ. It wheezes into life as his fingers spread over the keys and the chords of "Oh Come all ye Faithful" blare out.

Mr Heaney knows how to hold a tremulous key. Winnie stands beside her husband, her alto soprano harmonising with his tenor notes. Joyce and Mary join their parents, while Rhona hands Ross over to his dad and then joins her two sisters.

Four, then five-part harmonies merge into play. Past years of choir and family singing melt away any minor irritations. Sisters take cues from each other as Mr Heaney glances round. The Choirmaster of old is still in charge.

It's beautiful.

Entrancing.

Worthy of another *Songs of Praise.*

We three brothers-in-law glance approvingly at each other as our collective spouses reach a crescendo of harmonies that ends in a glorious vocal chord.

Mr Heaney lingers on the bass notes as we all breathe out… and recover.

The phone rings in the hall.

"I'll get it." I'm nearest. I edge out the door while my in-laws congratulate each other. Deservedly.

I pick up the receiver. “The Heaney household. A Merry Christmas! Who’s calling?”

“And how the Devil are you, John? Iain here, just to let you and the old folks know… They’ve got a brand-new Grandson. Iain Heaney the third has just arrived on Earth. Mother and her seven-pound baby are fine. Happy Christmas to you all. I’ve got to get back to rest of the bunch. It’s chaos here. We’ll see you all soon.”

I opened the living room door with a grin. “Apparently the Heaney clan just got bigger! Mum and Baby Iain the third are both well, but Iain the second is kind of busy and says Happy Christmas to us all.”

“That’s great news.” Mr Heaney stands up from the organ stool and moves to the fireplace. He lifts his glass in front of him. “There’s nothing like a new baby to bring joy to a family. Here’s a toast to my namesake!”

We all stand up for a rousing, “Here’s to Baby Iain!”

The three kids excitedly jump up and down as I look at Mary’s bright, happy eyes. A beaming smile as she looks at the girls and boys, then over to Baby Ross, now wrapped in his shawl propped up on the settee. Then she looks at me.

And lingers.

Now I know what Joyce meant about a broody look…

Chapter 42
Hijacking the Chef

"Damned machine's not working again!" Mary thumped the buttons on one of the most expensive pieces of kit of her still fledgling catering business: an Ansaphone machine which, in those days, had to be rented from the phone company. At £23 a month it was a big financial commitment. And along with the obligatory yellow pages advert any start up business was apparently enhanced and given credibility. Much like today's ubiquitous web sites that can make the smallest enterprise look like a major corporation.

"I've called the phone company. The engineer will be out ASAP they said," Mary shouted upstairs to me as I languished in a Saturday afternoon bath. Luxury...

"They answered the phone on a Saturday?" I shouted back surprised. I had expected them to use one of their own contraptions at the weekend.

"Apparently, we've got the gold-plated seven days a week rental contract. Bloody salesman never told me I could have got it cheaper," Mary answered back. "Well, are we going to help the band out? Seeing as how I've got no Saturday function and you've wangled a day off..."

....

The applause was long and loud. Wee Robbie, sounding ever more like a rasping Rod Stewart, with Joe Slyder, who had now officially adopted the stage name 'Funky Summers' and could make the lead guitar sing, while Arge, the South African bass guitarist kept a beat that really turned on the crowds.

"Ballroom Blitz" was the finale of their last encore and the lads started to pack up their gear. I pitched in to help as an unofficial roadie, while Mary was chatting to one of the hotel staff. The band members eyed her warily.

"So, what do you think? Have the band managed to get the residency for the summer?" Mary was talking to the entertainments manager of the large hotel in Renfrew.

The tuxedo-dressed boss looked at Mary, whose very short rock chic outfit belied her true vocation as a cooking-obsessed caterer.

One of Mary's many quirky attributes was an enjoyment of role playing, so here she was, acting out the part of rock band manager. Just for fun…

"Yeah. Well… Ok… The crowd seemed to take to them. Takings are up. You've gorra deal," the manager drawled in a very Glasgow version of a mid-Atlantic accent.

"Great." Mary turned and grinned at the band who'd never actually entrusted her with any kind of responsibility. They just loved her for her sense of fun and her brilliant cooking.

"That'll save them taking all their equipment back every night, means we've got an empty van for a change."

"Great. So, let's talk money," the tuxedo drawled.

"Yes, well…" Role playing was one thing. Financial responsibilities weren't so much fun. "See the drummer over there. He's the man who can beat the numbers better than me," Mary smiled while gesturing to George, the only sensible drummer there ever was, to take over.

All part of the seventies; Glam rock was still 'in' and the sixties legacy of enjoy life for the moment was still very much the vibe.

We'd had a hectic day helping our friends to get their gear to the gig. The band's van, a very old ex-parcel delivery vehicle, had suffered yet another calamitous outing when the driver's sliding door had decided to break free and slide completely out of its rail, just as they were trying to pull away at traffic lights. It clattered onto the bonnet of a mini going the other direction. The mini driver jammed on his brakes, causing a bit of a pile up, culminating in an orange and green Corporation double-decker bus crunching into the nose of the band's van. Lots of angry passengers and assorted drivers gesticulating while the band members struggled dragging the heavy door off the mini and trying to set it back on its rails. They finally gave up and chucked it in the back. Sheer slapstick. Like slow motion rock 'n' roll. Thankfully no one was hurt.

Hence Mary and I being involved in their Plan B.

Halfway through my Saturday morning: “Any chance of you guys using your van to take us to the Imperial tonight?” Joe nee Funky was on the phone.

“You might get some free grub ’cos you’re with the band. It’s a big dinner dance. We’re hoping to get a residency out of it.”

Being the first of our crowd to get married in our very early twenties meant our freedom to have folk to our wee house in Campsie was very much appreciated. Especially as Mary was forever trying out new recipes. Who said there’s no such thing as a free lunch? Our chums knew exactly where to get them! So, the chance to enjoy a hotel dinner at no expense via the band was a bit of a carrot…

It turned out the complementary grub that had been hinted at was just wishful thinking. As the evening wore on, we found ourselves feeling more and more peckish. Crisps and roasted nuts can only ever postpone the need for proper food.

After her successful negotiations with the wannabe American manager, Mary turned her sights on her next challenge.

The gear was packed away into an ante room much faster than the usual van loading, the band were gathered round a table already occupied by some kitchen staff and the inevitable couple of well-made up groupies. The dinner we never got being long gone.

“So, you’re a proper chef then?” Mary asked the Mediterranean-looking young man in whites, who was trying to tell Wee Robbie how much he’d enjoyed the music.

“Sorry, mate. Canny unnerstaun’ a word yer sayin’.” Wee Robbie’s linguistic skills were somewhat limited to speaking a particular form of Glaswegian. And if you hadn’t been brought up in his segment of Maryhill, even other Glaswegians needed a translator. Strangely, when he was singing, Wee Robbie had almost perfect diction.

The chef waved his arms in the air. “I sorry. My English no good.”

“Nae, bother,” Robbie was generous. “Ma English is rubbish tae.”

“Excuse me,” the West End educated Mary interjected. And then spoke very slowly: “Where… are… you… from?”

"I from Italia, Signorina. My name ees Giovanni. I come here three weeks ago, to cook. I was trained in the best hotels in Roma!"

Mary's eyes grew even larger. "So you're a real Italian chef!" Inspiration sparked. "And you're finished your shift?"

"Si, Signorina. The kitchen porters… They clean."

"So, do you really enjoy cooking?" Mary's plan was hatching.

"Oh, si, Signorina… It is… how you say?... my passion".

"Have you seen much of our beautiful country since you arrived?"

"No no, Signorina. I too busy. I work all day till late. I will see some time. Maybe tomorrow. I have my first day off." Giovanni shrugged his shoulders.

Suddenly there was an annoyance of noise as the bar staff started shifting tables and chairs and shouting at the stragglers still in the bar.

"IT'S A QUARTER PAST TEN! HUV YE NAE HAMES TAE GO TAE!"

Being 'with the band' gave us special unspoken rights. Even more so if the band was sitting with the staff. We could have sat and drank for at least another twenty minutes! However, I was driving and even in those days it would have been foolhardy to drive what I knew would be a van full of merry musicians and assorted hangers on all the way from Renfrew to Lennoxtown pre-motorways.

There was a huddled confab among Mary and the bunch as the dregs of the drinks were finished and the prices of carry outs were negotiated.

Funky and Wee Robbie stood behind Giovanni. Mary stood in front of him.

"We'd like to help you get to know Scottish people and culture better," Mary said, still speaking slowly.

The Italian looked puzzled.

"How'd ye like tae see a wee bit of countryside?" Robbie tried to help.

"I sorry. I no' understand." He shrugged.

“We’ve decided to take you home with us,” Mary smiled benignly.

“I sorry. I still no’ understand”

There seemed to be a general shuffling out through the back doors to the van and I found myself in the driver’s seat with Mary climbing in beside me. In the back there was quite a crowd tumbling around the badly carpeted floor. I could hear some broken Italian but the consensus was: “I sorry, I no’ understand.”

It was after midnight when we pulled up outside our house. A lot of shushing and shooshing as I opened the front door. I glanced back and noted the anxiety in Giovanni’s eyes as he looked up and down the road. No idea where he was. Surrounded by a bunch of mildly intoxicated musical Scots. Going into a house of complete strangers. That’s what he gets for leaving home!

Sarah, watching for us coming home, appeared with an excited Buster.

Buster waggled his rear end and grinned as he was patted and petted by familiar faces. Giovanni looked even more fretful.

We crowded into the house while Mary went through to the kitchen. Robbie and co were making themselves at home by opening some of the carry out while Funky sat at the piano and started tinkling some of the band’s repertoire.

Arge was entwined on the couch with one of the blond groupies while Giovanni stood in the middle of the room looking like the proverbial scared rabbit. Sensible George, the only one of the band with a car, had gone home to his mum’s.

“Right then, my Italian master. You’re still on cooking duty!” Mary put her arms around the bewildered chef and virtually dragged him into the kitchen.

There, Giovanni was confronted by a heap of raw chicken pieces, bags of pasta, and a pile of fresh vegetables. Part of the next night’s Mary Caters function. He looked stunned.

“You wanna me cook? But it’s a middle of a night.”

"Why else would we kidnap you? We're starving. And I'm desperate to learn some new Italian recipes." Mary smiled sweetly while she chopped the vegetables with her favourite sharp knife.

"When's that grub gonnae be ready?" a gruff voice from the living room called, cutting through the melodic acoustic sounds of guitar and piano blues.

"Ok.Ok. I cook! I cook!" Giovanni had seen the light. "Wherra the herbs and spices?"

Half an hour later we all tucked into one of the best Italian pasta dishes I've ever eaten. Especially at one o'clock in the morning.

For dessert the lads emptied a few more cans before collapsing around the living room in various postures. Once the couch and chairs were taken, the floor doubled up as the bed of last resort. Blankets were shared, but the alcohol, Italian food, and the earlier adrenalin of a successful gig made for deep sleeps all round.

Except for Giovanni. He lay down nervously. Kept one eye opened as though ready for something terrible.

Mary and I were comfortably upstairs in our bed when the doorbell rang. Buster barked loudly. I looked at the clock. 8.30am. Early for visitors.

Mary gathered her wits and dressing gown round her and staggered downstairs to open the door.

"Ansaphone Engineer. Your machine's not working?" The smartly uniformed young man was holding a tool kit.

"It's Sunday morning!" Mary was astounded.

"You're paying for the Executive Contract, ma'am. Guaranteed seven days a week service." The young engineer was very professional. "Where's your machine?"

"Erm through here." Mary pushed the living room door and felt the dead weight of a sleeping musician move as she heaved the door open enough to step through.

Mary pointed across the prone bodies virtually covering the floor to the machine at the other corner of the room. Buster was waggling and trying to introduce himself.

As the young engineer gingerly stepped over and between the bodies, while trying to pat the dog on his head, some of the hung-over forms were beginning to grumble and stir. He began to lose some of his professionalism.

“Eh, missus… if you’ve got so many folk here, why the hell do you need an Ansaphone?” he asked logically.

He became even more bemused when one of the figures rose hesitantly and in a strong Italian accent nervously stage whispered, “Help me… I am prisoner… they kidnap me for food!”

The engineer’s eyes widened as he looked at Mary who smiled back delectably and managed a fair version of a Mediterranean shrug. “Don’t worry about it… we just fancied an Italian take away”.

The stirring bunch on the couches and floor raised a weak laugh. The technician managed to weave whatever magic it took to make his machine work again, while Mary produced a heaped platter of Mr Drummond’s morning rolls, filled with Scottish delicacies of square sausage, fried eggs, smoked bacon, haggis, and even some black pudding.

“There you are, Giovanni. A real taste of Scotland. It’s maybe not as healthy as your delicious pasta last night, but by God, it tastes good of a morning!” Mary passed plates around as hungry hands grabbed the hot filled rolls and found grateful mouths ready to chomp.

Robbie turned to Giovanni who was devouring a roll and bacon and egg. “Seein’ as how it’s yer first day aff, we’ll take ye up the Campsies an’ ye can see most of Glasgow from the top. Fancy that?”

“I sorry, I no’ understand.”

Robbie rolled his eyes in mock despair. “Haw, Mary. Whit a catchphrase! Now Ah need even more Irn Bru to wash down this great Scottish grub!”

Chapter 43
Buster's Holiday.

"You've got a summer residency in Jersey?" I was impressed.

"Yep. The manager of the Jersey hotel saw us playing in Renfrew and asked George if we were free this summer. It's a great big hotel on the beach. Got a swimming pool and everything!" Joe aka Funky was quite excited. And no wonder.

Mary butted in: "I think I should get some credit here… Who was that girl who negotiated that Renfrew deal? Ahem!"

Funky was sitting in our living room. He'd rushed over in the band's van to tell us his news. His excitement was infectious.

"That's fantastic!" I said. "We'll maybe come and visit you. I've never been to Jersey." I looked at Mary who was nodding her head vigorously. Her dark permed curls bouncing. "I'm all for that. We could make it our summer holiday. And I could maybe negotiate the band a world tour, eh?"

Funky laughed. "I think George might have a say about that. But yes. It would be brilliant if you could come over. I mean lounging about by the pool every day might get a bit boring eventually!"

The following Sunday when we were over at my mum and dad's for a visit, we mentioned that we were planning the trip.

"Good for Joe and his chums, they must be very good. I've never heard them play," Mum said.

I reminded her, "That's not quite true, Mum. Joe and Robbie were playing at the barbeque last year, remember?"

Her face darkened. "Mmmm. We'll just never mind talking about that if you don't mind… Anyone like another cup of tea?"

Sniggers all round.

Alan piped up. "Could I come too? I could pay my way. Now I'm a fully-fledged office worker. I've been saving a bit and I'll be due holiday pay." Alan had recently started a job in the admin office of the Electricity Board in Glasgow. A nice little nine to five number. And well paid for an eighteen-year-old.

I looked at Mary who nodded. "Of course you can, Alan. That would be great. All we've got to do is decide the dates and book some digs. I think the hotel they're playing at will be way too pricey for us."

Alan's grin got even bigger. "Smashing. This'll be my first holiday without Mum and Dad. Apart from the odd school trip of course. It means we can go to the night clubs and casinos and beach parties…"

Mum took the bait. "Just you don't be so foolish, Alan!" She turned to me. "You'll look after him won't you, John."

"Alan's a big boy, Mum. I'll look after him when he lets me. Ok? I'm depending on Mary to look after me. Isn't that right, Mary?"

"Yeah yeah. So you are."

We managed to book flights fairly easily, though they weren't cheap, leaving our modest budget even leaner when trying to find accommodation. After scouring countless newspaper ads in this pre-internet era I finally found a reasonably priced guest house not too far from the band's luxury hotel on the outskirts of St Hellier.

"I can give you a family room for the first week, Mr Dickson. But I'm fully booked after that," the Jersey landlady explained.

Tired of making expensive long-distance phone calls and reckoning we'd easily find another hotel or B&B once we were there, I told the landlady to please book us in and agreed to send a cheque for our deposit.

"So, you've booked *half* a holiday then?" Dad was a bit sceptical about our plans.

Alan liked the idea. "I said we could sleep on the beach, didn't I?"

"You said we could *party* on the beach," Mary distinguished.

"Doh! And then you'd fall asleep of course!" Alan was being logical.

Ever the optimist I said, "I'll ask Joe to keep an eye out for digs once they're there. It'll be fine. You'll see. Just a wee adventure…"

Of course, Buster would have to be taken care of. A couple of days before we left, we put the catering van into the garage for a proper service. This left Mary without transport to take Buster to the kennels.

"No problem. I can get there by bus. It'll be fun."

While Buster was a marvellous pet who was great with all our young nephews and nieces, everyone except me found him to be quite a handful. Consequently, after a while we had run out of friends and relatives who were prepared to look after him while we went on holiday.

Especially after the episode when he'd chased Rhona's cat all over their house, waking up Graham, who hadn't been told Buster would be lodging. We dropped him off early one Saturday morning. Graham was abruptly abreast of the situation when both animals clambered over his sleeping form, barking and hissing as the dog put his full weight onto his solar plexus while springing to catch Tabby who was just milliseconds ahead of him…

To get out of repeating the bedroom scene Rhona highly recommended kennels run by her neighbours on the south side of the city. *And* we'd get a discount!

Mary planned her journey well. This meant taking the blue bus into the old Dundas Street station, walking through the centre of town to the Waterloo Street terminal which served the south of the city. Then finding a bus to take them to the kennels in faraway Philipshill.

Buster dragged Mary to the bus stop where a few people were waiting. Buster never understood queues. So, when the Route Master rear entry bus arrived and they were still last in the queue, he yanked the lead out of Mary's hand, wriggled past everyone, and jumped onto the bus. He was determined to be first!

Mary lowered her head and shuffled on behind everyone else; discovering her pet languidly sprawled over the length of the bench seats just inside the lower deck. Pretending to ignore him, she walked past and sat up at the front behind the driver.

Once he'd seen where Mary was seated, Buster decided he should join her. But to keep her in sight he used the most direct route, bounding over all the seats… *And* the passengers who were sitting on them!

He then perched on the aisle seat beside Mary excitedly nuzzling into her neck. She was trapped!

The bus conductress arrived. She said Buster would have to sit on the floor. So, Mary tried pushing him off the seat. He started to growl (well, would you like to sit on a pile of sweetie wrappings and chewing gum?).

So, she gave up trying to move him.

The conductress bristled. “Well, you’ll just have to pay a fare for him!”

“Ok,” Mary sighed. “Fair enough. I’ll have a return for me and a single for the dog then please?”

“I don’t blame you for not wanting to bring him back.” She raised her eyebrows as she took her money, and then clicked her machine to produce the tickets.

As she was handing them over to Mary, Buster snatched them out of her hand.

Sucked them between his lips.

And swallowed them…

“Ouch!” the conductress yelped.

Mary giggled, and asked the conductress what she was going to do. She’d paid for two tickets and needed her return to get back home.

Buster looked ponderously from the conductress to Mary and licked his chops, satisfied drools beginning to form at the back of his grinning lips.

“Well. You’ll just have to buy another ticket, my dear. It was your dog what ate it!” She turned and strutted down the aisle with Buster and Mary staring at her rear.

The next stop an inspector came on. Mary saw the conductress pointing at them as he came up the aisle to investigate.

Mary agreed with what had happened but she needed another ticket for her return journey.

The Inspector looked at the conductress. "Why *did* you give the tickets to the dog?"

At this injustice she yelled: "Do I look daft? The dog just grabbed them!"

Mary made big eyes to the inspector: "Either way, she definitely didn't give them to me…"

The Inspector looked as if he was having a bad day and carefully gave her a receipt for the missing ticket. But Buster would *have* to lie on the floor.

"Ok," Mary smiled. "Thank you."

The conductress glowered. The Inspector departed.

Buster stayed on the seat. Well, it *had* been paid for…

They arrived in Glasgow. Hot and busy. Between bus stations Mary decided to go into a cafe for a snack and a coffee.

Buster trotted in with Mary and politely sat under the table on the nice clean floor.

When her snack arrived, she noticed he'd lain down on the cool tiles. *Good dog.* Or so she thought.

There were two men sitting about three tables across from her. Buster started crawling towards them. *He'll be begging a chip.*

So wrong…

Seconds later four pigeons flapping noisily flew up from beneath the men's table. Their basket was on the floor, and Buster, clever dog that he was, had managed to muzzle the door open.

Instant panic…

People screaming. Doors slamming shut.

Buster was, of course, trying to catch the pigeons, and the pigeons, terrified, were dropping messages all over the shop...

Chaos ensued as the pigeon owners clambered over tables and chairs with Buster barking encouragement. Mercifully the owners caught the birds before Mary's pet committed avian homicide.

Unfortunately, the homing pigeons missed their train which would have taken them to the south of England, from where they would have raced home. Incidentally, Mary learned, *very loudly*, one of them had won the £1000 prize the previous year!

The cafe had to close to clean the indiscriminate pigeon mess.

Buster ended up with an old-fashioned kick on the rump and Mary found herself ejected from the cafe as they closed the doors behind her.

Without her coffee…

She made her way, dragging Buster, to Waterloo Street Terminal. Another queue. Mary decided this time *she* would be first and Buster could follow.

They got on the single decker bus and made for the long back seat. Trying to stay out of the way…

Mary sat next to the window and Buster clambered onto the seat beside her.

So far, so good. If the conductor was going to make Buster sit on the floor Mary decided she would break down and cry.

Luckily for them he was a dog lover and patted him on the head and let him stay where he was.

The coach quickly filled with passengers, including a young couple who sat in the seat in front of them. Buster ignored them, he was more interested in looking out of the window and Mary was in his way.

He was squashing her so hard against the corner of the bus she let him change sides to get a better view.

It was quite a long journey, and very hot, so Buster was panting a lot.

The young man in front turned round, "You're a fine specimen!" as he tickled Buster's ears.

This was Buster's cue for fun. He was now pretty bored not being able to stick his head out the window.

He began playfully chewing at the young man's forearm. He was also enjoying the game, until two of the buttons on the sleeve of his jacket stuck between the dog's teeth.

He tried to wrench his arm free.

Buster enjoyed this. This was proper play!

The young man was getting worried as Buster growled and pulled at the sleeve.

His girlfriend wasn't at all happy. "Will you let the dog go? Now!" as she glared at Mary who shrugged uselessly, suppressing a laugh.

They both started to fluster as their stop came closer…

The young man stood up wriggling out of his jacket with Buster getting more and more excited and really pulling in earnest.

The couple shuffled into the aisle, so Buster jumped over the back of their seat to continue the game.

By this time Mary was in a helpless fit of laughter.

"It's our stop, for God's sake!" the girlfriend shouted as the bus came to a halt.

Her boyfriend gave one mighty yank of his jacket, sending his sleeve buttons scattering. They ran down the aisle and jumped out of the front door.

Buster ran after them and reached the door just as the driver slammed it shut on his nose.

He yelped… The fun was over.

The driver wasn't a dog lover and threw Buster and Mary off the bus at the next stop. They had to walk the rest of the way to the kennels.

They finally arrived. The kennel maid, sensitive to such partings, said Mary could take her pet into a side-kennel/room to say her goodbyes to him.

"No thanks. This'll do. We'll part right here. I'm now officially on a dog-free holiday!"

Chapter 44
The French Connection

The plane took off and I felt the familiar grip on my left arm as Mary transformed her slim hands into a tightening tourniquet slowing all blood flow to my fingers. I looked at my lovely young wife and saw again the tightly shut eyes and her lips mouthing frantic prayers. Thankfully she hadn't reached the stage of shouting them out loud… yet. I'd have kept my fingers crossed if they weren't already numb.

Alan looked away from the window. "What's with Mary? You ok, Mary?" He reached over to tap her.

I slapped his hand hard. "Just leave her alone!" I hissed. "She'll be fine once we land. But for God's sake, don't disturb her. It's not worth it!"

Alan rubbed his hand. "This is a great start to a fun holiday. With my fun big brother and sister-in-law! I'll just look out the window then. Will I?"

We landed safely, of course, in St Heliers Airport where Mary came back to life. She was as bright and cheerful as ever, until she spotted the newspaper headlines in the terminal shop.

JERSEY FULL!

Best Summer Ever for Island's Tourist Industry.

Alan laughed. "The beaches better be good!"

I worried

Mary gave me a look and shrugged.

We heaved the three heavy suitcases onto the trolley and pushed our way out to the arrivals area.

"Well, Hello youz fellow Glaswegians. Welcome to the sunny Island of Jersey! Yessiree!"

Funky and Wee Robbie were waiting for us with open arms, dressed in their stage clothes of white braided fringe jackets with embroidered epaulettes.

Alan, Mary and I stopped and stared. Stunned!

"What's with the cowboy look, guys? Whatever happened to rock 'n' roll?"

"I could do with a coffee, guys." Mary led us all across the terminal.

Funky explained. "Well, he who pays the piper calls the tune, as they say. Only, here in Jersey, it's literal. Turns out the hotel manager's a fanatical Country and Western fan. We didnae know that till we got here of course. Rattlin' all the way down south in that van of ours. Three punctures and a new shock absorber tae get here!"

"Took us two days and an eight-hour ferry crossing. In the middle of loading our stuff into the hotel the manager starts asking about our Country and Western set list. We didnae know what he was talking about till we looked at George…"

Robbie took up the tale: "His face went bright red. Then he admitted it: 'I was going to tell you before we got here, but Ah thought you might decide no' to come. An' Ah packed in ma job for this gig. An' we're here now…' Arge nearly walloped him. Ah nearly walloped him myself!"

I was astounded. "So, what did you all do? How come you never told us? I'm not sure we'd have come all the way here to listen to two weeks of Country and Western, you know!"

Funky shrugged. "Once we were here, we couldn't afford to go back. We made George buy the outfits, and they cost a few bob as you can see. All white leather and proper matching boots. Neat, eh? Learning the songs took a couple of days. The manager gave us a list. To be quite honest, it's a piece of piss. And now we're managing to infiltrate some proper music. And *that's* when the punters fill the floor. So, it's kind of working out. Plus, we've got these nice new jackets. And George is awfy nice to us. The icing on the cake is we get paid cash every week. So, life's not at all bad."

Once we'd assimilated the band's change of identity and musicology we piled into the familiar rickety van and they drove us to our guest house.

Then I remembered. “Hey, Funky. Did you have a look for any digs for next week like I asked you? The paper says *Jersey is full!* Doesn’t look promising.”

Looking a bit guilty he answered. “Well… afraid not. Been kinda busy. I went across on the Hydrofoil to St Malo in France last week for the couple of days that we had free. It was brilliant! Found a nice Petite Hotel that had silk sheets and everything. You could always go there for a few days.”

Alan chipped in: “This travelling lark sounds like fun after all. I quite fancy a trip to France.”

Mary had a thought. “If it’s anything like Paris, we can’t afford it. That was a nightmare. We had to drive all the way back to the Isle of Wight to find some sanity.”

“No, it’s nothing like Paris.” Funky was reassuring. “It’s a medieval walled town. Quite pretty actually. It’s got a harbour and lots of little narrow streets. You’ll love it.” He gestured to Mary.

So, after a bit more chat we decided that we had a plan and relaxed into the first week of our holiday.

The guest house was nice and clean and not too far from Hotel Du Mer where the band were playing five nights a week. They were off that night so Funky and Robbie suggested they’d give us the guided tour…

The tour didn’t last much past the second pub where we were bemused by the game of Bar Skittles. A bit like a table top version of ten pin bowling only you swing the ball which is attached to an overhead wire. Very moreish. Especially after a couple of beers.

While Robbie and Funky and I were setting up yet another game, Mary went looking for Alan. She found him in the ‘snug bar’ next door. Sitting playing cards with a bunch of locals. He looked anxious.

Mary, wearing short shorts and a summer top stood watching the game for a few minutes. Alan was being fleeced. “What’s that you’re playing, guys?”

One of the locals, a narrow-faced guy in his mid-twenties, looked her up and down then said: “We’re playing five card stud. Ever played?”

Mary shook her head. “Always willing to learn. Can you show me?”

One of the other players nodded as Alan handed his cards over to the dealer. “Erm. That’s me rooked, guys. I’m going to see if I can cadge a pint next door. Bye then.” With a hang dog look he dragged his feet through to join us.

“What’s up, Alan?” I asked.

“I was playing cards with those guys next door. I’ve lost a good few quid. I feel bloody stupid. And now Mary’s playing with them.” He looked worried.

Robbie squared his shoulders and stuck his chin out. “You want me to sort them, John?”

“Don’t be daft. Mary’ll sort them fine. It’s your shot, Funky.”

In the meantime, Mary, giggling as she fumbled with the cards, managed to lose in the first three rounds. Then she asked the players: “Can I have a go at dishing them out? I think I get it now.”

“Here you go, babe. Enjoy yourself. You sure you understand how it works?”

Mary took the cards, shuffled them gingerly, and then slowly dealt the cards to each player. First card face down, then a card face up and the antes went into the pot. More cards were dealt carefully. And the game settled down. Mary won a few pounds.

“This is great!” She smiled all round. “Want another game?”

“Ok, babe. You’re on the ball. Try and speed it up a bit though.”

Mary speeded up the dealing just a bit and managed to win that game as well. She burst into a giggling fit. “That’s amazing. Must be beginner’s luck. Can we keep on going? This is great fun.”

Another player won a small pot in the third game but Mary cleaned up in the fourth. “I think I better quit while I’m ahead, guys.” She wriggled her way out from behind the table clutching her winnings. All eyes on her short shorts.

"Bye, guys, see you again.”

A moment later she came through to the skittle bar. “A good idea if we leave now,” she whispered in my ear.

I took her lead, downed the remains of my beer and motioned to the rest. "I think it's time to go back to the digs." The other three looked puzzled but didn't argue.

Walking briskly a couple of streets later Mary asked Alan, "So how much did you lose in there?"

Alan's shoulders slumped even lower. "Twenty quid, I think. How much did you lose?"

Mary laughed. "Oh, I never lose at cards! My Uncle Bill, God rest him, Aunt Peggy's man, was a bit of a 'rascal' shall we say. He taught me how to shuffle cards 'properly' when I was about twelve. Though that's the first time I've really needed to use that skill. Here's your twenty quid back. That means I'm a fiver up! Not bad, eh? And by the way... Don't be such a sucker again, Alan."

Alan stopped and stared at her. "You're amazing, Mary!" He gave her a big hug and looked at me. "You knew!"

"Oh aye. I don't play cards with Mary. Not since she managed to double her housekeeping the first week we were married!"

After a fun and relaxing week, we were ready for the next stage of our adventure. We managed to pack enough clothing for the three of us into one big orange case and left the other two cases in the tiny flat the band had been allocated.

We'd checked the timetable of the Hydrofoil service and booked tickets for the one o'clock sailing which would get us to St Malo just after two.

It was exciting boarding the futuristic Hydrofoil. Laid out like a spacious aeroplane internally, only with much bigger windows.

"Hey, this is cool!" Alan was a happy chappie as he settled down beside one of the windows. "Will you be ok, Mary?"

"I'm fine on boats and trains and buses. It's those bloody machines that don't belong in the sky I can't take. No, this should be fun."

The sleek ship loaded up quite quickly as the departure time approached.

Two o'clock arrived and passed and nothing happened. The full craft just sat in the water, mildly swaying. Then an announcement.

"Our apologies, ladies and gentlemen. We have a technical problem which we're working on. We hope to leave as soon as possible. We're sorry for any inconvenience. Please remain in your seats.'

"I thought it was just planes that had technical problems," Mary commented.

Despite murmurings from the dozens of passengers, we had to sit in our seats and wait. We'd gone through the duty-free shop and customs. Rules are rules and we weren't allowed to wait on shore. So time ticked by. Boredom turned to anxiety as the minutes turned to hours! Three and a half of them, before it finally departed! In that time Mary had threatened to open the duty-free whisky we'd bought and we'd spent a small fortune on expensive snacks from the tiny shop on board.

Once the ship had lifted out of the water and was zooming along at 40 knots, it was exhilarating. But by then we just wanted to get onto French land and get settled.

It was almost 6 o'clock when we heaved the heavy suitcase down the ramp and onto the quay. A pretty harbour with lots of small boats moored in the basin and many rowing boats and dinghies scattered around the whole area. It was very colourful, but it was already darkening and I was anxious to find somewhere, at least for that night.

The pretty tourist information building just outside the quay had closed ten minutes earlier. "That's handy," Mary sighed. "Still, it looks very touristy. We'll be fine."

St Malo is quite hilly, especially when carrying an over-filled suitcase. Only one handle straining with the weight. This was long before someone came up with the excellent idea of putting wheels on them. A great invention, the wheel…

There were lots of hotels up lots of streets. But none of them had any vacancies. *Plien* was the sign in almost all windows. Very disheartening.

"Let's stop for a drink and come up with a plan." I finally suggested as we traipsed past a welcoming cafe full of merry people who all had beds to go back to.

We back-tracked to the cafe and ordered some beers and toasties. We were starving, having had nothing proper to eat since late morning. We were just too scared to stop long enough to buy a proper meal.

I had the embryo of a plan. “Look, this bloody suitcase is holding us back. We’re walking about one mile an hour even with Alan and me carrying it between us. I think we should hide it somewhere then go back for it once we find a hotel.” Pretty desperate but by now it was nine o’clock and the streets were thinning out.

Mary looked a tad haggard. “I remember noticing a rowing boat down at the harbour, with an upside-down dinghy in the middle of it. No one’s going to use either of those boats tonight.”

Alan spoke up. “That means we’ve got to lug that monster all the way back down those streets. Then lug it back up to whatever hotel we do find. Eh?”

As leader I made a decision… “At least we’ll be able to move quickly. We can try going down different streets. We might strike it lucky before we have to dump the case.”

This wasn’t going to be any kind of lucky day. The *Travel Gods* were against us!

We staggered back to the harbour. “I’m sure that bloody case is heavier than it was!” Alan was getting fed up. He was tired and hungry and had a cold coming on. He’d been snuffling for the last hour.

“Attishoo!” Just to prove the point…

It was now pretty dark down by the harbour. A few street lamps left big pools of darkness. There were dozens of boats along the curve of the quay. Mary strained her eyes.

“There it is. Right in that dark corner. It’ll be safe there.”

Relieved to be getting rid of the case we stumbled past the other boats. Alan and I cursing as we bumped our legs on the awkward surfaces and tripped over the sailing debris lying in the shadows.

We reached our target. A high-sided rowing boat with a dull red dinghy’s keel sticking up in the middle of the boat.

I took charge. “Right. If you both lift the dinghy up on one side, I’ll lug the case into the boat. Ready?”

The dinghy wasn't too heavy and after a cursory glance around the quay in case we were being watched by potential knicker thieves, Alan and Mary pulled the dinghy up to reveal complete darkness beneath it.

I hefted the suitcase up to chest height and tossed it into the darkness.

Splash!

Gurgle gurgle as the suitcase sank into water that could be any depth…

Mary and Alan looked at my face and burst out laughing.

"Well, that'll make it lighter, eh?" Alan quipped.

I gave up. *This was not a good day!*

"To Hell with it!" I said. "The clothes will be soaked now anyway. At least we're not lugging it anymore. Let's start walking."

The upshot was we trudged for another couple of hours while the town emptied of people. Noises off echoed around the dimly lit, high-walled, narrow streets, giving a sinister feel to our tired and stressed bodies.

Finally, we made it to our last resort, the Hotel de Police at the top of the town. Mary tried all her womanly charms including weeping copiously to see if the Gendarme would be kind enough to give us a cell for the night. No luck there either.

"What if we smash some windows? They'd have to arrest us then! Eh?" Alan was getting desperate.

The Gendarme was sympathetic and explained we'd turned up on one of France's major public holidays. "All of Paris come to St Malo this weekend." The best he could do was to allow us to sit on the waiting bench opposite his counter.

That bench must have been the narrowest I've ever sat on. No more than four inches wide. Presumably designed to put lingerers off. But we had nowhere else to go. I had failed to provide a roof for my family. We had even failed to go to jail! All we could do was to sit in misery until daylight listening to Alan's sneezing fits.

At 6am sharp a new Gendarme appeared and brusquely shooed us out of his station. We were virtually vagrants. Dishevelled, unkempt and bone weary. The thought of all our best clothes lying submerged in our stupid hiding place didn't help to cheer us up.

Still. It was a new day as we walked back down to the harbour. We fished the sodden case out from under the dinghy and sure enough. It wasn't any lighter. We carried it dripping all the way through the marina to the Tourist information building.

"It says here it opens at nine. Nearly three hours away to wait." Mary looked as bedraggled as I felt. We were all drained and exhausted.

Thump! We dumped the warped and sodden suitcase on to the steps surrounding the building. Opening the case to be confronted by the soaking mass of holiday clothing.

"I think we should make the most of the time before the tourist office opens." I tried to motivate my 'team.' "See the ornate metalwork on all the office windows? How's about we hang up our clothes on them. The sun's getting warmer, so they'll dry out a bit."

Action is always better than sitting around moping. So, we pulled out our wet clothes, wrung them as dry as we could, and hung them up all over the decorative window bars.

Mary laughed, as she surveyed our handiwork. "You realise we're now gypsies. And, our dirty washing is literally hanging out in public!"

Alan shouted from the other end of the building: "There's a baker's opening across the road. Anyone fancy coffee and croissants?"

Food and a hot drink can fairly cheer you up. We pitched camp until the Tourist Office was opened by a very nice lady who looked at our encampment in astonishment until we did our best to explain our predicament.

Once inside the tourist office, she explained that St Malo was still full.

"What about hiring a car? Zen you can go anywhere. Zer are plenty of pensionnes and hotels further inland."

We looked at each other. “That’s a brilliant idea!” Alan’s eyes brightened. “Can I drive? Maybe there’s a French safari park we can visit…”

“Ha ha! You think? I’ll bet you’re too young to drive a hired car. So that knocks that idea right on the head! But hiring a car is a good idea, seeing as how we’ve saved the costs of a night’s digs. Good job the police didn’t charge us.”

“Alors.” The tourist lady explained. “Zer is a car rental place just two blocks away.” As she pointed it out on a local map.

“Merci, Madam. You have been very helpful.” Mary shook her hand.

“Enjoy the rest of your trip. Au revoir.”

An hour later we were all packed up. Our not quite so sodden clothes jammed back into the not quite ruined suitcase. The case itself squeezed in beside Alan on the back seat of our rented Citroën 2CV.

Fifty bouncing miles later we arrived in the town of Rennes, where we stopped outside the first hostel we came across.

The receptionist took us upstairs to show us the modestly priced ‘family room.’

“Look at all those beds!” Alan exclaimed, looking at the two double and four single beds spread around the very large, bright room.

“I didn’t realize French families were quite so large but we’ll take it please.” I turned to the smiling concierge.

One more heave of the blasted suitcase up the stairs to the room, I pulled the outside shutters closed, before we collapsed onto two of the many beds.

“Nighty-night folks, we’ll get up in time for dinner, ok?” I said as I drifted off into one of the deepest sleeps ever.

It was more like supper, by the time we all came to. But we were refreshed and managed to actually enjoy the next few days gently exploring the pretty countryside of Brittany, before bouncing back to St Malo the day before our flight home.

Thankfully, the hydrofoil was fully operational and sped us back to Jersey in a jiffy. We staggered up to the band's digs dragging the rapidly disintegrating suitcase. I knocked on the door and Funky finally opened it, bleary-eyed from the previous night's gig.

"How was St Malo, then? Did your beds have silk sheets too?"

Mary glowered. "More like splinters in our backsides!"

"Eh?" said Funky.

Chapter 45
Kids?

“Katie told me she’s expecting this morning.” Mary was sitting next to me in the kitchen. We were just finishing off a delicious Irish stew, the very same as my Granny used to make it. Lumps of potatoes and lamb fighting for floating space with the carrots and onions and sprinkles of parsley. Autumn had arrived with a chill breeze, so Mary had rustled up the stew while working her shift in Country Fayre. My fork stopped halfway to my mouth: “Really? That’s amazing! Helen in The Buy In told me today that she’s pregnant! Is this some kind of conspiracy?

Mary shook her head in disbelief. “So, when’s Helen due then? Katie reckons she’s three months gone. She’s talking April or May.”

“Just about the same for Helen. They don’t know each other, do they? That’ll be fun come next April or maybe even March when they’ll both be missing.” My mind started figuring out how we were going to cover for them both. Sometimes life gets complicated.

Mary looked thoughtful. “I’m sure we’ll manage. Everyone will pull together. It’s for a happy reason they’ll be off. Maybe get my dad to do a shift in the shop? Or ask Thomas to come in on his day off from McColl’s…”

“Now I know you’re joking. I love your dad to bits and he’s fine playing the Maître D’ at a function… As for Thomas? You know he’s pretty busy. Seems to be thriving in corporate land. He was telling me he had to cover for the Area Manager last week when she was off sick. I somehow don’t think he’ll have time to be doing a shift in The Buy In.”

“Good for Thomas. I’m glad he’s doing well.” Mary still looked pensive as she pushed the potatoes around her bowl. She stabbed a piece of lamb with her fork, picked it off, and passed it down to Buster who was in his usual position, lying under the table.

Satisfied chomping duly commenced.

What’s going on? Giving Buster food from the table is one of Mary’s red line no-no’s.

"You ok, Mary? Anything else happen today? You sick or something?"

She laid her cutlery down. Her shoulders slumped uncharacteristically. Her bottom lip trembled. "Iain and Maureen came into the tearoom today with wee Iain. Big Iain had some business errand to do in Kirkintilloch and managed to take Maureen and the baby with him while the other kids are at school. It was great to see them. Wee Iain's just adorable." Her eyes were welling up. What's going on?

"He was so bright! All the customers were making a fuss over him. He wanted out of his carry cot so he could crawl all over the shop. He's ten months old now. Goes like the clappers. That's when Katie told us she's expecting, and Maureen was so-o understanding. Full of congratulations and overflowing with advice… And then she just looked at me… She didn't say anything… Just a look of absolute kindness that said, 'It's so sad you haven't had this joy.' I glanced at Katie and she had the same look. And she's three years younger than me!"

I got up from the table and moved round towards my trembling wife. I gave her a big squeezy hug.

"Come on, Sweetheart, I'll do the dishes and we'll both take Buster out for his walk, eh?"

Mary gathered herself, wiped her tears, and looked at me with those big, big eyes. "Ok, a bit of fresh air will be good," she said in a small voice.

I clattered the dishes into the sink and rinsed them through while Buster ran excitedly between Mary and me. He must have heard the words *Buster* and *walk* in the same sentence.

Wrapped up well against the autumn bluster I held onto Buster's lead as we walked across the Crow Road and along St Machan's Way towards the open ground surrounding the primary school.

I pulled Mary into my side. "So, all this baby talk getting to you then?"

She pulled in tighter. "We've been married nearly four years now and you know we've never done any kind of 'family planning.' So how come I'm not pregnant?" She stopped. Turned her head and looked up at me. Sadness in her eyes. "There must be something wrong. Joyce and James have three kids, while Iain and Maureen seem to be going for more than a hat trick. You're one of five boys with lots of cousins on your side of the fence. Although Rhona and Graham have adopted. They've never said what the problem was. Gotta accept their privacy."

We reached the open ground, with the school football pitches playing host to a few dog walkers letting their pets off the leash. I unfastened Buster's and he was off like a shot. Racing over to parry with the springer spaniel he'd got to know over the last few months.

I felt thoughtful, and actually kind of grown up. We'd always agreed we'd simply wait and see what happens… But nothing had happened. *Maybe it was time to try a bit harder?*

I stopped and pulled Mary towards me: "Well, Sweetheart, I know it should all be romantic and natural, but if we have to go down the medical route to give nature a hand? That's what we should do. Are you ready for this next chapter? Do you really want to have a baby? All those nappy changes that you've never had to do 'cos you were the youngest. While I, on the other hand, have been a big brother since I was two. I hope you know what you're letting yourself in for." I was trying to keep it light.

She gave me a squeeze. "I'm fine. This isn't like my usual self. It was wee Iain. Such a great wee boy. I just felt an ache that I'd never really felt before. It's never mattered. I mean, we're two busy people. And we've got Buster and all his mischief. But…" She gave a deep sigh.

I called to Buster, who just ignored me as he and his pal raced each other up and down the pitch.

"You realise you're going to be prodded and poked as well as me, Mister?" Mary punched me playfully in my midriff. I hadn't really thought about that. Goody goody, that'll be fun.

I took a deep breath: "Ok. So we have a plan. You set the ball rolling with the doctor and I'll just do what I'm told. I love you, Mary. Let's hope they find a magic wand."

After a long, lingering kiss Mary pulled away. "I love you too, Mister. But look over there. You better get after our pet. His spaniel pal's gone and he seems to have got that poor lady trying to hold on to her white poodle into a proper fankle!"

"Oh no! And now we want to have kids. Are you mad, woman?"

"BUSTER!"

Chapter 46

How Much Are Your Balls, John?

Mary contacted our GP a few days later to start the investigative process. It all sounded so clinical. She was told we'd both have to go through a number of tests and they might well be inconclusive. It could simply not be our time yet… However, Dr Armstrong, after giving Mary a preliminary examination, set the ball rolling with a warning that it would probably take a good few months. So it was best if we just carried on with our lives as normal. That seemed like good advice, so we did our best to put it to the back of our minds. Like the saying goes "Keep Calm and Carry On."

But some days were different…

I was working in The Buy In on a midweek afternoon when I noticed the leather-jacketed stranger. His body language looked suspicious. Loitering at the video section, occasionally glancing towards me. I decided to just stick where I was and stay by the till.

It had been fairly quiet afternoon. Helen, my pregnant workmate, was in the back store putting stock away while I minded the counter.

We'd changed the layout of the shop over the summer to make it more spacious and bright. And also to make room for a selection of videos which were suddenly all the rage. With two large front windows with the door between them, on entering the shop the counter was on your left and newspapers and magazines to your right, with a couple of gondolas of sweets and crisps in the middle of the floor. The video display was beside the magazines.

Suddenly, the stranger turned round and started weaving his way between the gondolas. A stocky thick set twenty something. Matted hair and unshaven. A bit shorter than me and looking as if he's been enjoying an early refreshment, or three… He headed straight towards me. A foot away from the counter he pulled a nasty looking knife out of his pocket and held it pointing to the ceiling.

"Open the till!" his voice rasped roughly.

The large heavy metal cash register sat high between us. I felt my adrenalin whooshing up as he brought his right arm down and pointed the knife at my face while his left hand reached over and blindly pressed the till buttons in an inept attempt to open the cash drawer.

Anger welled as I smelled the whiff of stale alcohol. *You're not getting my bloody hard-earned takings,* I thought, as I instinctively grabbed both of his wrists. The wannabe robber's eyes widened with surprise as I gripped harder than I knew I could. I battered both hands down on the rigid top of the till as he tried to pull his hands free.

I gripped and squeezed even tighter as I crashed his forearms again and again. The fingers on his right hand finally loosened and the knife clattered to the floor. Result!

I held on to both wrists as Helen, alerted by the noise of the scuffle, appeared in the back shop doorway.

"Oh my God!" she shouted as she took in the scene.

I walked the robber in a grotesque line dance along the length of the glass display counter towards the back shop.

"Call the police now, Helen," I said as I tried to think what to do with the now wilting robber.

Still holding both wrists as tightly as ever, I came round from behind the glass counter and pushed him against the birthday card rack next to the back shop door.

I could hear Helen talking to the emergency operator. "We've got an armed robber in the shop. And I'm four months pregnant! The boss has got him up against the cards. Will you hurry up?"

The shop had a high ceiling, and in trying to utilise all available display space we had suspended brush poles by chains and, using butcher's hooks, had hung bulky items such as toy prams, kiddy-trikes, and bags of footballs from the wooden poles.

Being rather preoccupied dealing with what was turning out to be a loser of a robber, I hadn't noticed one of our regular customers coming up behind me. Until I felt a tap on my back.

Mrs McClure hadn't realised what was going on and I heard her busybody familiar voice asking the back of my head, "How much are your balls, John?"

I had an almost overwhelming urge to burst out laughing at the absurdity of the situation. Mrs McClure was one of those customers who lived in her own bubble. Oblivious to anyone else. She'd sometimes come bustling in jabbering to her grandchildren and I'd often had to stop her coming right to the front of the queue as she barged past more patient folk.

"I'm a bit busy just now," was all I could manage. My foe grunted as he feebly struggled. His obviously excessive Dutch courage now really taking its toll.

"The police are on their way." Helen was back in the doorway. "They said could you hold him till they get here".

"I'm shorry… I'm shorry… Let me go, please." The would-be robber was looking more and more pitiful as he slumped more than struggled.

"No chance, chum," I said as I dragged him into the back shop. Ah, there's the solution, I thought as I bundled him into our small toilet, pulled the door closed, and held on to the handle. I think he was glad of the opportunity to have a sit down!

Moments later a mass of blue lights flashing outside the shop announced the arrival of the Calvary.

The store was suddenly full of large policemen busily taking statements and hauling the handcuffed chastened culprit out of the shop and into one of the police cars.

After Helen and I had told them our stories, the shop swiftly emptied and Helen suggested a wee cup of tea would do us both good. And do her bump no harm either. A good idea. I concurred and let her fill the kettle.

As I wandered through the back shop door and back behind the counter an impatient familiar voice piped up…

"You *still* huvnae told me how much yer balls are, John!"

Chapter 47
The Moskvitch Moment

Generally, life carried on back in good old Campsie, while The Buy In continued to tread water, even with the odd moment of excitement.

Mary was still enjoying the catering side of life, although she was getting a bit tired of the tearoom. It had never really lived up to our earlier hopes. And here we were actively thinking about having children. Although that might never happen… All of a sudden uncertainty seemed to have taken over

"You know the McGonagall sisters who live up the hill?" Mary asked me over dinner. I racked my brains. "Are they the twins that still try to look identical? They still like dressing the same even though they're in their forties. Although, last time I saw them, one was definitely a dress size larger than her sister… I've always thought of them as a bit weird.

"That's them. They came into the tearoom today and after a bit of beating around the bush, they kind of offered to buy the business! I was a bit taken aback. I thought they were more of the 'ladies who lunch' type who live in the new houses. Apparently, they want to turn it into a 'proper restaurant.' "

"Really? Are they serious?" Did they make you an actual offer?

Now that could solve a couple of potential problems.

"Not quite the offer we couldn't refuse. But enough to pay off the bills." Mary looked perplexed.

"Why don't you give them a call and we'll have a chat tomorrow."

The tearoom had become such a big part of our lives. And Buster's. Thinking back to the start of it, one of the big problems had always been what to do about Buster?

Mary's use of our neighbours had had mixed results. Sarah had got a bit better at handling Buster after the early funeral debacle. She'd take Buster out for walks. But sometimes Buster's boisterousness still got a bit too much for her and he'd break free…

It soon became apparent that Buster was quite a clever dog. He could think things through. He got the hang of where the important places in his life were. Mary was astonished the first time he arrived in the tearoom on his own, trailing his lead. He'd been up the high park and decided he fancied a tearoom biscuit. Then another day he ran back out of the tearoom, jumped on the platform of the double-decker bus as it pulled away from the bus stop a few yards from the shop.

"Where do you think you're going?" Bunty, the bustling regular conductress, accosted him.

Buster sat there and looked at her. No woofs, no barking. Two stops later he was home. Very quickly he became a regular feature. And, he was never charged a fare!

Perhaps the intelligence was in his blood. His official Kennel Club name was Clachan of Campsie, very posh. Apparently, his grandfather belonged to Princess Anne… even posher.

Far better bred than the likes of us human mongrels.

Sometimes, Mary would take him down to the tearoom and a neighbour would walk him home. Inevitably he'd get a treat, a biscuit or a bag of crisps. The customers loved him. He was a good-looking animal and a very friendly beast.

Occasionally I'd get away early and come home via the tearoom. After a bit Buster would follow me out to my van, my pride and joy. A brand new Moskvitch, a Russian built, cheap but distinctive vehicle. He'd jump through the open passenger window and sit proudly on the seat, head hanging out waiting for the wind.

My Moskvitch was a sexy bright beige and one day that caused a problem.

On a quiet afternoon, when I *wasn't* home early, Buster was lurking at the door of the tearoom, hoping for treats from incoming customers. Looking to his right he spotted an identical beige Moskvitch van carefully coming along the virtually deserted road. The driver, an out-of-town lady who was slowly looking for an address, was trying to read street numbers through her open windows…

Buster was excited at the prospect of his master coming home early and maybe taking him for an extra walk, so he ran towards the slow-moving vehicle and joyfully jumped through the passenger window, where he plonked his considerable weight on to the seat. Then, as was his wont, he hung his large grinning head out the window and waited for the wind…

The lady driver, however, was taken a tad by surprise. The sudden clambering of a six stone grinning golden Labrador hurtling through her van window and expertly twisting its body to land perfectly on the passenger seat was, to say the least, unexpected. The whiff of dog breath, as Buster whirled his slobbering head round, leaving a thin trail of drool across her shoulders, was an additional bewildering shock. She frantically heaved on the steering wheel and jammed on the brakes… She wasn't going fast, but it was too late to stop the crunch as the van swerved into Buster's favourite bus stop lurking on the pavement just yards from the tearoom.

Buster didn't hesitate. He sensed trouble. So, he jumped out of the window and galloped up the main street aiming for home, where he knew he would be welcomed by our neighbours if not by us. No waiting for Bunty on the bus that day!

The crunch of the van hitting the bus stop was, of course, heard in the tearoom, so Mary, tea towel in hand, rushed out just in time to see Buster disappearing over the horizon…

Uh oh…

"Are you alright? Are you hurt?" Mary asked the middle-aged woman who was sitting bolt upright staring at the spot where Buster's galloping hind quarters had vanished.

"There was a big dog!" the driver spluttered. "A big dog with a big head!".

"Pardon?" Mary said "Did you hit a dog? Is that why you crashed? Are you ok? Is the dog ok?"

"No, no, no!" She stared wide-eyed at Mary. Then she looked inwards. "Of course I'm ok. He was sitting there right beside me!" She pointed to the empty passenger seat.

"Ah, *your* dog." Mary sounded relieved. "Do you want to come in and have a cup of tea?"

"I don't have a dog! Are ye daft?'" the woman's voice had risen. "This bloody dog jumped through my window and sat on my seat!"

"Really?" Mary thought hard. *Can an insurance company sue a dog's owner for causing an accident? Maybe…*

"Where is this mysterious dog?" Mary asked innocently.

"He ran away!" The woman was pointing to the nothingness on the horizon.

"Oh dear," said Mary. "Are you sure you don't want a cup of tea? There'll be no charge."

"What am I going to tell my husband? What is he going to tell the insurance company? Who would believe it?"

The stricken woman extricated herself from the van; she shook her head as Mary comfortingly held her shoulders and quietly brushed Buster's familiar drool from her coat.

"You'll be fine," Mary soothed. "Come on in. You'll feel better once you've had that cuppa. Don't worry. I believe you. Would you like a biscuit with your tea?"

…………………………………………………………………………

"Yep, I well remember that day." Mary laughed. "That poor woman. She tried to call her husband from the tearoom, to get me to back up her story, but he wasn't in the office. When she finally found the courage to go back behind the wheel, she was like a scared rabbit. Staring everywhere for the ghostly window hopping Labrador."

I finished my tea. "Maybe these twin sisters have arrived at just the right time. Seeing as how we seem to have reached a bit of a crossroads."

"I didn't want to bring it up, but… I heard back from the clinic today." Mary pursed her lips.

I held my breath: "And?"

"Ach, it's all so inconclusive. He wouldn't… or couldn't give me a definitive answer. Talking about percentages and probabilities versus possibilities. I don't know. It's frustrating." She looked at me and gave me a small smile. "What about you? When are your results due?"

My head felt a bit numb. Uncertainty uncertainty. Not where I like to be. “Sometime next week. I’ve got an appointment with Dr Armstrong. Maybe we should both go. What you think?”

“Yes, let’s go together. Then we’ll talk to the twin ladies afterwards. Ok?”

Good. A wee bit of a plan.

Chapter 48
Decisions Decisions

"It's good to see the both of you." Dr Armstrong was a kindly avuncular man, in his mid-fifties. He looked as if he should have been holding a pipe in his hand.

We sat down on the two chairs beside his desk. The fingers of Mary's left hand laced my right hand's fingers. I gave a gentle squeeze.

Dr Armstrong looked up from our files. He pursed his lips and smiled encouragingly.

"You are two pretty fit young people. Neither of you has any disease or particular abnormality. So there's nothing to worry about on that score." He hesitated… long enough: "However, while it's quite possible you could both produce a healthy baby, I'm afraid the probabilities are a good deal lower than the average."

Mary squeezed my hand as she turned to me. I recognised her brave face. I know I was wearing mine.

The doctor continued: "Now, there are surgical and medical procedures we can perform, that might well enhance your probabilities of having children. So long as you realise that there are no guarantees, and it will take a considerable amount of time and commitment from you both. You'll have to talk to each other and decide what you want to do. There's no immediate hurry. Time's still on your side." He sighed. "I'm sorry to be the bearer of such news."

Mary nodded. "So, it looks like we have to come to terms with this new reality." I met her eyes and held on to her hand, a shade tighter. "That's the right phrase: 'come to terms with it.' Ok, Doctor, you've given us a lot to think about."

He stood up and shook both of our hands. "You are two fine young people, who I'm sure would make fine parents. If you really want that to happen, I know you'll find a way. Good luck to you both."

I felt the urge to push my shoulders back as we walked out of the surgery. I reached for Mary's hand as I saw her looking at the half a dozen or so children fidgeting in the waiting room, as we walked towards the door. *Aye aye aye…*

Mary's strong. We're both strong. We'll deal with this…

"I think you were right in calling it a crossroads," Mary said as I let Buster off the lead. We were walking towards the old abandoned railway line, just beyond the nail factory at the bottom of the village.

"We have to make decisions," I said. "We've an opportunity to sell Country Fayre. That might never come again. But Mary Caters as a part-time business still does ok, and I know you still get a buzz from feeding those hungry faces. I think it's worth holding on to. But we'd have to find somewhere else with a kitchen and storage."

My mind was on practical, business stuff. Stuff where we had an element of control. Not this 'new reality' of not having babies. That seemed hard, and beyond our control.

Mary stopped me as we reached the old line. Spindly trees creaked in the breeze. Buster wasn't far away. She turned me round and held both my hands. "Did you know Rhona and Graham have applied to adopt another baby?"

I felt a little dizzy. What was she saying?

Mary stared at me. I recognised that same unblinking stare from way back. Right back at the beginning. Two teenagers sitting at the Formica-covered table in the Bundoran Club. Challenging one another to blink first.

I held her stare as I contemplated the pros and cons of adopting a child. *That's a major commitment. In a way, much more than a couple just having a baby. That happens every day. But there's maybe a kiddie who needs a new mum and dad… And there's maybe a couple… a good couple, who could be good for that kiddie… Could we be that couple? Could we be that mum and dad?*

We said nothing.

Just held each other's hands and looked deep…

Then I blinked.

“So… we’re going to adopt some wee wean, are we?” I found myself nervously smiling. This was uncharted territory.

“Well, you hate being indecisive. So let’s make some decisions.”

“Let’s take Buster to the Swan for a treat. I could do with a pint and a plan.

I looked round for Buster. He was unusually close by. Maybe he felt the mood.

“Hi, Buster. Do you want one of Jock’s pies?” He woofed and waggled his rear end as we turned and walked up to the comfort zone of the Swan Inn.

Chapter 49
Clean Break

"There's a queue of folk wanting to view the house! It's mental! What should I do?" Mary was shouting down the phone as I was trying to serve Mrs McClure and her noisy grandkids, who were taking forever to choose their ten-pence mixtures.

"Ach, we shouldn't have put the address in the paper. We should have got an estate agent after all… Sorry, Mrs McClure, you want a quarter of soor plooms for Mr McClure? That'll be fine… Hi, Mary, you'll have to manage. I've got my own queue here. I'll try and come home early. Hang on in there!"

An hour later I had extricated myself from The Buy In and was on my way home.

A queue of buyers? Must be too cheap.

It's all very well being decisive if you know what you're doing, I thought, as I worried about Mary coping with a bunch of strangers traipsing through the house. It had all seemed so straightforward. Once we had accepted the 'Dolly Twins' offer, as Mary had named them, we had a bunch of things to do.

After our soul-searching chat that night and later in the Swan, we'd decided it was best to go for a clean break: sell the tearoom and our little house and find another house with a big enough kitchen and garage to carry on with Mary Caters. But the hardest part, especially for Mary, was the realisation that we'd have to move back to Glasgow, where she'd discovered, the chances of a successful adoption should be greater. Simply put, they had more children looking for parents.

Once we'd thought out our plans and made the deal with the Dolly Twins, I unearthed a whole new burst of energy. "Right, now that's been dealt with I'll check out houses for sale not too far from The Buy In." Two days later, after driving around looking for 'For Sale' boards I found a three-bed semi with a garage that ticked all our boxes. A knock on the door, a wander round the house: the living room was twice the size of ours; the kitchen was next to the side door of the garage, with a nice wee garden back and front. Three rooms and a bathroom upstairs, all with room to swing the proverbial cat. Perfect! A quick phone call to our in-family lawyer, James, and the offer was accepted.

Just one problem… Mary hadn't seen the house…

"You've put in an offer for our new home and I haven't even seen it. I don't even know where Garrowhill is? What if I don't like it? How could you, John?"

Uh oh.

"Well… we'd talked about the kind of place we were looking for and this one fits the bill. It's in a nice area, shops and pubs down the road. Ten minutes from The Buy In. Two primary schools within walking distance…"

She glowered. "That's a low shot!"

I put my hands up, palms out. "Sorry, Mary, I was just trying to be efficient. The main thing is it was a fixed price, 'cos the sellers, who're retiring, have bought their new house already, so they'd reduced the price… And they had another viewer due to see it later today. It was just lucky timing. So I called James from their phone."

That lit a fuse: "You what? And he thought that was fine, did he? Never mind the little woman, us big men can make the big decisions! Have either of you ever heard of Women's Lib? Those Victorian attitudes are well gone. This is the bloody 1970s. Wait till I call Joyce. God help James tonight!" With that she stomped into the kitchen and slid the door shut with a bang.

Oh, please don't smash that glass door; we have to sell this place now.

The next day, I took the day off and made sure Mary had time off from the tearoom. It hadn't been an easy night… "Right, let's see what you think about this Garrowhill house. If you really hate it, I'm sure James could do something," I said, more in hope than knowledge.

Mary was still not a happy lady. Brow furrowed. "We'll take Buster too. And if he doesn't like it, it's not going to happen!"

My God. The bloody dog has the power of veto!

"Yes, dear. C'mon, Buster, fancy some new walkies?"

As we approached Garrowhill, I carefully drove round the side streets of the new house. Happening on small wooded parklands and tennis courts. Then, having briefly explored the previous day, I drove a couple of streets away from Springhill Road, where our potential future lay. And there was a big patch of open ground. Perfect for dog walking. People were throwing sticks for their dogs. I pulled in and, avoiding Mary's eyes, I turned my head round to talk to Buster. "Fancy some walkies, Buster?" Stupid question.

"Don't think you're that clever, Mister. Buster can wait until we've seen this 'perfect' house in the middle of this suburban jungle."

I'd been rumbled.

Two minutes later, leaving a disappointed Buster in the van, we were inside the house. Mrs Brown, the owner, very pleased to see us, gave us the tour. Then she offered us a cup of tea.

"So, what do you think, Mrs Dickson? I was a bit surprised your husband put in his offer without speaking to you yesterday. He must *really* know what you like. And *you* must really trust his judgement. You take milk and sugar?"

Mary swallowed hard. I actually trembled as I waited for the sparks to fly. "Mary doesn't take milk, thanks." I nodded to our hostess.

"Excuse me." Mary was very controlled, but I could sense the magma bursting to explode beneath the surface. My turn to swallow hard. "I'm quite capable of speaking for myself, John! That's correct. I don't take milk, thanks. But my husband does. Yes, he does know what I like, as I know what he likes, such as milk in his tea. And other things… However, one of the main things I like is to know what's going on." She stared coldly at me then paused. I held my breath, while Mrs Brown looked tense. Her cup rattled on its saucer. Just a bit.

Should I speak?

Nah…

"So, I was even more surprised than you were, Mrs Brown, when John came home last night to tell me we'd bought your house." She glared at me. "I was quite angry, wasn't I?"

I nodded numbly but held her gaze. I managed not to let my cup and saucer rattle… Victory.

Mrs Brown looked even more uncomfortable as Mary carried on. "However, what I find myself most annoyed about…" she breathed very deeply, then looked around… "is that he was right! This house is just what we're looking for in the next stage in our lives." She glowered at me again. "Grrr. But I hate that you're right!"

Mrs Brown looked a little less tense. She placed her cup and saucer on the coffee table.

As did I. "Would it be ok if we brought our dog, Buster, in for a few moments, Mrs Brown? Apparently, he has the power of veto…" I smiled at Mary, who shook her head. *Thin ice, my man.*

Buster strained at the lead as I walked him up the short, steep drive. Thankfully, he didn't do any 'business' in the front garden, but bounded right into the house, where he ran up and down the stairs and in and out of the hall and lounge before settling down with the bowl of water thoughtfully provided by our hostess.

Mary ruffled his ears as Mrs Brown, now visibly relaxed asked: "And so… what do you think of the house, Buster?"

"Woof!" Buster waggled his rear end and grinned. Deal done!

Chapter 50

On the Way to a Burn's Night

A few weeks later it was all sorted. The Campsie house was sold to the first of many viewers who came through the door. My copying the Garrowhill vendor's concept of 'first legal offer of a fixed price' had worked too well as a draw. Maybe we could have got a little more if we'd been patient. But we, or rather I, were being *decisive*.

So here we were, back in the city we were born in. A bit more living space and close enough to The Buy In that I could again pop home for lunch. Yay!

Buster had been introduced to the locals in the Clachan Bar. They loved his party piece of running behind the bar and stealing packets of crisps, then bringing them to the front and bursting them open. He was in a home from home. Quite a few characters there: from the ice cream van guy who always wore what looked like an inside out sheepskin coat, to the morose-looking shopkeeper who spent every night pumping ten pence pieces into the one-armed bandit. Then there were the three old duffers who Mary managed to introduce to her mum and Big Aunt Peggy in a moment of madness.

The Clachan could be reached in five minutes by walking down the road. Or via Buster's preferred route across the large area of open ground beside the railway line, something else we hadn't had in Campsie. (Though we did miss the country air and the view from the back garden.) We discovered we could go by train to the west end of Glasgow. Marvellous! We were back to being City Slickers. Or rather; Suburban Slickers.

Mary had a good long chat with Rhona about adoptions. Sister to sister. I stayed away. Then I got my briefing, sitting across the table in our new house. Mary had a pile of pamphlets and leaflets in front of her.

Here we go. Here we go…

"Rhona says there are two routes to adoption. We can apply through the Church like they have, but we'd have to be pretty much involved in our local parish and we're brand new here. The other factor is the Church has a whole extra layer of rules and commitments that I don't think you and I would be comfortable with. Do you agree?"

I thought back, "The last time I was in church was the day of our wedding. It'd be just a tad hypocritical to expect them to help us now. I'm not sure I'd want to go down the religious route anyway. A baby isn't born with a religion, even if the parents have strong beliefs."

Mary shrugged. "I don't entirely agree with you there. But it's really important that we both agree to follow one route. Yes?"

"Yip. And that route is?"

"I've read all the leaflets and been to the library as well as talking to Rhona. What we have to do is contact the Social Work department, because they're the people who deal with the mums who're giving up their children for adoption…"

Mary's eyes welled up as she spoke. "That's so sad, isn't it? It makes me feel as if we're taking advantage of some poor soul's misfortune. Can we do this, John?"

I knew how she felt. Somehow, saying the words "Mums giving up their children" changed the concept of solving our problem into the reality of some young woman's life being so impossible she has to give up her child. How hard must that be?

I looked at Mary. "You're right to feel sad. I feel sad as well, thinking about the plight of these mums. On the other hand, we're offering a solution. We're here to help. Our job is to give a child a home. Our job is to do our best to look after that child and make him or her as happy as we can. Do *you* think we can do that?"

Mary was startled. "Of course we can! I know it'll mean big changes for us and the way we live. But I think we're adaptable. That's all depending on whether the Social Workers, or whoever, reckon we're suitable for the role. Rhona says that's the hardest part!"

I was surprised. "Really? Well, I'm not worried about that. I think it's time to light that touch paper. Do you want to make the call or should I?"

Mary gathered her leaflets. "I think I'll make that call." She smiled serenely. "Love you, John. You'll make a great dad."

A week or so later the first of many forms came through the door. The big message was that this process would not be quick, or certain. So, in the meantime, carry on with your life as normal. So, we did…

I was enjoying my easier commute to The Buy In while Mary organised the catering business to work from home. Her old catering van had finally given up on her, so we'd decided to go for a different transport solution. Mary bought a big old Nissan estate that could seat seven folk with a tow bar. Meanwhile, I arranged for a local coachbuilder to create a small trailer that could live in our new drive when it wasn't being used for catering functions. And I could occasionally use it for the Cash and Carry.

Mary Caters had by now earned a great reputation: "Best steak pie I've ever tasted," was often genuinely spluttered by her appreciative guests as they toasted the bride and groom, or maybe even their lately departed.

We sorted out the single garage beside the house as a store for all the catering stuff. You know; dishes and cutlery and pots and pans. Tons of it. It was all very heavy and I was usually the lucky one who got to pack the new 'wee trailer' before any catering do.

The trailer was really a small business compromise. It could carry a van load but cost nothing when not in use. It fitted onto the quite steep drive beside the house and looked like a mid-blue horsebox for a dwarf horse. The rear door opened down from the top and formed a short sharp ramp. Once you'd manoeuvred yourself inside, your back nearly broke positioning the heavy plastic bread trays absolutely full of wally dishes, as well as containers of, literally, home-made steak pies, tatties and veg.

I'd strained my back a bit, so one Saturday in January I'd managed to persuade Alan to help me out with the loading. Alan had recently changed jobs. He'd discovered that while his white-collar job at the Electricity Board was a 'cushy number,' he could earn a good deal more working as a bus driver for Glasgow Corporation. So, he'd joined up and he loved it. As a bonus he even became really proficient at playing snooker, as there was a full-sized table in the rest area of the bus garage, just up from Mum and Dad's house in Riddrie.

We'd been out for a beer the night before and I knew he was due to work a 'split shift' the next day. Before he started the second half, I reckoned he could pop down to Garrowhill. He duly obliged. After we piled the last crates into the trailer, Alan gasped “That’s a pint or two ye owe me. I’ve gotta go, folk could be waiting to catch my bus.”

This particular Saturday, Mary had a Burns’ Supper of 150 hungry guests to cater for in faraway Auchinairn Bowling Club. So, the trailer was more than usually laden as the guests were due to get a first course of haggis which was packed in even more ‘borrowed’ bread crates perched on the top of the pile, completely filling the interior of the trailer.

Mary gathered her troops, a motley mixed crew of new East End gems and some of her lasses from Campsie. The staff still included the sonsiest lassie and chief cook, Thelma, who busily held the kitchen together. Out front she’d still retained the services of the ferocious ‘Big Jessie’ as Head Waitress.

While Mary went over her itinerary and checklist with her staff, I manoeuvred her American-sized Japanese estate, perfectly designed to transport a full team of gaggling waitresses and kitchen staff, into position. This meant blocking the narrow suburban street while I lowered the oh-so-heavy trailer onto the ball joint at the rear of the car.

“Get your backside into it!” I recognised Big Jessie’s exhortation. As I hurried, Mary and the wild bunch were jabbering at each other and squeezing the eight various-sized bottoms into the six seats that didn’t include the driver’s. At least I had a seat to myself…

Finally, we set off. Slowly lumbering up Barrachnie Road, then west along Edinburgh Road.

It was around 4 o’clock. Everything was fine. The girls were noisily swapping gossip and looking forward to the wee ‘refreshment’ Mary would treat them to after the venue’s kitchen was prepared and all the tables were laid out and set. For all they were a bit of a rough crowd they were remarkably professional in creating a great function and feeding all those hungry faces with tasty hot food and a bit of banter. The proof was in the hefty tips.

The lights at the junction of Edinburgh Road and Gartcraig Road were at red. I slowly came to a stop. I had been towing trailers since I was seventeen when I’d helped Big Peter out and regarded myself as a pretty competent driver, conscious of the need to take your time and avoid sudden acceleration or braking. There was a lot of fragile cargo behind me in the dwarf horsebox. And I didn't want Big Jessie shouting at me for a broken dish…

Even if I was technically the boss, that didn't stop me being terrified of her…

The lights changed to green. I turned the corner into Gartcraig Road which is fairly wide and started to pull away after the turn.

There were screams and shouts from the far reaches of the back of the car. "Whit are ye shoutin' about?" says me.

Big Jessie retorted, "Ya stupid lookin' Galloot!"

I looked back to my left, and between the backs of all their heads I caught a glimpse of the trailer lurching under its own steam, aiming straight for the front of a parked Gas Board Transit van.

Nothing could stop it. As I jammed on the brakes with the car load of assorted women screaming in disharmony, I caught sight of the trailer, with its front jockey wheel crunching itself under the bumper of the van. The short revolving pole which lifts and drops the jockey wheel folded back on itself to form a kind of grotesque barb which, as it wedged under the crumpling nose of the van, forced me to realise this wasn't going to be our easiest gig.

Then it didn't get any better.

"Look out!" somebody shouted, "Quick… Catch them!"

The crash of the trailer into the van had twisted its chassis and the rear ramp door flew open, crunching down on the road. Mayhem ensued. The sound of hundreds of those precious wally dishes shattering simultaneously was almost drowned out by the screeching of the girls as they clambered out of the car and heroically tried to catch the dozens of individually sized, perfectly round, homemade haggises as they rolled down the road, bursting and exploding as they were caught under the wheels of passing cars. The motorists and their passengers were just a wee bit confused by the sight of a bunch of formally dressed waitresses in their black and whites running down the road chasing strange wee balls.

Then the day took on an even more surreal note as everything and everyone came to a dazed stop and we contemplated how we were going to fix this tricky situation.

How were we going to get the trailer out from under the van? How were we going to deal with the angry van driver who was just emerging from his house with a half-eaten jammy piece in his hand? What about all those hungry faces that would soon start trickling into the bowling club? Where were we gonna get another 150 individually made haggises in a hurry?

As I was standing uselessly in the middle of the road, a number 6 Glasgow Corporation bus in all its green and orange glory slowly came to a stop right beside me and the door flapped open. There was my wee brother Alan, on his split shift, sitting in the driver's seat and looking out at the scenes of chaos and destruction, and he could see how much trouble we were in.

Big Jessie looked at the near-empty bus, and recognising Alan from previous encounters, shouted, "Howz about bussin' us tae Auchinairn, Alan?"

Alan looked thoughtful. "I don't think so, my inspector widnae like it. But I'll soon be finishin' ma shift."

He looked around at the mess on the road, glanced at my slumped shoulders, then grinned. "Fancy a pint and a haggis supper?"

I got the irony, and so wanted to just say yes. However, I had to dredge up the energy to organise a plan B, and deal with the trailer and the van driver who was not a happy chappie.

Thankfully, everything that happens in life isn't always bad. One of our East End waitresses, a spirited teenager called Wee Angela, shouted: "Shuggy! How's yer Mammy?" The angry van driver looked at Angela in her professional garb and realised he was staring at his Aunty Nellie's sister's niece, who prided herself in being Big Jessie's apprentice…

Sorted!

So, after a promise of severe compensation and just a bit of persuasion from Big Jessie and Angela, our newest best friend let us transfer the salvageable items from the trailer into his disfigured van. A second whirlwind of blacks and whites ensued; the trailer was emptied and wrestled from under the van.

Eventually our sorry convoy limped into Auchinairn, just a tad late. We'd emptied every butcher's haggis stock en route. Then Mary and her team had to work their magic, utilising the hall's assorted dishes and mixing the shop bought substitutes with what remained of the originals. The customers never did know the adventures their grinning waitresses had gone through just to feed their hungry faces.

The proof was in the hefty tips…

Chapter 51

Change Isn't So Easy

"There's a letter from the Social Work Department!" Mary shouted up the stairs as I was brushing my teeth.

"Open it, then. I'll be down in a minute." I rinsed out my mouth and pulled on a jumper.

Mary was sitting at the table. "It says here a Social Worker has been appointed to deal with our adoption application. A Mr Jamie McDuff will contact us to arrange a preliminary meeting."

She looked up at me. "So, we've got our own social worker eh?"

"Who'd have thought?" I replied. "Jamie McDuff? Not a name that oozes confidence. Well, that's the ball rolling. This time next year we could be a bigger family! That includes Buster of course."

At the sound of his name Buster lifted his head and cocked his ears inquisitively. *Walkies? You haven't said walkies.*

"In the meantime, life carries on. You've got nothing till Saturday, have you?"

Mary looked around. "That's right. I think I might just whizz round the house and make it nice and shiny, just in case this Jamie makes a surprise appearance." She gave me an anxious look. "Actually, I'm a wee bit nervous. What if they don't want us? That would be terrible. I haven't talked about it to anybody except Rhona. Have you told anyone?

I shook my head. "Remember, when we spoke about it, we said let's keep it private for now. But I think I might like to let Mum and Dad know. What do you think?" Mary nodded as she re-read the letter again.

The prospect of some stranger called Jamie coming into our house to judge us was an uncomfortable feeling. I suppose we're going to have to go through the pain to get the gain, I philosophised. Sighing, I turned round and went back upstairs to get dressed for the day ahead.

The time came a couple of weeks later. The doorbell rang. Mary had a tray of her best china and biscuits sitting on the coffee table. She'd dressed as 'Mumsy' as she could, with a light cotton full skirt and a puff-sleeved blouse. I gave her the thumbs up as I went to the door. The new term 'yummy Mummy' came to mind.

"Hello, I'm Jamie McDuff, your appointed social worker. You must be John. I'm very pleased to meet you. I shook his hand then ushered him into the living room. Mary was standing by the fireplace with her hands behind her. Not her normal posture. *She's nervous.*

Mary gave him her widest smile as she shook hands while trying not to be too obvious in sizing up our judge and jury. I was just coming in behind him. Jamie looked rather young, I thought. He was strangely wearing a pair of denim dungarees with a dishevelled corduroy jacket over a chequered shirt. Bright red socks peeked above his dessert boots.

How people dress normally doesn't matter to me in the slightest. Maybe it was because his purpose in our lives was to come to a conclusion as to whether Mary and I were good enough to be allowed to become parents, triggered an instinctive urge to judge *him.* All I knew about him was that he wore unconventional clothing. And bizarrely, that rankled, considering I'd had aspirations of hippiness just a few years previously.

We all sat down and Mary served tea. I managed not to say, "Do you want to be mother?" as she poured Darjeeling from our best china teapot.

Jamie rummaged in his satchel and pulled out our file. It was thin. "Just so you know… I'm not here to judge you." He looked from Mary to me. *Really?* "My role in this process is to engage with you both. We *will* have to talk quite deeply about your current life. Your backgrounds, how you relate to your parents and siblings. How much you know about the adoption process, and what you think being parents actually entails. What are your hopes and dreams…?" He went on, glancing at his notes as he spoke.

Mary and I listened carefully to his every word, looking at each other as he spoke.

After about ten minutes I had to interrupt. "I think we understand the necessity of the process, Jamie. But it might help if we get to know *you* a bit better." Jamie sat back, his face neutral. I went on: "How many adoptive parents have you managed to match with suitable children?" As if I had a choice as to whom our social worker would be…

Mary glanced at me but said nothing. She looked at him intensely. Jamie sat upright. "Actually, you and Mary are my second potential adoptive couple. I recently placed a little baby girl, but of course, I can't divulge any confidential information."

"So, you're quite new to this then? Do you enjoy it?" I asked, carefully. *Do we want to be dealt with by a newbie?*

Jamie relaxed. "To tell you the truth, this is maybe the best job in social work. We haven't really spoken yet about your case, but here I am, in a nice house, sitting having a delicious cup of tea poured from a china teapot. This is not the kind of environment most social workers find themselves, on a day-to-day basis. And, the best bit is, if it all works out, we get a definite result. The child has a new, loving home. The adoptive parents have a new family, and the natural mothers, and occasionally, the natural father, have a chance to move on with their lives. So yes. I enjoy it." He opened a Blue Riband and picked up his teacup.

"That's a good answer, Jamie." Mary smiled and nodded to me.

Once the tea and biscuits were done, Jamie started the form filling in earnest. He explained that this was just the beginning.

"So, to pass muster against all your criteria, how long is this process going to take before we know if we are going to be acceptable to this panel you've told us about?" He'd been sitting there for two hours, and I was feeling just a bit numb.

Mary was just as interested in that answer. "My worry is that there's some wee toddler living out there, in some form of Limbo, and they're destined to be living here with us, but they're growing up without us."

Jamie looked taken aback: "Sorry, Mary, you mentioned a toddler. Why?"

I tried to nudge her foot without Jamie noticing… Mary and I had had this conversation…

Mary took a deep breath. "John and I have talked about this endlessly, as you can imagine. And I've decided I would rather have a wee boy or girl who's not a baby. I have a picture in my mind of a two or three-year-old toddler… who needs a mother even more than a baby… 'Cos new babies are certain to be snapped up." She gulped.

Jamie's training kicked in. "That's fine Mary. At the moment it's all hypothetical." He looked at me." And how do you feel, John? Do you not want a baby either?" His voice moved up a notch.

I'd been worried about this. And here we were, having to deal with it on the first day.

I shook my head. "I have no objection to us having as near to a new-born baby as we can. On the other hand, I would welcome some young child who'd maybe been through the mill. I think this is where your professionalism is going to come into its own, Jamie."

Jamie called it a day after that. Packed up his paraphernalia, shook our hands, and told us he'd contact us about his next appointment. *Oh dear.* We're *not 'normal,' he'll have to talk to his superiors. But we won't get to talk to them…*

We shut the door after him.

Mary opened her arms. "I need a hug!" I did too.

We'd popped into Mum and Dad's during the day when we knew they'd be on their own. Phil and Andy were both in high school. Alan was out and about on the Number 6. And Thomas was actually busy leaving home!

"So, what's this about Thomas?" Mary asked, as Mum placed a plate of ham and eggs in front of Dad. He'd always managed to stick to his routine of coming home for lunch every day. And he always had his plateful of hot food served to him. Every now and then Mum erupted. But the next day his lunch would be ready and waiting for him.

"It's actually quite exciting," Mum replied, taking her seat across the table from Dad, who was concentrating on masticating his ham and eggs. "He's found a flat in Kirkintilloch, round the corner from his friend, Dennis. He's moving in over the weekend. I think he was going to talk to you about using your wee trailer for shifting furniture? Help yourself to tea and toast, there're loads." She picked up her knife and fork and attacked her own lunch.

"That's big news." I said. "In a couple of years, you'll be rattling around in this big house." I felt strangely nervous. Mary was messing around with the kettle beside the sink. She turned to me and raised her eyebrows. Well?

I breathed… “Well, we’ve kind of got news too…” Mum’s head spun towards Mary who slowly shook her head.

Dad interrupted his chewing. “News? What’s going on then?”

Mary rescued me. “A few months ago, John and I decided to investigate why we haven’t had any babies.” Her eyes caught mine. I looked at Mum. Dad concentrated on buttering his toast. “We didn’t want to tell anyone. Not till we found out.” She bit her lip.

I took up the story: “The bottom line is… we’re very unlikely to have any children… naturally.” There…It’s out! Phew.

Dad stopped chewing his toast. He looked from me to Mary. “So, whose fault is it then?”

Mum’s shoulders fell. “Jackie!” Dad shook his head in bewilderment.

Mary sat down and poured tea for her and me. “John and I made a pact. We know the medical reason why we probably can’t have children. And we agreed never to say who’s at ‘fault.’ ‘Cos it’s nobody’s *‘fault.’* Ok?” She supped her tea. Dad picked up his toast and kept his eyes down.

My turn. “The main reason we’ve popped in today is to let you guys know that we’ve decided to go for adoption. We saw our social worker for the first time yesterday.”

Mum blinked. She looked at Dad, who’d actually stopped eating.

There was a moment’s silence as they took in the concept.

Mum almost shouted; “That’s wonderful! What a wonderful way to react to what must have been devastating news.” She rose from her kitchen chair. “C’mere you two.” We both stood up awkwardly and she hugged us so tightly we could hardly breathe.

“Ok, Mum… It’s ok.” I extricated myself from her grip, as she continued to hug Mary. “I’m so proud of you. Both of you.” She turned to Dad, who’d gone back to finishing his tea. “What do you think, Jackie?”

Dad put his cup back in its saucer. "Do you realise how much it costs to have weans? I mean, I can tell you. We've had five of you. Having weans is a very expensive hobby. Now, we never *planned* any of you. You just happened."

Mum's arms were in the air as she interjected. "For God's sake, Jackie. What are you saying?"

"I'm just stating the obvious." He stared at Mum then looked at Mary then me. "You're not daft, and neither are you." He pointed towards Mary. "If you're going to adopt a child, be prepared for the expenses involved. When a baby turns up in the natural order of things, you have to cope… But you're literally asking for it. That said, I'm sure you know what you're doing. So, good luck with it." He stood up and shook my hand, then Mary's. Mum glared at him. There would be sparks when we'd gone…

We left after giving them strict instructions not to tell anyone, as there was an enormous amount of uncertainty ahead.

"Your dad's something else, isn't he?" Mary said as we drove back home.

"As Mum says, 'Sometimes he's at his Jackiest!' I'll bet, if and when we've got our new wee baby, or toddler, or whatever, he'll be the first to want to play. I remember climbing on his back, pretending he was a horse, while Thomas ran around us on his trike. I was the cowboy and he was the Indian. Then it was Thomas's turn. Although that was a long time ago. Maybe he's just got grumpier."

"I think grumpy fits the bill." Mary grinned. "It's not a big deal. The big deal is going through the 'process.' Oh, I hate that word! It's so, so, bureaucratic. This ought to be a joyful experience." She hunched down in the passenger seat.

Five months and many visits from Jamie later, the doorbell rang. Mary answered it. "Hi, Jamie, you coming to check the contents of our fridge again? I've made sure it's full of fresh fruit and vegetables this time… Not a drop of beer to be seen!"

Jamie chuckled as he walked into the living room. "Very funny, Mary. I know you were having some of your musical friends up last time.

It was never a problem. I've just never seen a fridge *completely* full of beer before… No, that's not true. There were a couple of bottles of Lanliq for, what was his name? Aye… Wee Robbie. He must be quite a character. Hello, John. How are you?"

I shook his hand. "I'm fine, Jamie. Are we any further forward? This has been quite a marathon."

We all sat down, again. Jamie pulled out our file. A lot thicker now, I noticed. "I've got good news and I've got not so good news." He looked from Mary to me.

Okay?

"The good news is that the panel think the two of you would make excellent adoptive parents." He smiled.

And the sting in the tail?

"The not so good news is that they don't understand Mary's insistence in not wanting to adopt a baby. Apparently, this is a first. And I'll be honest, I find it hard to grasp, and I've got to know the both of you pretty well over the last few months."

Mary had her fists to her mouth. "Does that mean… does that mean… we've been rejected?" Saucer eyes staring from Jamie to me.

I felt a sickening ball forming in the pit of my stomach. 'S'not fair!

Jamie looked uncomfortable. "That's not quite where we're at."

I had to butt in," Not quite? Is this some kind of cruel game? You've asked us to delve into the innermost corners of our souls. Opinionate about every member of our families. Hypothesise about how we might react if our unknown child runs in front of a car. Open up about our deepest hopes and dreams. And we bloody well have! What's the problem? Mary is offering to look after and rear a child that's not a baby? You don't have to 'get it.' You just have to say… Thank you!" I sat back on the settee. *Calm it, John.*

I could see Jamie's training kicking in as he spoke in a very calm voice: "I understand why you're upset. But, I'm on your side. Please believe me. Unfortunately, the panel don't know you the way I've come to know you."

Mary's eyes were welling up as she poured another cup of tea. "So, what more are we supposed to do? We're empty. You've emptied us. "

Jamie tried his best not to say, "Calm down, dear." But his hands said it. "What my line manager has proposed is that both of you go before a Resolution Panel and explain to them, rather than me, how and why you should be accepted as adoptive parents"

"Eh? And who's going to be on this 'Resolution Panel'? Even more social workers? This is ridiculous!"

Cool it, John. Breathe…

Mary tried to lighten the tone. "That sounds like fun. Should I practice my dancing? I do a mean eight-some reel all on my own. It usually brings the house down!" I laughed out loud. I had seen it a number of times.

Jamie scratched his head: "I know this is not what you'd hoped for by this point, but this will be the last stage of the approval process. I know you hate that word, Mary." He looked at me. "The panel meets next Tuesday at 2pm. Is that a suitable time?"

Chapter 52

The Panel Game

"Well," I ventured. "The worst-case scenario is that they say no. And that means we'll be free to have a nice comfy life, just the two of us. The world would be our oyster. We don't have to put ourselves through this, you know, Mary."

We were in the waiting area, outside the boardroom of the social work department. A grey, soulless office block in the centre of the city. Artificial plants in the corner of the room. Chipped table in front of the sagging leatherette sofa.

Jamie had briefed us before we came in. "Everything in my report, which I've let you see, and *that* could cost me my job, advises the panel to accept your application." He looked at Mary, pleadingly. "You'll somehow have to get them to understand why you don't want a baby…" Mary nodded and sat tall.

I asked: "And tell me again, who's on this panel?"

Jamie sighed. His training was well stretched. "There are four senior social workers. Three of them have extensive experience of adoption cases… And a city councillor who's on the Social Work Committee." He grimaced.

I shook my head: So, we've to be judged, not just by a bloody phalanx of social workers but a bloody local politician as well. And all this is voluntary, we must be mad!

The double doors opened and Jamie led us in. He would take notes but wasn't allowed to speak.

We sat down. Two against five.

Two grey-haired women and three grey-haired men.

All wearing artificial smiles.

The cityscape was visible through the large window behind them. The one in the middle introduced himself as the chair and explained that as the politician, he represented the people of Glasgow, but he would be guided by his professional colleagues.

That's comforting.

One of the grey-haired women offered a thin smile and spoke: "We realise this is a bit of an ordeal for you both, but as custodians of the most vulnerable people in our society, especially children, who are not able to grow up in a normal, natural family, it's our duty to be especially careful where, and with whom, we place those children. We can't afford to make mistakes." The others nodded sagely

One of the grey-haired men lifted our report. The one we shouldn't have seen. "Mr McDuff, your social worker has done a very thorough job in compiling this report. We've all read it with great interest." He looked across at his colleagues who all nodded sagely. "You come across as a bright, ambitious couple who would rise to the challenge of looking after a little one. And do your best to give that child a loving home." They all nodded sagely. "Unfortunately, there is one major sticking point…" He looked at his colleagues, then straight at Mary. "Why *don't* you want to adopt a baby, Mrs Dickson?"

They all leaned forward as Mary cleared her throat: "I'm here, sorry, we're here," she smiled at me, "because nearly a year ago we discovered we're very unlikely to be able to have children naturally. However, after an awful lot of thought, and talk, and more talk, we decided that we have a lot to offer a child. It would be a waste of our talents and experience if we didn't have a chance to pass on what we know, and who we are. So, we have put ourselves through your 'process,' a word I have come to detest, to be judged on whether society, that is, you, think we are fit and proper people to be allowed to become 'unnatural' parents." She paused to take a drink of water. I smiled in encouragement.

"Your question is why don't I want a baby? I have a number of reasons: I don't want to feel I'm pursuing the next best thing to the natural baby I'm not going to have. There's something fake about waiting for someone else to have their baby, so that we can have it. But mainly, the positive reason that I want a toddler is because it's possible that no-one else wants them. And they've probably been through the mill. *And*, if we're given a toddler that leaves a baby for some other adoptive couple. I also think a toddler might need a new mother and father more than a new-born baby. That's quite a few reasons."

I squeezed her hand.

The grey heads conferred. The politician spoke. “We hear what you say. One of the practical problems we have is that the application form doesn’t have a box for two- to five-year-olds… If we ticked the zero to five-year-olds box, would that be a solution?”

Then he winked…

Mary and I looked at each other, and then faced the panel…

And nodded…

Sagely.

Chapter 53

Buster's Room Service.

"It's arrived! It's arrived!" Mary excitedly tore open the envelope from the Social Work Department. "We are delighted to inform you that you have been accepted as potential adoptive parents. Your case worker, Jamie McDuff, will be in touch to explain the next stage of the adoption process. (I still hate that word!) Please understand: we can give no timescale as to when a suitable child may be placed with you. We appreciate your patience and understanding."

Her face beamed as she grabbed and hugged me. "There we go, Sweetheart." I grinned. "We *are* going to be parents! Hopefully in the not-too-distant future."

Mary sat down with a contemplative sigh. "This whole experience is like a bureaucratic pregnancy. Its six months since we first applied. But I don't have a due date yet! Right then, let's relax… and breathe!"

I felt a tremendous sense of relief and was so happy for Mary. The tension had been telling on her; and me too, probably. Now all we had to do was depend on Oor Jamie to fight our corner in the depths of the social work world that decided who are the best adoptive parents for a particular child. All we need now is patience…

Mary smiled and unexpectedly waved an opened envelope at me.

What's this?

"I haven't told you about this, have I?" She almost sing-songed, teasingly.

"No, you haven't. Although I suspect it's a good thing, or you wouldn't have that grin on your face."

"Well, you know how I get the catering magazines and trade journals, to keep up-to-date with when Steak Pie Dinners are going to be the trendiest dish on the menu?"

"Uh-huh?"

"Well, I entered a competition…" She held her breath… "And won! A weekend break for two at the five-star Peebles Hydro Hotel! One of the biggest, poshest hotels in Scotland. And… Roll them drums… It's to include a tour of their kitchens conducted by their Head Chef Ian MacFarlane! How good is that? Apparently, the kitchens are the size of a football pitch!"

I was genuinely amazed. "When did this happen? Why didn't you tell me? We could have done with some good news."

"I actually got the letter the day before the panel day. I couldn't bear to think about anything so frivolous at that point. But now we know we're on the list we can relax for a bit. Fancy a free luxury weekend, Mister?" she asked with a wink.

"It all sounds brilliant. Wait a minute. What about Buster? You know nobody will want to look after him, and kennels are so-o expensive. Remember the bill for Phillipshill? Almost as dear as the Jersey hotel. I wonder if the Hydro let's dogs stay? Just ask them when you're making the booking, yeh? How's about next weekend. I noticed you've got nothing in the *Mary Caters* diary. We sure could do with some relaxation…"

Later Mary gave me the lowdown. "I've checked with the hotel. They're quite happy to let a six-stone adventurous Golden Labrador reside in their fine establishment. The lady I spoke with sounded quite enthusiastic when I told her that Buster's parentage included one of Princess Anne's Labradors. I didn't bother to explain that his pedigree is a damn sight purer than us mongrels. That's next weekend sorted." She put her arms around me and gave me a loving hug.

Aye, roll on Friday…

It was a fine spring day as we drove the big estate down the twisting country roads. Buster liked the big Nissan as it had an unusual feature. The side window of the luggage area rolled down electrically, presumably designed to ease loading the shopping, but Buster loved having his own window to stick his head out of and catch the breeze. Drools whisked away in the wind… Passing motorists giving a double take…

"Wow, this is some place." I was really impressed with the scale and the grandeur of the hotel as we drove up to the magnificent front entrance. Buster jumped out of the car and blended right into the setting.

He was a handsome dog. And a very happy dog once he saw the open countryside all around. His rear end waggled delightedly. "Woof!" he barked in appreciation.

The reception was all mahogany and inlaid leather, the young lady behind the desk the epitome of efficiency and professionalism. "Ah, Mr and Mrs Dickson, welcome to the Peebles Hydro, my name is Lynne. Here are your room keys. We've arranged your tour of the kitchens just before lunch tomorrow, so you should see the team in full flow. Chef MacFarlane will be expecting you. And what a lovely Labrador you are. What's his name?" She smiled engagingly.

"This is Buster," Mary answered. "We were wondering what arrangements there are for feeding him? Do you have a kennels area or something? I don't fancy taking him into dinner with us." She laughed.

Lynne smiled. "I'm afraid that wouldn't be possible. Dogs on leads are allowed in all the public areas except for the dining room, for obvious reasons. As for feeding him? You'll find an extensive pet menu in your room. Simply call room service with your, or rather Buster's choice, and his food will be delivered shortly afterwards."

I was impressed yet again. "That's some service on offer. I'm sure Buster will appreciate it as much as we do. Thanks, Lynne. Right, Mary, let's dump our luggage then go for a wander."

"No need, sir. Your luggage will be delivered to your room." *Ding.* She pressed the desk bell and a porter appeared from across the hall.

"Thanks, Conner. Please take Mr and Mrs Dicksons' luggage to room 242." Lynne smiled again.

"Oh, I could live here for a while if it was always free," Mary muttered as we followed our porter along the wide corridor to our room.

"You better give him a tip. He'll be expecting it. I've seen it in the movies." Mary whispered as we followed Conner into our room where he was opening our one big case, (not the washed-out case from St Malo) after placing it on the luggage rack.

“How much?” I whispered back as I fumbled through my loose change.

“Give him fifty pence. Don’t look mean…”

I gasped. *Fifty pence?* Mary plucked one from my open palm and gave it to the porter. “Thank you, madam. Sir.” he nodded and left closing the door silently.

“That’s nearly two pints of lager in the Clachan!” I complained. “I thought this was a *free* weekend.” Mary laughed me off as she felt the king-size bed then looked out of the window. “Look at that view. Those rolling hills. Reminds me of our Campsies. I do miss them.” I put my arm around her waist. “Let’s appreciate the here and now. Shall we? Where’s Buster? Ah. He’s exploring the bathroom. Time we went for a wee walk, I think.”

Later on, we went back to the room to freshen up before dinner. “Let’s have a go at Buster’s room service.” I picked up the phone.

Sure enough, ten minutes later there was a knock on the door. When I opened it, the formally dressed waitress, a pretty blond girl, entered carrying a domed platter. Buster jumped up from the rug, excited by the aroma as the waitress laid the platter on the floor beside the settee, then lifted the dome with a flourish. The best presented dog’s dinner I ever saw was laid for Buster’s delectation. A bowl of cubed beef and chicken, a bowl of dried cereals, and a bowl of water. All presented in gleaming stainless steel.

“All that dog’s dinner needs now is a glass of Chablis and a napkin,” Mary joked as Buster made short shrift of his luxury meal. The waitress was just leaving the room as he went over and sniffed her legs.

“I think he’s looking for more,” I said. “C’mon, Buster; sit down. There’s a good dog.” The waitress gingerly patted him on the head as he came over to me.

“Thanks, sir. I’m a wee bit scared of dogs. But you have to do whatever the boss tells you.”

She smiled nervously as I tried to reassure her, “Buster’s just trying to tell you that you are his new best friend for bringing him this marvellous dinner. He’s never seen anything like it either. His idea of a treat is catching a pie in a pub! Thanks very much, Lilly." I'd noticed her name badge as I fumbled for a tip. *How much is a dog's dinner worth?*

We enjoyed a lovely meal. The food was superb, the service quiet perfection. An enormous dining room that somehow managed to make us feel we were in an intimate setting. "Yep, if this is how the other half live, I'm quite enjoying this wee shot of it." I tucked into delicious profiteroles before we started on the coffee and brandy. Ahhh…

"I'm quite excited about this tour of the kitchens," Mary said at breakfast the next day. "We'll just leave Buster in the room with one of those fancy dinners. Ok?"

After a stroll round the grounds we headed back to the room. Buster would be hungry, so I called room service. "There might be a bit of a delay, sir, there was a large wedding in one of our function rooms and we're getting a lot of room service calls at the moment. If you'd like to leave your dog in the room, the waitress will let herself in. It'll save you waiting."

"That sounds reasonable. Right, Mary, let's go see the kitchen of your dreams… and my nightmares."

Fifteen minutes later we were being personally shown round the phenomenally large kitchens by the Head Chef, Ian MacFarlane, a bustling baritone of a man with a booming voice obviously honed to make sure his instructions were well understood. "So, you have your own catering business in Glasgow, I understand," he shouted at Mary, who took a step back. "We'll start with the food prep area. I'll wager it's a little larger than your own." He chuckled loudly, leading us into a busy corner of stainless-steel tables and sinks about three times the size of our home kitchen. Mary was suitably impressed and nodded to the white-suited team all chopping and scraping away.

In the meantime, Buster had been waiting for his fancy food for a bit longer than he was expecting. He was hungry, and when he heard the knock on the door, he answered with his customary "Woof!" When the door didn't open, he went up to it. He could smell the food outside. He started pawing at the door.

"Buster… Buster…" He heard the tremulous voice of the waitress through the door.

"Woof!" he answered.

The handle turned and the door slowly opened. “Sit down, Buster…please.” Lilly nervously inched into the room, holding another platter. Buster liked what he smelled. The waitress managed to lay the platter on the floor and lifted the dome without the flourish of yesterday.

“Woof!” Buster started bolting the food down as the waitress stood transfixed, wondering if this was a good time to try and conquer her fear of dogs. Buster was obviously a nice dog. He wasn’t going to do her any harm. But he was awfully big, and he looked very muscular as he gobbled down his posh breakfast. She should have sidled out of the room and left him to it. She didn’t. She tried to pat his head nervously as he was eating. “Woof!” She got a fright and backed into the phone table. The phone fell on the floor with a clatter. Buster was distracted. *I’m busy*. He finished the food as Lilly put the phone back on the table. “Woof! Woof!” Buster would like more please. *That was delicious!*

Buster was now between the waitress and the door. The girl was too frightened to push past the barking dog. She had the phone in her hand so she decided to call for help. She called room service…

“WOULD MR OR MRS DICKSON PLEASE GO TO RECEPTION, THANK YOU,” the loudspeakers boomed out throughout all the public areas.

But we were down in the kitchen, with Mary enjoying being shown the size and capacity of the gigantic walk-in refrigerators and freezers. Then we went on to the sou-chef area where one of Chef MacFarlane’s deputies, a young French chef named Jacques, gave a demonstration of how to prepare a stilton and mustard sauce to go with their award-winning pork and apple link sausages. Mary was in a cook’s seventh heaven.

“WOULD MR OR MRS DICKSON PLEASE GO TO RECEPTION, THANK YOU.”

“Sorry, Lilly, the guests haven’t gone to reception; they must be out of the building somewhere. We’re sending someone up just now.”

Lilly was staring at Buster who was now lying on the carpet thinking about having an after-breakfast snooze. But still, between her and the door… Finally it opened and her colleague, Blair came in. He looked at his distressed, pretty blond colleague. “What’s all the fuss, Lilly? Want a hug?”

Buster climbed to his feet. He'd spotted his chance, and, running between Blair's legs, scarpered out of the door. Blair looked back along the corridor at the galloping Labrador and weighed up his options… Lilly needs more attention; she's had a bad time. I'm sure I can help her…

Meanwhile, Buster was thinking*; Where are they? They left me with that crying girl…*

A door opened halfway along the corridor and a couple came through. Buster nudged between them and ran down the stairs. "Was that dog on its own?" the nudgee said.

He came down to the first landing and found himself at the top of the balustraded main staircase leading down to the ground floor. He sniffed the air. *I don't smell them. I'll go down there, they can't be far away.*

He loped down the stairs into the reception area and looked around. *Not here. I'll try through there.*

Lynne, the receptionist, spots the lovely golden Labrador walking through the reception area unaccompanied. "That's the Dicksons' dog," she says to her colleague, who's helping her check out a party of ten American golfers. Golf bags and suitcases everywhere. Chequered trousers louder than their voices.

"Hello, Buster. Where's Mummy and Daddy?" Lynne calls across the wide desk at the dog, which has no chance of hearing her over the din of the departing American golfers.

"Nah! There's no way that was an eagle, Charlie! I saw that little pick up just off the fairway. What am I? A Schmuck?"

Buster stopped and took stock. He looked around and spotted a couple of other dogs sitting with their people. He decided to join them. The two Chihuahuas were pleased to have a new friend sniffing at their nether ends. Unfortunately, their owner wasn't so happy. "Who the Hell belongs to this dog?" the tiny dogs' Master called while Buster circled his legs. He tried to hold both dogs high enough that the Labrador couldn't get his curious nose close to his two miniatures. They might get even more excited.

"Buster! Come here." Lynne moved from behind her desk. She had decided that her colleague would have to cope with the Americans as she prioritised this strangely loose dog. *It seemed so normal, yesterday.*

"Conner, can you help me please?" Lynne called across to the porter's desk. Unfortunately, Conner was involved with three American golfers insisting he should deal with their luggage before he did anything else. He shrugged. Lynne sighed. Buster ran.

He'd spotted the main front doors. A large golfer pushed open the heavy glass door to see if the coach had arrived. Buster darted past him. *Maybe they're outside. We had a nice stroll earlier and I could do with a pee.*

"WOULD MR OR MRS DICKSON PLEASE COME TO RECEPTION, URGENTLY, THANK YOU?"

Lynne had run back to the reception desk to make the announcement. She hadn't known about the previous crisis in the Dicksons' room with Lilly. That announcement had come from the room service department and she'd been too busy with the Americans to pay attention to it.

"Who are these Dicksons? They seem to be very popular." An elderly lady asked her companion as they were sitting in the foyer enjoying the bustle.

"I don't know, maybe they've got something to do with that lonesome Lab. Smart dog. He just went out by himself."

Nope, don't see them out here I'll run along this path. No wait a minute, that tree looks inviting…

Lynne, meanwhile, had organised a posse of housekeepers and other porters who had just started their shift. "The dog went out himself, I've just discovered there was a commotion in his room and he escaped. He's called Buster. A golden Labrador. We can't have him getting lost. His owners would rightly complain. Please find him and bring him back. Ok? Fetch!"

Buster was just finishing his business at the tree when he heard his name. "There he is! Buster!" Not recognising the voices, he thought he'd run away from them, down the slope and around the end of the building.

There was another large double door. It opened as a man pushing a laundry basket wheeled it towards a white van. “Hi, Doggy, you’re a fine specimen. Where’s your master? Wait, you can’t go in there!” Buster whizzed past him, through the flapping rubber doors and into the laundry area.

Running past rows and rows of bed linen, Buster spotted another door. This one was jammed open. He headed there. As he got closer, he smelled food…

“There you are. I’ve done it. Taste that, John. Stilton and mustard sauce as good as Jacques!” Mary lifted a spoon to my mouth. It was superb. Even before lunch.

“It’s quite a hubbub down here, Jacques. Is it always as busy just before lunch?” The general noise level seemed to have risen in the last couple of moments.

Jacques looked around. “Ce n’est pas normal. Quelque chose ne va pas.”

“What did he say?” Mary looked at me. I shook my head.

We stared across the work stations to the other end of the kitchen. There was definitely something going on. Shouts and banging, and a lot of restlessness.

Then I heard that word…

“BUSTER!!”

Mary and I looked at each other. Our hearts sank.

I threaded my way between the counters and workstations, trying not to bump or bang into all the hard-working chefs and cooks. The commotion seemed to be moving towards the serving hatches, where the waiters were given their completed orders to be taken impeccably through to the diners. Lunch had now started and there was a queue of waiters at the other side of the hatch.

Buster was still managing to evade capture as he darted between passageways and underneath counters, while the posse of housekeepers and porters tried to organise a pincer movement. Then I spotted our dog, scarpering into the serving area. All the serving chefs froze in horror. A dog in the kitchen? Guard the food!

"Buster! Stay!" I shouted.

But Buster knew he was in trouble. He cocked his ears, just as the door at the side of the serving area opened and the Maître D' came through. "What's all this I hear about a dog in the kitchen?"

Buster took his chance and squeezed between the perfectly creased trouser legs. *Where to now?*

The queue of waiters' usual routine was upset as Buster weaved between their legs. Another door opened as the waiter at the head of the queue took his fully laden tray, held head high, through to the restaurant. Buster grabbed his chance and bolted for that escape.

Unfortunately, he didn't manage to slip so smoothly between this waiter's legs. He stumbled as Buster's heavy paw pressed on his patent leather shoe. The dog tried to get out of his way but it was too late.

The heavy platter slowly slid out of his hands, finding a trajectory that sent the plates of sausages and stilton and mustard sauce straight towards the nearest table, where two elderly ladies, dressed in their finest lunching outfits, were treated to an airborne tasting of Chef Jacques' delicious creation, as the plates bounced off their condiments and spread deliciousness all over them.

Instant chaos as the waiter tried to wipe down the lunching ladies. I'd managed to get through the serving area, past the bewildered staff, and into the restaurant. Buster had stopped when he'd heard the crash of the platter.

"BUSTER!! SIT!!" I yelled.

This time it worked. He stayed still as I grabbed his collar. "How did you get out of the room?" I asked him loudly enough that the diners would know that *some* of the responsibility for the chaos wasn't mine. Mary came through seconds later along with the posse of housekeepers and porters.

"WOULD MR OR MRS DICKSON PLEASE COME TO RECEPTION, URGENTLY, THANK YOU?"

"I think that for us, Mary," I said. One of the elderly ladies, cleaning the stilton and mustard sauce off her specs, looked up at us: "So, you're the Dicksons they've been shouting for. Nice dog… Smart. Might respond to a little more training?"

Chapter 54

Hopes and Dreams

"Jamie's here, Mary," I called as I answered the door. "You get out of my way, Buster. I still haven't forgiven you for the Hydro." Jamie threw me a curious look. "Too long a story, Jamie. Come on through."

We sat in our usual positions round the coffee table. Mary had the china tea set out; it had become a bit of a ritual. "I'll be Mother." Mary smiled ruefully as she poured the tea into the floral cups.

Jamie gave a small smile." Maybe sooner than we'd hoped, if things don't go wildly wrong…"

"What?" Mary almost dropped the teapot. "You wouldn't joke with us, Jamie!" Her face had gone very pale. I suddenly felt tense. "Jamie, what is this? You told us it could take months, maybe years before a suitable placement is possible…" Mary and I both stared at him.

"Well, to start with… there is nothing definite about this…"

"What the Hell does that mean?" *Don't mess with us!*

"I feel it's right that you both know there is a possibility of a placement. There are many uncertainties, as we've discussed many times, but there is a child who is due to be placed on the adoption list. And I think you'd make his perfect parents."

"Him?? A boy??" Mary jumped on the word.

I took a deep breath. "Ok, Jamie, we're flattered at your description of us as his 'perfect parents.' But the very mixed message is that you talking about 'many uncertainties' in the same breath. Please explain the situation. We now know there's a boy. Can you tell us his age?" I looked at Mary's face, her fists over her mouth.

Jamie put on his 'I've been trained for this' look. "Ok. I know you hate the word, Mary, but there is a process." Mary sighed audibly. "There's a young boy, he's two years and five months old." Mary's eyes widened enormously. "He's currently placed with the foster parents he's been living with for the last fifteen months. However, the fostering situation was always going to be temporary, and it's been decided to try and find him a permanent home. And that's where I've been fighting your corner." He smiled. I slumped into the couch. *This is all so difficult. So many people involved. He has to fight our corner. This shouldn't be a battle.*

He continued while we came to terms with this new situation: "The child has his own case worker. Essentially, I have to convince her that you are the right adoptive parents for the child. I've been on that case since the day after the panel."

"So, what happens next?" Mary asked. There was more colour in her cheeks, I noticed.

"The next stage is that I leave you an edited background report about the child. You have the right to say 'no thank you,' and that will not be held against you. However, effectively, this child is probably the closest you're going to get to exactly what you've been hoping for." He was talking to Mary. She smiled, graciously.

"Once you've read over Stephen's report." *We have a name!!* "I'll arrange, if you want, to have an initial chance to meet the child in the foster parents' home."

Mary spoke up. "What if he doesn't like us? In a way, it's really his decision?"

I butted in. "If that's the case, that's right and proper. But Bloody Hell! It's not easy is it? We've got to impress a bloody two-and-a-half-year-old. And we thought being judged by social workers and politicians was tough?" Mary laughed nervously.

Jamie left us the report and told us to call him if and when we were ready to move onto the next stage. He also gave us a photo of a little boy, sitting on a trike, looking right into the camera. My heart jumped.

By the time we had digested the report and pored over that photo, we really needed to meet little Stephen.

The meeting was set up. The most un-spontaneous get together I've ever been involved in. We had to go to the foster parent's house. Mr and Mrs Black lived just a few miles away. They had two children of their own and had been fostering for over five years. Stephen was their sixth placement but by far the longest, at fifteen months.

"I'm so nervous." Mary confided as we sat outside the foster parent's semi-detached house in a quiet suburban street. "What if he just ignores us? He's just a wee boy. This must be very stressful for him too." I pretended not to be nervous as we walked up the drive.

The door opened before I pressed the bell. "John and Mary? Come in, come in. It's a very artificial kind of situation, isn't it? I'm Bill, by the way." Mr Black was doing his best to put us at our ease. He showed us into the living room. There, surrounded by a homely Mrs Black and three social workers, was a little boy, sitting alone in the middle of the carpet… surrounded by a pool of Lego…

Introductions were made to all the parties involved. Annoyingly there were only two chairs empty in the small living room. Both were dining chairs at opposite ends of the room, so Mary and I couldn't sit together. *You'd have thought the professionals would have organised that…*

Mrs Black tried to break the ice. "Hi, Stephen, this is John and that's Mary. They've come to visit you. Would you like to say hello?" She smiled encouragingly. Stephen looked up from his Lego. "Hello." Then he went back to building his house.

I looked over at Mary, who smiled awkwardly.

The tension in the room was palpable. *We need movement.* I hunkered down on the floor and motioned to Mary to do the same. *This was a dance. We were being observed. We had to perform. Our judges were taking notes. Would watching my wife giving birth be more stressful?*

"Hi, Stephen, we've brought you a couple of presents." *So, what's wrong with a bit of bribery?*

I brought out the two cool toy cars we'd brought with us. Not too expensive. A grade up from pocket money toys. We'd agonised over the purchase of these cars. An 'E'-Type Jaguar and a fire engine with detachable ladders. They were still in their boxes, and Stephen was very patient while I unpacked them.

Playing toy cars with your potential two-and-a-half-year-old son with three social workers and a couple of foster parents looking on sounds very odd… It wasn't. It felt natural. We zoomed in and out of the Lego obstacle course we built and finally parked both vehicles beside the trike we'd seen in the photo. Mary and I glanced at each other as we climbed back onto our respective chairs. There was an air of 'that'll do' in the room.

"Did you enjoy that, Stephen?" Kirsty, his case worker, asked.

"Aye. Funny," he answered.

Then more pointed questions…

Stephanie, the Black's social worker, asked the killer: "Do you like Mary and John, Stephen?"

Oh God!!! What if he says No?

"Yes." More politely. "They're fun."

A general nodding of heads all round as Mary and I sat stiffly.

Then…

Stephen clambered up from his Lego. Picked up the 'E'Type Jag. Walked over to me… And climbed up on my knees and cooried in… It felt so natural as I took the car from him and made it fly through the air. He sat up and laughed when I let it land on his sleeve. I looked across at Mary. We smiled and nodded.

The tension melted away as we played until Stephen eventually climbed down and we said our bye-byes.

A flurry of social worker's chatter outside the Black's house that we could see from the car, and Jamie contacted us later to arrange our next meeting. We were to be allowed to take Stephen out for an hour on our own. We decided to take Buster along and introduce him.

It was love at first sight. Buster had always got on well with children (when he wasn't snatching their ice cream cones). Stephen and Buster were about the same height. So, we went for a walk in the nearby park, where the highlight was Stephen riding on Buster's back as if he was a miniature horse, while I nearly broke my back holding him safely. Mary was in stitches at our antics. Great fun.

"So, what are your hopes and dreams about Stephen if the adoption goes through?" Jamie asked Mary yet one more thought-provoking question.

Mary didn't hesitate. "I'm looking forward to being surprised in maybe a few months or maybe even years from now when Stephen finally calls me 'Mummy.' That'll be a good day."

A few days later the phone rang in The Buy In. It was Jamie. "I was at your house but there was nobody in."

"That's right. Mary's over at her mum's as it's her birthday. Any word yet?" I closed the back door. We'd still only told Rhona and my mum and dad. It all seemed so private. And we'd been warned so many times that it could all unravel.

"I've got good news. We have a handover date! A month from today on the twenty-eighth of June. I'll come and see you both and we'll go over the arrangements. Congratulations. You might want to call Mary's mum's." He laughed. I jumped up and down with excitement before dialling the Heaney's number.

xxxxxxxxxxxxxxxxxxxxxxxxxxxxxxxxxxxxxxxxxxxxxxxxxxxxxx

"I think it's time to tell folk now," Mary said later that day once we'd got over the shock. "I found myself holding back from telling Mum and Aunt Peggy today. I'd like us to be together when we tell people. Am I being daft?" She laid her head on my shoulder.

"Tell you what!" She sat up. "We haven't had a housewarming party here yet. And once Stephen's here it won't really be suitable. At least for a while… Why don't we hold a midsummer bash come housewarming on say…" she flicked through her diary… "Saturday the nineteenth. If this heat wave keeps up, we'll mostly be out in the garden. We can announce our impending parenthood, then everyone knows at the same time. Plus, it'll be our 'final fling' as a childless couple, eh, Mister?" She sealed it with a kiss. How could I refuse?

A flurry of phone calls later and Mary had the day all planned. Everyone who'd played a part in our recent life had been invited. She'd even managed to enrol Big Jessie and Thelma to help her set up the food and drink, catering trestle tables in the garden as the sun shone obligingly as it had done for the previous month. Talk of drought down south didn't really affect us in sunny Glasgow. We'd always have big Loch Katrine to quench our thirst.

Mum and Dad and my wee brothers were first to arrive in mid-afternoon. Mum came over to me and gave me a hug. "I'm so-o happy for you both. I can't wait to meet our first Grandson. Even your dad's excited, aren't you, Jackie?" Dad rolled his eyes, and then gripped my hand. "Just watch those pennies, John. But well done to you both. You must have said something right." Mary gave him a hug.

"What's going on?" Thomas butted in. "What's with all the handshakes and hugs? How come you never shake my hand, Dad?" He grinned and shook his head.

Alan had a strange long parcel with him. "This is for later to celebrate midsummer's day. I know it's not actually today, but that's why we're here. Yeh?"

Phil and Andy were armed with large water pistols. "If this gets boring, we're just going to have a water fight!"

Mum's head swivelled. "I told you not to bring those guns. They're too big." Both boys laughed and ran round the back.

"It's going to be a busy day, Mary. I hope you're well-prepared. Remember this is your idea…" I passed the blame as I went out the back to check on the drinks and have a word with Big Jessie and Thelma.

"And where have you been hiding, Mr Dickson. You've no' been to any of our gigs for ages!" The familiar voice of Wee Robbie came from between the house and the garage. "We've brought the guitars. Do you want us inside or out? Aw, there she is! Mary, my darlin', you're looking fantastic, if a little less rock chic. Whit's this with the flouncy skirt. Ah preferred those hot pants you used to wear."

"Thanks, Robbie. You're such a flatterer!" Mary flounced over to him and Funky who was just behind, holding both guitars. "Hiya, Mary. Quite a crowd you've got gathering. I just saw Jim and Hannah pulling up. Hannah looks like she might be dropping a baby any minute. She wants to be careful in this heat… I think I saw your sister, Joyce, and her family parking round the corner. Lots of kids, eh. Aye, I suppose we're getting to that age. Eh? But it'll no' be me for quite a while. Life is still Rock and Roll!"

Finally, Rhona and Graham arrived with Ross, now a big brother to three-month-old Calumn, coorying into his carry cot. "Well done with the weather, you two. Great day for an announcement…" Rhona grinned mischievously.

"Shush, Rhona. We're waiting for our mum and dad first. Ah, here they are. I hope they don't complain about the price of the taxi."

The Heaney clan were all here as Iain and Maureen and their kids arrived from the wilds of East Kilbride, tumbling out of their minibus. "Best car I've ever had," Iain explains to his dad as the weans go chasing after Andy and Phil, shooting each other with the water guns up at the top of the back garden.

Mary nudged me. "Now's the time. How're we going to do this? Inside or out?"

"It's too sunny to be inside. Plus, they might not all fit. Here we go…" We walked round to the back garden where Funky and Robbie were gently playing that old classic "Summertime" while Big Jessie and Thelma were handing out drinks.

Mary and I walked to the middle of the garden and stood together. "Excuse me, folks. Mary and I have a wee announcement to make. Harrumph." My mum and dad were standing beside Rhona. A slightly smug look on Mum's face, I noticed.

Mary held my hand. We'd decided she could do the talking: "There's quite a few weans here today, as you can see. Phil, Andy! Put the guns down for a minute! Please? And John and I would like all you precious people to know that we're about to become the new proud parents of a wee boy called Stephen."

Surprised looks all round. "You're looking remarkably slim, Mary. When's the baby due?" Big Jessie called from behind the table.

Uh oh. They haven't got it.

I was about to complete the story when Mrs Heaney interrupted: "What was that, you said, Mary? How do you know it's a boy?"

Aunt Peggy butted in. "Ya deaf 'owl Bugger. She's no' pregnant! They're adopting. Same as Rhona and Graham. That right, Mary?" Mary nodded nervously as I took up the tale. I could tell everyone was bursting with questions. "We know he's called Stephen, because that's how he was introduced to us. And Big Peggy's right. We'll be adopting Stephen in the very near future"

"So, you've met him then?" Hannah's eyes were full of wonder. I nodded as she spoke, "I wish I could be introduced to my little one before we have to take responsibility… That's a plus! Congratulations, by the way! That's wonderful news!"

The dam burst. Everyone was shaking our hands and giving us hugs and the warmest wishes.

"So, what age is this little boy?" Mr Heaney asked.

"He's two and a half, Dad," Mary answered. "He can talk and walk and even ride on Buster's back. Is that right, Buster?" she called as he was lurking under the trestle tables hoping for scraps of crisps and biscuits.

"Woof!" he seemed to reply, but maybe it was the chocolate biscuit little Trinity had just sneaked past her mum.

Big Jim Lang and Funky came over. Jim slapped me on the back. "You've managed to keep this big news pretty secret. Even when you and Mary were up for dinner a couple of weeks ago. I mean, we would have kept Hannah's pregnancy a secret too. But I don't think we'd have got away with it." He nodded in his wife's direction. She was due within the next two weeks.

Funky raised a glass. "Congratulations, young man. I think it might be a wee while now before we three can think of planning another camping trip, eh? Well, I can go anytime. Not being encumbered with any offspring," he said smugly.

Jim nodded, "I don't think you'll be doing any camping anytime soon, unless someone invents a tent with an amplifier that you can plug into!"

Thomas and Alan joined us with Phil and Andy. "So, John. When's this wee guy coming on the scene?" Alan was doing the talking. "Does that mean we'll be his uncles?" He looked at our brothers. "Absolutely!" I said "You'll be Uncle Alan! And you, Andy. You'll be *Uncle* Andy. How cool is that?"

Thomas asked seriously, "So when does it all happen? When does he actually belong to you and Mary?"

"We've been given a 'handover' date of twenty-eighth June. Ten days from now. We're due to see him once more before then, when we'll bring him here for an hour or so. It's all part of what they call a gradualist approach."

By now I had quite a crowd around me, all wishing us well and asking a thousand and one questions. Then Alan took the mood up a gear.

"This is a cause for celebration!" he said, unwrapping the long parcel he'd brought with him earlier. "Look what I've got. I found them in Dad's garage, left over from Guy Fawkes." He revealed two large rockets and a couple of launching tubes."

Dad came over when he saw his stock on display. "What on earth do you think you're doing?" He frowned at Alan. "They were in the garage. How come they're here?"

Alan picked up the big fireworks. "Well, I was gonna celebrate midsummer. But now… I'm gonna celebrate becoming Uncle Alan! Want to light one, Dad?"

Everyone burst out laughing as he strolled through the crowd to the back of the garden where there was a little raised area. Pushing the heavy-duty launching tubes into the ground, he loaded the rockets then stood beside them, matches in hand.

"Right, folks! Pay attention! Everybody stay well back. This is my way of saying congratulations on the adoption of wee Stephen to my big brother and his smashing wife, Mary. Hip hip!" With that he lit the fuse, and as the crowd shouted "HOORAY!" both rockets whooshed into the air and exploded with a burst of coloured lights.

Woof! Woof! Buster joined in, and we partied till the sun went down and even a wee bit later…

Chapter 55
What's Going On?

"Hello, Jamie. We weren't expecting you today, anything wrong?" Jamie looked strained as he came inside the house just as I was about to leave for work. "Jamie's here, Mary," I shouted upstairs where Mary was having a shower.

"I'll be right down. What's up?" Mary clattered downstairs moments later, housecoat pulled tight. Jamie was standing in the middle of the room, looking uncomfortable.

"I don't like the look on your face, Jamie. What's going on?" I said as Mary reached for my hand.

Jamie sighed. "It shouldn't be a major problem, but the Blacks aren't at home. And won't be there next Monday when the handover was supposed to happen."

Mary gasped: "What do you mean they're not at home? Where on Earth are they? Where's our Stephen? Have they run away? For God's sake, I can feel my heart thumping!" She staggered to the couch and sat down. Her tears were beginning to bubble up as I tried to take it in: "Jamie, when did you find this out? Are they not supposed to let their case worker know if they change plans? I'm worried they simply can't bear to part with Stephen. What the hell happens then?"

Jamie raised his palms and began to speak, but Mary burst out: "Oh no, John! Don't even say those words. Please! Please! Please!" She turned her pleading eyes to Jamie.

"I just found out this morning, that's why I came straight here. Apparently, they're all in Blackpool on a family holiday. I'm not sure yet when they'll be back..."

I sat down beside Mary. I could feel my heart pumping too. I felt powerless. I gulped. "Sit down, Jamie. We have to know what's going on after all we've been through to get to this stage. Are they allowed to just up sticks and skip the country, less than a week before a foster child's arranged handover? Will this uncertainty not be upsetting for Stephen? Who's dealing with this?"

Jamie did his best to answer, but I could see he wasn't happy either. "Kirsty and Stephanie have been talking to each other. Apparently, Stephanie got a call from Mrs Black last night from Blackpool. It's a last-minute holiday… They got a bargain… The weather's really nice…" He shook his head in spite of his training.

"Wish you were here? We'll send you a funny postcard? Give me a break!" I was trying not to be angry. "So, I presume next Monday's handover is postponed. Do you realise we've told both of our families about all this, Jamie? We thought you knew what you were doing! When will we know what's going to happen?"

"I'm just so-o worried they might never come back! What if they have friends or relatives there? Are the adoption laws the same in England? Could they try and keep Stephen? Oh God! Oh God!" Mary was losing it.

Jamie stood up. "I'm going straight from here to the office. As soon as I have more information, I'll call you. That's the best I can do, Mary. I'm so sorry. Will you be in the shop, John?" I nodded. *Won't be doing much work though.*

Once Jamie left, I tried to comfort Mary. "We've met the Blacks three times now, Mary. I can't believe they would do something really stupid; they've got their own kids to think of too. Let's hope it's just a glitch. Give us a hug. It'll be alright. Just a chunk of life's roller coaster. Eh?"

Of course I spent the next few hours hovering around the door to the back shop waiting for the phone to ring. When it did it was Mary, desperate to know if Jamie had called.

At five-to-five the phone rang again. I jumped on it: "Hello, John, Jamie here. Just to keep you in the loop. Stephanie managed to talk to the Blacks. They said they'll be back at the end of next week, so we've postponed the handover till a week on Monday. Will that be ok?" *How can I say no?*

"Well, we don't have any other option do we, Jamie. I don't suppose the Blacks could be persuaded to come home sooner? We still don't know why they suddenly went down south. Do you? It's very disconcerting. Mary's at her wit's end… and no wonder!"

A hesitation, “I do know why, John. But I’m not at liberty to say. I’m sorry again, you and Mary try to relax for this extra week, and I’ll call you next Friday to confirm the new arrangements.”

“Relax? Oh, that *will* be easy. Do we have anything more to worry about, Jamie? Can you give me your word that we’re not going to get any more rotten surprises?”

Jamie replied: “Alright, John. I give you my word. It’ll all be fine on the day…”

When I got home, Rhona and her boys were with Mary. And Thomas and Alan had driven down in Thomas’s new company car. They were all being very supportive.

I told them the gist about what Jamie had said, and we all concluded we’d simply have to be patient. It was out of our hands.

Thomas had an idea: “Listen, John and you too Mary. The best thing you can do is to try and put it all to the back of your mind for a wee bit. Did you know that Phil and Andy are helping out Big Peter this weekend? He called Dad looking for help out of the blue. He figured they’re old enough to work now they’re teenagers.”

“Eh? Really? How come? Is he still doing the same old stuff? Gala days and balloons and stuff? My God, I remember those sodden wet days down the Barras. I don’t miss them. What’s this got to do with the adoption situation?” I was puzzled.

Mary looked bewildered as Thomas continued: “It’s not really got anything to do with the adoption. It’s just that Alan and I had said to Phil and Andy we might show up, just to annoy them… I just thought you two could come along as well. A bit of a distraction… All five brothers plus Mary all together for a change. What do you think?”

Mary gave Thomas a wee smile. “Thanks, Thomas… I’m not sure if I feel like that. Where is it?”

Alan spoke up “It’s in Burntisland in Fife. A gala day beside the beach. The weather’s to be a real scorcher. It would do you good to have a walk along the beach licking an ice cream cone… Go on! Better than moping about here!”

I looked at Mary and nodded: "Ok, guys. That's a good idea. I wouldn't mind seeing the old stall again, and it'll be fun to see them two sprogs doing some work for a change." I was in a better mood now.

So, on the Saturday, Mary and I loaded up the big Nissan; Thomas and Alan in the back seat, with Buster sticking his head out of his own private window, we motored over the country roads to the Kingdom of Fife.

The sun was high in the sky and it was a sweltering day. Crowds of pale-skinned torsos risking blistering sunburn as we threaded our way through the outer edges of the carnival, set up to support the gala day. I held Buster's lead as there were a number of loose dogs wandering in and around the brightly coloured stalls.

"There they are!" Alan shouted as we spotted the old blue trailer, easily picked out by the clouds of gas balloons bouncing and whirling above the roof of the mobile stall. They were busy. Andy had quite a queue of folk waiting for balloons to be inflated, while a cowboy-hatted Phil was drumming up more trade: "Get your furry monkeys here! Buy two and you might end up with three!" He was obviously enjoying himself.

"Business looks brisk." I said to my two youngest brothers. "Where's Big Peter? He used to be on my top all day when I was working for him."

"Aye, well," Andy answered. "It looks like we're damn sight better workers than you ever were then. Eh? He went away to get some lunch. He knows we'll be fine, now I've finally mastered tying knots in the balloons… Here you are, Missus, tie the balloon onto the kiddie's arm. The boss doesn't give refunds for the ones that fly away!"

"I think you both look very smart." Mary grinned as Phil convinced a customer to buy a bow and arrow as well as a cowboy gun. "What's the point in fighting by yourself? They'll give you more peace if their battling each other. Isn't that right, Andy? That's how we kept out of our mum's hair… We just knocked lumps out of each other! Do you want to see my bruises, Missus?" The customer gave up and handed Phil the cash before walking away laughing.

"Right, wee brothers, you're doing an excellent job. So, we big yins are going to go for a stroll along the beach, then enjoy Mary's well-prepared picnic in a nice grassy spot. We'll see you both later. Enjoy working!" Alan waved to the only Dicksons working that day, apart from poor old Dad. We made our way towards the beach, past the tug of war going on in the main ring. Buster could smell the sea and was keen to have a dip.

"We'll wander along the beach for a bit. Have the picnic, then come back and give them some abuse. Ok?" Thomas had a plan.

Leaving the noise and hubbub behind us, the sea was glistening in the sun, as we strolled along the prom. "Look, there's a couple of those new oil rigs." Alan pointed to the dark structures floating far out on the horizon "Don't know if I fancy working out there in stormy weather. I think I'll stick to the buses for a bit. I'm thinking of entering a snooker competition, with all the practice I've been getting. Might win a few bob."

Mary and I were enjoying the small talk, away from the intensity of the last few months. We worked our way down to the sand, and I let Buster off the lead. He scampered into the shallows, splashing and cavorting in glorious freedom. There were a number of families picnicking on the sand. Parasols shading babies and toddlers in push chairs. Mums and dads playing Frisbees with older children.

"That'll soon be us, Sweetheart. Not long to go now. Once we get through the formalities, I say we take Stephen away for a few days. How about the Lake District? We had a great weekend there, didn't we? Remember the Drunken Duck Inn and that fantastic king-sized bed? We could maybe go back there." I held Mary's hand. Thomas and Alan were walking ahead of us, laughing at some story being told.

Suddenly, Buster ran out of the water and headed for a family group sitting in the shade of the prom wall. *Oh no! He'll soak them…* "BUSTER! COME HERE!" I shouted as he bounded up to the family. I could make out the silhouettes of a couple of adults and two or three kids, one of them sitting up in a push chair. Buster had headed straight towards it and put his head on the kiddie's lap, his tail wagging happily...

"What's he doing?" Mary wondered as we picked up our pace and walked over towards them.

"Oh my God!" Mary exclaimed. "That's Stephen! Our Stephen! In the pushchair!"

Surely not. They're in Blackpool. Makes no sense. But I hurried up as the adults pulled themselves out of their fold-away beach chairs. It was true! *That's Mr and Mrs Black.*

Whit?

Mary reached them before me. Then stood stock still. *What do you say? We can't upset Stephen*. Mrs Black spoke. Nervously… "Erm, hello, Mary… and you, John. Fancy meeting you here. Look, Stephen. Here's Mary and John come to see you again. And they've brought Buster too. You like Buster, don't you? And I can see he likes the way you're tickling his ears." She gave us a pleading look as she bent down and stroked Stephen's hair, lovingly.

Mary still hadn't said anything. *She's still in shock. I think I am too.* I had to say something. "Aye, hello, Bill, Jean. And hello to you, Stephen. Are you having a fun day out at the beach?" He waved at me… "Can I have a word, Bill?" I walked a few feet away. He followed.

"I'm sorry, John. This is all a bit awkward, meeting you and Mary like this." He wrung his hands and wiped them on his shorts.

"We were told you were in Blackpool? How come?" *This is so off the wall!*

"The truth is… That's what we told the social workers. We didnae want them coming over here and pestering us… It's just that… Well…Jean's finding it very hard…giving up Stephen… He's been with us for over a year and he's such a great wee boy. Ah'm awfully sorry. We shouldn't have put you through this extra anguish."

I looked over at Mary who had regained her composure and was actually introducing Stephen to his new uncles, Thomas and Alan, both of whom were acting daft and making Stephen laugh. The Black's other two children were trying to dry Buster with what looked like a wet towel. *This is all so bizarre…*

"So, the next time we see you will definitely be next Monday morning then?" Mary looked hard at Mr and Mrs Black. They both nodded. Mr Black extended his hand and I shook it. "Well this way we got to meet your brothers. Foster parents usually never get to meet any extended family. They look like good lads… We'll see you Monday… Promise…"

"Well, that was a turn up for the books." Alan ventured as we wandered back towards the stall. "Phil and Andy are going to be so-o jealous. *We* got to meet Stephen first. Hey, hey."

I caught Mary's eye as I held my crossed fingers in the air. She matched me.

Chapter 56

The Final Hurdle

We'd had it out with Jamie. He'd had it out with his colleagues. Somebody had had it out with the Blacks. Everyone was CALM the day before the definite handover.

"Our last Sunday lunch as a couple without kids. I'm sure Stephen will get to love your roast beef as much as I do. I've double-checked upstairs. His room is still ready. I've lain on that bed quite a few times now. It's still comfy! The Batman wallpaper is still on the walls. The Thomas the Tank rug is still on the floor. Ok? Let's do our best to just enjoy this once-in-a-lifetime experience. You are gonna be an amazing mummy!"

Mary smiled and put her knife and fork down. "I'll do my best. I know you will too. It's been a bloody hard road to get to here but. Too many other people involved. Grrr! But we are where we are, as you say. Let's open that bottle of wine and toast our new future?"

I'll drink to that!

Monday morning 6am the phone rings beside our bed. "Hello, John. It's Helen. I'm awfy sorry but I'm not going to make it into work. I've been up all night with the baby. She's no' well. I think we're going to have to take her into Yorkhill."

"Right, Helen. Of course you have to look after wee Angela. I hope she's ok. But you've got the shop keys, haven't you? Barbara won't be able to open up then, will she?" *Ohhhhh Noooooo!*

"Sorry, John, I've really got to go. She's coughing again."

"No problem, Helen." Phone down: "Mary, I have to open the shop. I'll call someone once I'm there. I promise I'll be back here by nine."

Mary's eyes are enormous. "But… But… Today?"

I don't have time to answer as I jump out of the bed.

Grab clothes. Struggle into them. Pull hair over. Rush downstairs. Grab spare shop keys. Run out the door. Fire up the car. Race to the shop. Watch out for speed cops. Screech to a stop. Barbara's helping the Menzies guy unload the newspapers outside the shop… Sit for a moment and breathe… Open shop. Turn on the lights. Lug in the papers and sort them out. Throw up the window shutters. Open up the tills. Say hello to the early birds who always want their paper from the bottom of the pile. Deal with the newsboys. Check the morning rolls. Serve a few more customers. *I need to make some calls. Look at the bloody time! We've to be at the Blacks by half past nine!*

Mum comes along at quarter to nine. Dishevelled but here! "Gotta go. Gotta go. Thanks, Mum. Love you!" She doesn't get a chance to say, "Good Luck!"

Rush out to the car. Zoom down the road. Don't get a ticket by the skin of my teeth. Reach the house with a minute to spare. Mary comes tearing down the stairs, looking the Mumsiest of Mumsy Mums. Wonderfully!

"You promised you'd be here well before nine!"

"I didn't! I said I'd be here on time! And I am, so let's go. Have you got the new Lego and the flowers for the Blacks?"

"They're all in my bag. The flowers might be bashed!"

Oh God. This can't be the way to start a new life…

We rush along to the Blacks and arrive just in time. Jamie is waiting outside. "You look lovely, Mary. You ok, John?" I don't mention the previous three hours madness. He wouldn't understand.

Jamie presses the bell. Mary and I are holding hands behind him, trying to keep the nerves at bay. The door opens and Mr and Mrs Black are standing in the hall. Mrs Black has been crying. I feel a lump in my throat. *This must be so hard for them.*

Take a deep breath.

Say something:

"Hello again. A big day all round."

We squeeze into the narrow hallway and follow the Blacks and Jamie into the living room. It's a full house. The same three social workers plus *another* lady who's there as some kind of independent observer. Her title goes over our heads.

Mutterings of introductions as Mary and I stand slightly apart from everyone else. The tension is as thick as a pea-souper fog.

Stephen is sitting in the one easy chair. A good-looking wee boy who's the centre of everyone's attention. He's holding the cars we gave him on our first visit. He looks at us and grins.

"Hiya! This car goes fast." He clambers down to the floor and wheeches the car across the carpet.

Mrs Black is holding back tears. She bends down and picks up Stephen… For the last time.

She holds him tightly as Mr Black ruffles his hair. "You be good, Stephen. You're going to have great fun in your new house with Buster, aren't you?"

Stephen squeezes his foster mum back. She kisses him on the cheek. He kisses her back.

Mary is standing very close. I can feel her shaking. I look at her and see the tears flowing down her cheeks.

Oh… This is so hard.

Kirsty steps forward. "You alright, Stephen? Ready to go with your new mum and dad?" He nods unsmilingly.

Stephen looks at us as Mrs Black steps towards us, her mouth closed tight. Mary moves forward, arms ready to take Stephen.

For a moment both women are holding their child. Then Mrs Black slowly lets go. She steps back and gives Stephen a feeble wave. Mr Black lays his hands on her shoulders.

"I think we should go now, John and Mary," Jamie says in a low voice. I reach out and shake Mr Black's hand then give Mrs Black a peck on the cheek and turn away, to move out of this fog of tension.

Fresh air beckons.

Mary holds Stephen on her hips while I hang on to the little suitcase holding his few precious possessions. We knew already there were pyjamas and summer clothes, a couple of favourite toys, and a one-eyed teddy he'd been given by his birth mother, two and a half years before.

"Right then. I'll walk you to the car." Jamie looks strained. *God knows how I look.*

We put Stephen into his car seat in the back of the car and strap him in. "Where's Buster?" he asks as Mary closes the passenger door.

"Oh, he's at home. We're going there now. You'll see him soon, Stephen. Are you ok?" He nods and settles into the car seat.

We wave to Jamie standing on the pavement. I see the shadows of the Blacks standing behind the venetian blinds. The lump comes back into my throat.

Five minutes from home Mary says, "Pull in at the local dairy. You never brought any rolls or milk from the shop. I'll pop in and get some here. You like milk don't you, Stephen?" She smiles over the front seat.

He answers, "Milk good. Ice Kispies?"

I give a wee laugh: "I think Stephen just placed his first breakfast order. The first of many, I suspect." Mary grins and waves as she closes the door.

That was exhausting. What a morning and it's not even ten o clock yet…

I sigh. Then Stephen's voice pipes up behind me: "Where's Mummy gone?"

I gulp and try not to show my shock. "Mummy's just in that shop over there. She'll be back in a minute. She's getting the milk and the Ice Kispies. Look, there she is."

Mary, billowing skirt and soft pastel blouse, holding a small bag of essentials, walks across the pavement and opens the car door. "See, Stephen. I told you. Here's Mummy now." Mary gives him her widest smile.

"Hiya, Mummy. You got Ice Kispies? Me a good boy…"

Mary looks at me in astonishment. "There you go… Stephen's been Mummying since you left the car." I exaggerate.

Once inside the house, we say hello to Buster, delighted with his new companion, who's dying to ride on his back as before. So, Daddy duly obliges, till Mummy gets the breakfast out and we all sit up around our family table for the first time.

"I love Ice Kispies." Stephen spoons up the cereal.

"Nothing wrong with your appetite, young man." Mary laughs.

The sun is shining so we go out to the back garden and take a few photos. A momentous day.

Mary says as we watch Stephen hanging on to Buster's collar, "I don't know about you but I'm shattered. Stephen must be tired too. It's been a very stressful day all round. Why don't we all lie down for a wee nap?"

"Great idea, Come on, Stephen. Let's see your new room. It's up the stairs."

"All right, Daddy. I'm coming." He startles me by giving me my new title. *Wow! I really am a daddy! It's official. Now I do feel grown up…*

We take him up to his room and show him the Batman wallpaper and the Thomas the Tank rug. Change him into the jammies out of his wee case and put the one-eyed teddy onto his pillow. "Just have a wee nap, Stephen. Mummy and Daddy are very tired".

I lift him up and lay him on the bed. His head on the pillow, Mary pulls the sheets up to his chin and gives him a kiss on the cheek. I follow suit. His eyes droop and he falls into an instant sleep. "He must be exhausted too."

We stand back and look at our Son, lying peacefully in his new bed. An overwhelming joy surges through me. I turn to Mary. "This feeling couldn't be bettered if we'd just won the pools!" I draw her to me and we kiss.

This… is as good as it gets!

Acknowledgements

My thanks go to everyone who has helped or encouraged me with this book. The members of Strathkelvin Writers Group who have read and commented on various chapters within the book. Their input has been very welcome. Special mention goes to Margot Aked and Theresa O'Hare who read the whole manuscript and whose constructive criticisms were very useful. I'd also like to thank Phil Smith, erstwhile editor of the venerable Scots Magazine who encouraged me to write the book while accepting stories for the magazine.

My thanks go to Miika Hanilla of Creativia Publishers for enabling the book to potentially reach a global audience. I just hope they can cope with some of the Glasgow vernacular spouted by one or two of the characters…

Of course, my main thanks go to Mary, my wife and best pal for almost half a century. Now you've read the book, you'll know how special she is. Special thanks goes to our brilliant son, Stephen, who makes an appearance towards the end of the book, and our amazing daughter, Kathleen, who will definitely feature in the sequel! (I'm working on it…)

About the Author

I was born in 1951 in the east end of Glasgow. The first of five sons. We lived in a new housing scheme; Ruchazie, on the edge of the city.

Dad worked hard in various jobs, supplemented with some buying and selling around Scotland. Eventually saving enough to take over the local newsagent's shop, where he managed to carve out a reasonable living for the next thirty years. Enough to support a wife, and eventually five boys.

After a few years we moved to a bigger house in Riddrie, a mile closer to the city, where, once I'd passed my 11 plus exam I was enrolled in St Mungo's Academy. A 'senior secondary' school which sprawled over four campuses near the city centre. It was an all-boys school, with fairly Victorian attitudes regarding learning and discipline. The teachers usually wore gowns and were not averse to throwing a wooden blackboard 'duster' across the class at talkative pupils. They would also punish pupils regularly by means of a leather 'strap' on outstretched palms. It was really sore! In spite of this harsh environment, I quite enjoyed my time at St Mungo's and made lifelong friends with some really good people.

Having succeeded in rising to the heights of mediocrity, with one Higher and three 'O'levels, I left school and entered the real world of work. Starting out as a not very good sales rep for a confectionery firm, then moving on to becoming a major newsagents chain's youngest ever branch manager, before opening my first shop at nineteen. None of that was plain sailing but it was a good grounding.

Over the years Mary and I have started a number of businesses (the early ones are in the book.) Mainly shops, such as Spar stores and catering businesses, although I did own a chocolate factory for a while…

We sold our final retail business a few years ago and I took up writing. I sent my first submission to the prestigious Scots Magazine (The oldest magazine in the world.).

It was a dramatic/humorous article describing my adventures in a camping trip as a teenager. To my delight, two days later I received an email saying they wanted to publish it! The Scots Magazine accepted a number of my stories and the then editor, Phil Smith, reckoned there was room for a book around our exploits. But to make sure that it featured Buster, our madcap Labrador.

So I did and '**Hopes and Dreams... and Buster Too!'** is the result. I'm currently working on the sequel.

I've since had a number of articles published in various magazines including a few quirky travel pieces in the Herald Scotland Saturday Magazine.

I enjoy the outdoors and have managed some big hikes over the years. Starting with the West Highland Way and later trekking the Inca Trail to Machu Picchu, before doing a couple of treks in the Himalayas, culminating in a three week trail to Everest Base Camp. All fantastic trips.

We have a son, daughter and two grandsons who keep us all busy. I'm very fortunate to have a large extended family, with quite a few of them living nearby. We have friends who go back to my first day in St Mungo's, as well as others who we see regularly. Bizarrely, they're nearly all called John! Hence the need to make some name changes in the book.

Overall I must say I've had a pretty full life, and still happy to be with Mary, the love of my life, for almost fifty years.